# Rediscovering the Books of God

# Inkblotitis
# Christianity's Dangerous Disease

## Book 2:
## Rediscovering the Books of God

## Greg Fay, Ph.D.

Lighthouse Christian Publishing
Savage, Minnesota

# Rediscovering the Books of God

Published by
Lighthouse Christian Publishing
SAN 257-4330
5531 Dufferin Drive
Savage, Minnesota, 55378
United States of America

www.lighthousechristianpublishing.com

# Contents

# Preface

Many books are available on how to read the Bible—too many, actually. So why should there be another one, and why would you want to read it? The answer is because this study boils down the most important concepts of effective Bible reading to a single, usable principle and shows you how to apply it in your own Bible reading. Divided into a two-volume set, *Inkblotitis: Christianity's Dangerous Disease* exposes a "serious illness" in today's church, coming from the way we read and use the Bible, and presents a common-sense, contextual method as a return to the inherent nature of the Bible as a collection or library of the books of God.

Briefly introducing the content, nature, and history of the Bible, Book 1 (*The Disintegration of the Bible*) reveals what we've done to the Bible by breaking it up into thousands of small, disconnected pieces that often function more like spiritual or theological "inkblots" than objective revelation of the word of God. This is inkblotitis: when our own subjective thoughts and feelings become the primary lens through which we interpret verses of scripture. (Is there anything more potentially harmful than substituting "what I think" for "what God thinks"?) Replacing the books of God with (disconnected) verses from the Bible is Christianity's dangerous disease—and most of us have it!

Book 2 (*Rediscovering the Books of God*) presents the solution or "treatment." My goal is to help you rediscover the books of God by changing the way you read the Bible. Like putting together a jigsaw puzzle, reading the Bible in context means learning to see/hear each verse as it fits into the shape and purpose(s) of the document it's a part of—that is, the individual Bible book as a whole (Matthew, Mark, Romans, etc.). Having a book-level perspective gives readers a Spirit-authored vantage point to understand the individual verses as part of their inspired picture, as they were originally intended.

At the risk of giving away the secret at the very beginning, the most important principle for understanding the words of scripture as they were originally intended (and thus for treating the serious, hidden illness of inkblotitis) is simply this: *Zoom Out!* Learning to zoom out to the book-level context of each Bible book is the key that opens the door to God's inspired library. I invite you to turn the key and enter his presence.

Numerous people played important roles in helping me with this book. Without going too far into the annals of my personal history, I'd like to express gratitude to the key women in my life, starting with my grandmother, Mavine Snyder, and my mother, Rachel Wallis. Like Lois and Eunice in the life of Timothy (2 Timothy 1:5), the faith that undergirds my work in the Bible first existed in these two strong women of faith in our family. I'm reminded at times that what they passed on to us spiritually came over years of tenacious and practical dedication to us. To illustrate, my mom went to work in a convenience store while I was in college so she could send me money—money used to a large extent to buy books on the Bible that became the building blocks of my personal library. Real faith and love express themselves in the daily grind of life on planet earth. Without the faith and love of my mother and grandmother, my pursuit of scripture would not have been possible.

I'd also like to thank my wife, Cheryl. In more ways than I can express, she has been with me through thick and thin, working hard—with this same sort of enduring, practical faith and love—in order to allow me to pursue God in his word. "Thank you" is infinitely insufficient.

A very special word of appreciation goes to Dr. Carroll D. Osburn, who was a professor of New Testament at Harding School of Theology in Memphis when I attended there. (Most recently, he was the Carmichael-Walling Distinguished Professor of New Testament Language and Literature at Abilene Christian University, from which he retired in 2004.) Dr. Osburn changed my life with the idea of learning to read the Bible in context. If there is anything good in this book, much of the credit goes to him. The bad—I'm sure there are things he would not like or agree with—belongs to me. Dr. Osburn rocked my world with his scholarly and persistent insistence that we learn to ask the right questions of the text, and in particular with the concept of how a verse or passage of scripture functions in the book as a whole. In the course of our studies—on the other hand—he also urged us not to "preach the method." I believe I understand what he meant and hope that the pages of this book do not violate that admonition, but simply elucidate a key idea of Bible reading as a means of pointing to *the Word* of God who gives life.

Several friends have been a great blessing in proofing and editing various versions of the manuscripts. In particular, I appreciate the consistent and thoughtful observations, both conceptual and stylistic, of Dr. Brian Casey and Norbert Herman. Their suggestions impacted and improved many portions of the text (Brian's keen eye for details of English writing has been invaluable throughout the process). Perhaps most valuable of all has been their encouraging interaction as friends.

Reading about God and experiencing him in the books of God (which is the Bible) is a gift beyond price tag. I pray that something in this book will encourage you to keep pulling the ribbon off the package and opening the gift of the words of life.

# Chapter 7

# Treatment:
# A New Way to Read the Bible

A serious illness is sweeping through Christianity today, and it comes from the most unexpected places—our Bibles, our churches, our small groups, our homes. The illness is a disintegrated, taken-apart, contextless Bible ("inkblotitis"), resulting in overly personal, subjective, and distorted uses of scripture. The treatment is an all-natural, over-the-counter, heavenly new drug—or actually, an age-old, fitness program—called SABR, resulting in the reintegration of the books of God.

If you've journeyed with me through the first half of this study, you understand what I just said. You know what "inkblotitis" is and what the acronym SABR means. If not, then perhaps a little catching up is in order.

"Inkblotitis" is the word we're using to describe the condition that results when a verse or set of verses from the Bible is taken out of its original context. It's reading and using the Bible in small, randomly selected pieces (verses or even chapters), which greatly increases the chances for all sorts of different (possibly wrong) interpretations—like Rorschach inkblots—and thus the name "inkblotitis." And it's by far the most common way of using the Bible today.

SABR stands for "Sequential Access Bible Reading." It means that instead of the inkblot-promoting "Random Access Bible Reading" (RABR) that dominates our culture today (where we jump around from verse to verse or pull a favorite verse or two out of their book-level context), we need to return to the inherent nature of the Bible as a collection of inspired, independent books that fit together as part of the library of God that we call the Bible. Reading the books of God sequentially means that we need to take each book of the Bible on its own terms and read it from beginning to end in order to

1

understand any individual verse or portion of that book (not necessarily in the order they appear in the Bible, though). In order to include the idea of perspective (that it should come from the context of the Bible book instead of the context of my thinking and feeling, primarily), I changed the acronym to mean "Summit Access Bible Reading," implying that when we finish reading a book from the Bible, we begin to position ourselves at the "summit," so to speak, so that we can have a Holy Spirit-inspired perspective on what the individual verses mean in context.

We closed the first half of the study with a related metaphor—The Zoom-Out Challenge. The Zoom-Out Challenge (ZOC) suggests that each verse from the Bible needs to be seen as a part of a larger whole, which is the book itself. Learning to zoom out, ultimately to the level of the book as a whole, is vital to the treatment of inkblotitis and what we're about to do in this part of our study. In the first half (*The Disintegration of the Bible*), I claimed that we currently use the Bible in pieces to such an extent that it has become a serious problem—one that I've described as an "illness" in the church of today. Serious illnesses need treatment. (If you haven't, I encourage you to read the first half of our study to get a fuller understanding of what I mean.)

Be assured that without treatment for the serious illness of inkblotitis as we might envision it, God is still God, he loves us, and he will work to save us, as always. This is not at issue. Our ability to hear and understand God's written word in scripture and the effectiveness of our witness to the world *are* at issue. This is why treatment is critically important. As sinful humans, we will never be completely healed of our tendencies, our freedom, to thwart the reception of God's word. In the end, only God can cure us. In the meantime, I believe that with the empowering help of God's Spirit, we can draw close to the Father and more freely receive his heart and mind through the written word—if we seek him there.

Treatment often involves change. For those of you who already listen to God as he speaks to us in the Bible and don't need to change the way you hear God in scripture, I trust that the information to come will help you see God even more clearly and be captured even more deeply by the breath of his Spirit in your hearts and minds. But for the rest of us, those of us who have been infected with the Bible-reading habits of our times, I pray that God will change the way we read the Bible.

For all of us, the key is respect and patience—the respect to sit at the feet of the Word, the patience not to interrupt.

# A Lost Bible

In the Old Testament book of 2 Kings (chapter 22; also in 2 Chronicles 34), the writer tells the story of Josiah (641-609 BC), who became king over Judah (the southern portion of Israel) when he was just eight years old. The Bible says, "He did what was right in the sight of the Lord, and walked in all the ways of his father David; he did not turn aside to the right or to the left" (2 Kings 22:2). Throughout the books of 1 and 2 Kings, statements like this—sometimes good, sometimes bad—provide descriptive (often introductory) summaries regarding the lives and actions of the kings. Highlights of the various kings then underscore the extent to which they followed or abandoned the teachings of the Lord. During a period of decay prior to Josiah in which the Jewish people turned away from following God (Josiah's grandfather Manasseh even adapted the Temple for the worship of idols), knowledge of the teachings and power of the word of God faded. As they quit using and depending on it, the Jewish leaders appear to have lost the word of God that had been revealed to them in the earliest books of the Bible. They literally lost "the book of the law." They lost the Bible.[1]

When he was just 18, Josiah sent his administrative secretary Shaphan to the Temple with a message for the high priest Hilkiah. Josiah wanted all the Temple funds to be used to "put the Temple back together," so to speak. It was in a state of disrepair, graphically symbolic of the spiritual climate of the time. Josiah was so set on repairing the house of the Lord that he told them to give all the Temple money to the carpenters, builders, masons, etc. and not even to keep track of how much it cost. Lo and behold! (to use an old Hebrew phrase), somewhere in the process, Hilkiah made an extraordinary discovery: "I have found the book of the law in the house of the Lord," Hilkiah said to Shaphan, the king's secretary. When Shaphan read the book to Josiah, the king tore his clothes (an ancient Jewish way of expressing great emotion and distress) and immediately sent a high-ranking delegation to the best source of the word of God anyone knew at the time (a prophetess named Huldah) to find out what God thought about losing his book (think spiritually here, not just literally). Because they had abandoned God and his words, the message delivered back to Josiah foretold of impending disaster upon the land and the people. God's message was different to Josiah, however: "'Because your heart was penitent, and you humbled yourself before the Lord . . ., because you have torn your clothes and wept before me, I also have heard you,' says the Lord" (22:19). God would delay his judgment. Josiah would live out his life and go to his grave in peace (a key word in Hebrew for overall well-being): "Your eyes will not see all the disaster that I will bring on this place" (22:20), the Lord said.

Josiah then gathered all the people—the elders, all the people of Judah, all the inhabitants of Jerusalem, the priests, the prophets, and all the people, both small and great. He got everyone and read to them the words of God from the book of God that had been lost in the Temple. The king and all the people then joined together in agreement to live by the teachings and commandments of the Lord. "The king stood by the pillar and made a covenant before the Lord, to follow the Lord, keeping his commandments, his decrees, and his statues, with all his heart and all his soul . . ." (23:3). The result: For a season, the idols were removed; the people, renewed; the land was cleansed. Led by King Josiah, they found God again because they found his word, which had been sitting, lost and dusty on a back shelf in a decaying building where God had once shown himself to his people. They found God again, not because they found the Bible physically—that was just the first step—but because they blew off the dust and read it, for the first time.

I believe we face a similar situation today. A major point of the first half of this study is to say there's more than one way to lose the Bible. The people of Josiah's time lost it as their culture and lifestyles gradually turned away from the teachings of scripture (the effects of that loss can be seen in 2 Kings). The Bible (or at least a portion of it) fell into such disuse that they actually forgot where it was (notice that individuals didn't have their own copies). Even good-hearted people, like Josiah, who might have followed God more closely had they known how, lost the ability to know God with clarity, conviction, and power because no one (except perhaps

Huldah) knew what God said. I believe we are on the verge of doing something similar—if we haven't already—ironically, by the opposite means.

In some ways, a disintegrated Bible is no better than a lost one, if, in fact, we don't hear and understand what God has said to us, regardless of the number of copies we have lying around. What message has God revealed (and is revealing) to us through the book of Genesis? . . . Exodus? . . . Leviticus? What message has God revealed to us through the book of Ruth or Isaiah? What message has God revealed to us through the book of Matthew? . . . Mark? . . . Romans? . . . Revelation? The extent to which we as Christians can't answer these questions is the extent to which we have lost the books of God. Inkblotitis is the modern day Bible lost in the Temple—personal and denominational temples built of isolated verses of scripture, taken-apart and reused bricks, fused together with various subjective ideas, beliefs, and experiences. The treatment—rediscovering how *not* to interrupt God when he's talking to us, learning to read the Bible within the marvelous conversations of each book—is Josiah finding it again. It's the beginning of the reintegration of scripture. May we blow off the dust and hear the secure and life-changing words of God again.[2]

# A New Way to Read the Bible

When Dr. Tischendorf found the ancient copy of the Bible known as codex Sinaiticus, the treasure in the trash the monks were burning to fuel the fires of the monastery, he felt it sacrilege to sleep, for he held in his hands a priceless treasure that took us closer to the original writings of scripture. When King Josiah found the book of the law of God in the Temple, he ripped open his clothes at the realization of what they had lost. With a rapid heartbeat (I suspect) and an intense purpose, he opened the book before the people; the heavy veil of evil that had settled across the land began to be lifted as they heard from God again. In spite of their negligence and their loss, they found the word of truth remained in force. God was still there. His power, undiminished. His commands, relevant and binding. His love, secure.

I believe that our present condition, the isolation of verses of scripture caused by the way we read and use the Bible (inkblotitis), calls for an awakening as precious and profound as these. Like Josiah, we need to find the word of God again—words and messages that for many people have become hidden through layers of time, tradition, and isolation. Like Tischendorf, we have the opportunity to find a sacred treasure of inestimable worth and potential. Rediscovering the messages and power of the Bible by learning to look at each book as it was originally intended will be for some a *discovery* of the Bible. For others, it will be a *rediscovery* so profound as to amount to meeting with God for the first time—at least, the first time in a long time. Although it may seem difficult at first, I believe that everyone who takes up the challenge of reading God's word as the books of God presents himself/herself with a chance to look upon the things of God more clearly than ever. . . . to hear them, perhaps, for the first time. Everyone who takes up the challenge presents himself/herself with a chance to enter into God's sacred library, check out a divinely inspired book, and hear God speak. . . . to be silent—perhaps to be silenced. . . . to be strengthened—perhaps to be saved.

The treatment for inkblotitis is to back up and hear God again, to forget what we think we know (so to speak), to take another

7

look, to zoom out before we zoom in, to see God's messages within the inspired book-level contexts in which they were originally given. Because we're comfortable with what we already think—where we are—and we're so used to reading and hearing the Bible in quotations and sound bites, listening to God's first conversations with his people will be for many no less than listening to him for the first time. At the very least, we'll have the opportunity to be renewed and refreshed by the life-giving power of God's Spirit. How excited would you be if you got an invitation to come into the throne-room of God and hear him speak? (Check your mail: the divine invitation has arrived, sealed and hand-delivered by Jesus on the cross.) This is the treatment for inkblotitis: to stop and listen to God.

Contrary to the subtitle of this chapter ("A *New* Way to Read the Bible"), reading the books of the Bible within their book-level contexts is not a new thing. It is, in fact, one of, if not *the*, most commonly "taught" ways of reading the Bible in the history of the church (at least in the last several hundred years). There have been others at various times and places, like the allegorical method of the early church Fathers, the doctrinal and Christocentric priorities of the Reformers, and the emotional and practical emphases of Pietism (as we talked about earlier). In general, though, the things I've been saying about how we ought to read the Bible are not new in theory. Pick up most any book on how to read the Bible, and there'll be some pages devoted to the concept of context. Problem is, we just haven't been successful at it—at least not in modern, popular church culture where Christians, by in large, seem to be less and less familiar with the larger content of each book. Exhortations about how we should read the Bible thus amount to "lip service" in the face of how we actually read and use it. That's why I spent so much time in the first half of this study on the *diagnosis* of inkblotitis as an illness in the church. The prevalence and danger of a fragmented Bible is one of the main reasons I've written this book. To overcome the token admonitions about reading the Bible in context and stop the momentous inertia of reading and using the Bible in pieces is the other. Or to put it more positively, the purpose of the rest of this book is to focus on the treatment: how to read the Bible in the contexts of

God's first conversations with his people, how to read . . . to *get* God's point(s).

Though it's not new in concept, a careful reading of the verses of the Bible within their own book-level contexts will be so different for most of us that it will amount to "a new way to read the Bible." This doesn't mean it has to become academic, non-devotional, or lifeless. On the contrary, it's commonsensical—simply different. It's focus and habit. That's all. And this is part of what makes this book unique. The degree of consistency to which we focus on learning to hear a verse or set of verses within its own literary and historical context makes the second part of this study different from other books on how to read the Bible. In other words, we will consistently and without apology ask the question concerning how a segment of text fits with the rest of the story or discourse. This is *The* (all-important) *Question*: how do these verses fit within (snap into, to use our puzzle analogy) the overall, big picture of the book we are reading. Not because the question is important—of itself, method means nothing—but because it's the best way to tune into God's original conversations with and messages to his people. Asking this of every piece of a Bible book is the core of how I believe we ought to go about reading the Bible today until it becomes natural to hear the verses in context again. That's what's important: hearing the passages as they were intended.

We must learn to think in terms of the picture we are looking at as we read a Bible book—everything finds its place within that picture. Of course, some of the connections to the immediate context will be general and vague at times, perhaps even minimal. Biblical documents were forged in the midst of real life, often at challenging, even critical times. Sometimes, they are very personal; the writers mention personal things, shared between them and the audience. Sometimes they deal briefly with isolated issues. But since words and sentences have meaning in relation to the words and sentences around them (the context), and since the writings of the Bible have intentional and inspired purposes, we will assume that the verses of a given book have a natural and meaningful relation to the rest of the book.

Like zooming in on a small point in a complex scene, the more we focus on the small pieces (as we do when we dislodge verses), the more fuzzy (out of focus) the surrounding image becomes. The more we lose sight of the bigger picture, moreover, the more we open ourselves to distortions of emphases and external leadings of all sorts. I'll say it again another way: the more we isolate individual verses and sets of verses, the more we lose the controlling currents of God's Spirit, streamed into these communications from God. (That's the first locale of Spirit-filled Bible reading, not my spirit.) The more we lose the controlling voice of God's Spirit, the more we interpret verses through the lenses of our own subjective interests and perceptions. Again: The more we turn scripture into inkblots, the more we risk seeing and following a reflection of ourselves instead of seeing and listening to God. The more we lose the fidelity of God in the sights and sounds of scripture, the more we forget the plans, purposes, and pleasures of God. The more we forget what pleases God, his directions for life, the more lost we are.

*The treatment for inkblotitis is to quit turning verses into inkblots and learn to read them in their book-level contexts.* More broadly: To read the books of the Bible as books—as connected pieces of various types of literature. The treatment is to quit using the Bible as if it were a pile of disconnected sayings or aphorisms or proverbs or prophecies or analogies or . . . spiritual fortune cookies. . . . to sit down with God and listen as he spoke with and to us. The challenge is to stop interrupting God when he's speaking to us and come to hear scripture within the defining moments of God's first conversations with his people. The treatment for inkblotitis, a new way to read the Bible, is to discover the power and focus inherent in the word of God by reading and hearing his word as he spoke it to us, book by book, as part of an incredible collection of the inspired books of God that we call the Bible. Like checking out a book from the library, we don't put it back on the shelf until we're done reading the whole thing.

# With a SABR

Throughout the course of this book, I've used several images to portray what I believe to be a better way to read the Bible. We've talked about reading the Bible as books, as part of God's inspired library, instead of reading the Bible as a single book or as individual verses—which in the end amounts to the same thing. We've talked about understanding verses as part of the interconnected literary and historical context of each book (the "book-level" context), with an emphasis on how the parts function within that whole (like a beating heart in a human body). We used "The Question" to highlight our need to grasp the organic nature of biblical writings. The puzzle analogy makes the concept concrete and practical with the image of how the pieces fit together to form one complex, easily discernible picture—when it's put together. I talked about the "Picture-Point" method of reading the Bible: once we see the put-together picture, we can point to any piece of the puzzle and the meaning is usually easy to see. "Zooming out" uses a lens or an electronic image to illustrate moving to a bigger or higher perspective. And finally, we used the analogy of sequential or summit access Bible reading (SABR) as opposed to the random access Bible reading that is so prevalent today.

All of these are basically different ways of saying the same thing: we should read the books of the Bible—as much as possible—as they were intended to be read and heard. Since they were written as separate books, at different times and places, so we should read them. Of course, there are questions and complications, but this approach will put us on a much more solid footing than the quicksand made of thousands of inkblots that the Bible has become.

Let's focus for a moment on one of the images to help move us into the second half of our journey: SABR. How do we go about putting together the pictures/puzzles of God's books? Instead of RABR (Random Access Bible Reading), we need SABR—Sequential Access Bible Reading. We need to start at the beginning and read to the end of each book, individually, as a book, as if we were trying to take in the whole of a painting, picture, or puzzle—a movie or a book. Once we've read all the way through the book and have begun to get an overview picture of the landscape—what's going on—we can then actually read with a sort of "random access." At least we can begin to look at each verse or set of versus in connection with the big picture. We can focus on the details of the picture without losing sight of the context; and just as Rorschach found with his inkblot testing (the head of a fox), once we see a holistic, big picture, all the parts begin to be seen as contributing to that whole. This is exactly what we want in Bible reading (the opposite of the Inkblot Test). Once we've read through the entire book, sequentially, then we can begin to focus more on the parts and how they fit together to create the landscape scene as a whole.

This suggests another sort of access or view when it comes to Bible reading. To keep our acronym (SABR), I'm calling it Summit Access Bible Reading. The summit is the view from the top of our experience of the book as a whole. This is the Book Picture: the picture or story of the book as a whole (again, like a movie, some things don't make much sense until you've seen the whole thing). It's a book-level perspective. It's our way of reconstructing and being a part of the world and setting of the book. The original audiences would have gotten the picture and the points as they heard the books read. They had the advantages of being there. They are part of the narrative world. We have the disadvantage of being separated from the settings in time, language, culture, etc.—what makes the Bible hard to understand. We have the advantage, however, of having our own copies, which allows us to look carefully at the content and design of the books, and to read them as many times as we like.

There are other legitimate perspectives or summits from which we can and need to understand Bible books. The second major, very important summit is the Bible as a whole: the Bible Picture or Bible-level context. Of course, we will want to integrate our reading and understanding of individual books with the other books in the Bible, but—as I've been suggesting all along—this needs to be done from a book-level perspective, not a verse-level perspective. Only when we know how a verse or set of verses works in its own book will we be in a good position and have a good perspective to relate it to other books in the Bible. If you're new to the Bible, doing this effectively takes time as you learn the overarching history and stories of the Bible, as opposed to just jumping around from one place in the Bible to another.

Thus, we have the book-level view/summit and the Bible-level view/summit, and there are others. For example, if a single author wrote several books, then a secondary perspective from which to view and interpret a passage of scripture is in comparison to other books written by that same individual in which he addresses the same subject or issue, since it is more likely that the perspective and meaning of words and passages will be similar. It makes more sense to interpret what Paul means by "grace," for example, by how Paul uses the word "grace" rather than John. We might call this the author-level perspective. These perspectives will grow and develop over time as a person becomes more and more grounded in the books of scripture.

For now our concern is with the book-level perspective because it's so important to all the others. In fact, I believe, that learning to read the Bible as books is the treatment for the spiritual illness of inkblotitis. And it's not a difficult concept at all. It's really very natural: just read it. Read the book, and the results will be transformative. It's an old way of reading the Bible—it's a new way of reading the Bible. And that's what happens when something gets lost. The word of God that Josiah found was there all along, but for him and his people, the day they found it was a new day. I hope and pray that a new day will dawn for many of us as we choose to hear the messages of God according to the meaning and purposes he intended when he inspired them by the Holy Spirit. When we do that, the words of the Bible pierce and reshape our hearts and lives with the living sword of the Spirit.

The emphasis on reading and understanding a Bible book within its own historical context is not meant to disregard or diminish the importance of what the verses are saying to us today as we read—to me, in my world, this day, this morning (that's why it is the "living" word of God). It gives us a clearer picture of what's most important and therefore most needful for our lives. If the verses of the

Bible don't speak to us today, then reading them historically is of little importance. In a sense, application is everything. Personal and community application of the Bible to our lives can thus be seen as another perspective or summit from which to view the messages of scripture. Summit 1 is the book picture; Summit 2, the Bible picture; Summit 3, my life picture. We might think of it as three summits on our ascent to intimate and ongoing communion with God—a tri-summit approach to Bible reading. (We'll talk more about these in the pages to come.) When we hear and understand what God tells us, believe and apply his word to our lives, then God lives in us and we in him. The goal of good Bible reading is to hear the word of God and be changed by it.

As you know, a saber (SABR) is a type of sword. For you *Star Wars* fans, we could envision a light saber. The new way of reading the Bible is simply another way of saying (let's go back and) receive the sword of the Spirit—the light saber of God. The new way of reading the Bible, the antidote for inkblotitis, is SABR. It's a sword. It's *the* sword, crafted and sharpened in the midst of real-life settings, theirs and ours. God spoke; God speaks. The treatment for Christianity's dangerous disease is to listen to God as he speaks, and he spoke in the books of the Bible.

Let's wander into the Temple of God—no, let's go with purpose and direction—and, like Josiah and his people, let's find the book of God. Let's blow off the dust, open it, begin to read, hear God speak, tear our clothes, repent and humble ourselves, and—like a brilliant sunrise on a quiet Easter morning—witness the wonder and majesty of the holy and gracious God and all he has for us in his kingdom. May his sword—more sharp and powerful than any sword or saber, even light sabers—may it pierce our souls and make us strong. May we find new life through the reintegration of God's books.

## Notes

1.  Or at least important portions of it (as we're not completely sure which "book of the law/covenant" Josiah found; some believe it was Deuteronomy).

2.  The 2 Kings' story of Josiah is not a story about inkblotitis. In a way, then, I just did one of the things I "railed" against earlier. I used the story of Josiah as a great big analogy. Is this really what the writer of 1 and 2 Kings meant for us to get from this story? To some extent, I think the answer is yes. Not specifically and directly, but basically and truthfully. Once we've read the books in their original contexts and sought to understand the writers' messages, comparisons with other portions of scripture are natural and helpful. See what I mean when I say that I'm not opposed to second and third level ways of using scripture and of the Bible-level perspective? I just think most of us jump to such analogical—often subjective—uses of scripture without knowing that we're doing it, before we've finished hearing God's primary message(s) in the books themselves. Were I to begin to take details of today's culture of inkblotitis and use these to interpret the story of Josiah, or—the other way around—were I to suggest that the story of Josiah is God's message to us today about inkblotitis, that the message of Huldah is the same to us as it was to Josiah, I would be in danger of excerpting (that is, punching out) these verses for my own momentary purposes and perhaps never taking the time to notice the particular truths revealed in 1 and 2 Kings.

### The Treatment Plan: A Look Ahead

- Context Rules
- Ten Rules of Good Bible Reading (Rules 1-3)
- Ten Rules of Good Bible Reading (Rules 4-10)
- Let's Do It: Reading Philemon (a letter)
- Let's Do It: Reading Mark (a narrative)
- Conclusion: A Plan for the Church

# Chapter 8

# Context Rules

## Divine Master . . . Pieces?

My son got married in the Church of the Recessional—a replica of Rudyard Kipling's home church in Rottingdean, England—in Forest Lawn Memorial Park in Glendale, California this last summer. While we were visiting before the wedding, he took us on a tour of the park, which has some impressive works of art, in addition to beautiful churches, a museum, an art gallery, ornate burial grounds, and a magnificent mausoleum. Some well-known people have found their final earthly resting place in this park. My daughter, who loves theatre and performing arts, became a little more interested as we visited the grave site of Walt Disney. Michael Jackson was laid to rest in the mausoleum. Forest Lawn is quite the place. "The Builder's Creed," which is on display in the park, starts with these lines:

I believe in a happy eternal life.

I believe those of us who are left behind should be glad in the certain belief that those gone before, who believed in him, have entered into that happier life.

I believe, most of all, in a Christ that smiles and loves you and me . . . .

Thus, New Year's Day, 1917, Hubert Eaton stood on a hilltop and envisioned a different kind of cemetery that these 55 acres (now over 300) could become. And he lived out that vision.

A huge picture caught my attention. Recessed but hard to miss in the Court of Freedom is a huge reproduction of the famous

17

painting by John Trumbull that resides in the rotunda of the Capitol in Washington, D.C. called *Declaration of Independence*. I'm sure you've seen it—or at least pictures of it. *The Signing of the Declaration of Independence* in Forest Lawn is 20 feet by 30 feet—three times the area of the original portrait. And here's the astonishing part: it's made of 700,000 pieces of Venetian glass tile. It's a mosaic—an amazingly beautiful, giant mosaic. If *The Signing of the Declaration of Independence* were blown into thousands of pieces—by, heaven forbid, a terrorist bomb or something—none of the individual pieces would mean much. Together they create a spectacular picture.[1] Apart, they're just shards.

Think what we do when we blow apart God's pictures, displayed to us in each individual book of the Bible. At the risk of sounding extreme, I'll venture a question: could it be that such is the work of a terrorist and/or perhaps our own subconscious declarations of independence? It's time to pick up the pieces and begin reassembling the divine masterpieces. Fortunately, they're still intact through the grace and power of God's Spirit. All we have to do is step back and look again.

# What Is a Context?

## "Context Rules"

The title of this chapter, "Context Rules," illustrates the point before we even begin to talk about it. What does it mean to say "context rules"? It depends on what you mean by "context" and on whether "rules" is a noun or a verb, doesn't it? . . . and on how I'm using the phrase. From a literary perspective, "context" refers to the words, sentences, and passages that surround another word or phrase. If you're talking about a place or an event—an historical perspective—the "context" is the surrounding set of circumstances that forms the environment of the event or action, sometimes called the setting.

It just so happens that I'm using the word "context" to refer to both, that is, with a double meaning: the historical set of circumstances within which and for which a book of the Bible was written; and the written words, sentences, and paragraphs that make up the book itself. These are the *historical* and the *literary* contexts. I combine the two throughout the pages of this book in the phrase "the book-level context." Both are important for understanding the meaning and purposes of a Bible book. (See how, even though the differences may appear to be subtle, the exact meaning an author gives a word or phrase becomes evident only in the context? Without reading various portions of this book, you wouldn't know how I'm using these terms, and without reading the whole book, you won't know for sure whether you might have missed some important nuance of my thesis or purpose.)

So when I say "context rules," am I referring to a *list of rules* regarding the context, or am I suggesting that the context *rules* or *controls* the meaning? Both. I intend to spend considerable time looking into the concept of how the literary and historical contexts shape and control the meaning of Bible verses. I also intend to give you a list of "rules" or principles for how to read verses within their book-level contexts. (I'm stretching a little here, as I really intend to give you some rules for good Bible reading in general.) Again, without some clarifying context, the double-meaning of my use of "context rules" would be uncertain.

## Where Do Words Get Their Meaning?

Basically, words get meaning from their historical and popular use as part of a language. (This is called "linguistics": the systematic study of language.) Thus, words have some quasi-definable meanings by themselves; otherwise, you wouldn't be able to look them up in the dictionary. Words *denote* things. As soon as you begin looking up words, however, it doesn't take long to see that many words have multiple *basic* meanings and all sorts of *shades* of meaning that we associate with them, sometimes referred to as their *connotations*. Words connote things—they can mean different things to different people. Think about what happens, then, when you translate from one language to another, as we do when the Bible is put into English. Not only do we have denotations and connotations of individual words or phrases, but also the denotations and connotations of the words and phrases used to translate them (in the receptor language). As languages evolve over time, moreover, things change. That's why living languages (languages that are in use today) are said to be fluid—they grow and change over time; new words and meanings have to be added to the dictionary all the time. So besides very broad and basic "dictionary" meanings, how do we know what someone means really or specifically when he or she use words to say or write something?

For example, what does the word "score" mean? And what does it mean "to score"? The meaning depends, doesn't it? How many ways are there "to score"? Scoring in football is completely different than scoring in—say—ping pong. But what kind of "football" are we talking about? Depends on whether you're American or English? And there are multiple ways to score in American football, but not in baseball (the only way is to have a base runner touch home plate). Every sport is different. On the other hand, if a high school teenager were asked if he "scored" after an evening out with the prom queen, the picture is quite different. And—to continue the relational (or should I say sexual) image—a young Don Juan might scratch a mark into the side of the bedpost or headboard to keep tally of his conquests. Teachers give us scores on tests; musicians write scores for movies and plays. Sometimes, the word refers to a degree of indebtedness (what you owe me), and I just might "even the score." Do you remember that a "score" can refer to a group of 20— "Four score and seven years ago . . ." How about a groove cut in wood for a rope, or a crease or perforation so you can fold or tear a piece of paper? It can refer to the state or facts of the present situation, or a successful robbery or drug deal. And there's more. By itself the word is pregnant with potential meanings, but we don't know the specific length, weight, health, even the sex of the child to be born. Bottom line: You have to have more context to know what's really intended.

Let's take another one. What does "stock" mean? There are many possibilities. My word processor dictionary brought up 38 options. A few common ones include the supply or amount of something (as in goods for sale), an investor's share of a company, a shortened form of "livestock," the broth of a soup or stew. And there are plenty of others. We really can't know what the word "stock" means without more context. So let's add a small amount of context. What does it mean to "water the stock"? Now we've used "stock" as a noun and added an action to it. If I'm in an agricultural setting, "watering the stock" probably has something to do with providing literal water to the collection of animals (as in giving the cattle or horses something to drink). I've read that the phrase originated as a way of increasing the weight of cattle before sale, which amounts to a completely different (underhanded) purpose than providing basic hydration. Another old use had to do with wetting cloth so as to add a lustrous appearance in wavy lines (as in to water silk). If I add water to a pot of soup, I also "water the stock"—more soup, less thickness and possibly flavor. Historically, companies would issue more shares of stock to artificially increase the capital stock of the company but diminish the value of an individual share; thus, "watering" or "weakening the stock." I've even seen the modern definition "to urinate (outdoors)." That's a meaning we wouldn't want to mix up with one of the others, unless, of course, your once lucrative "stock" no longer has any value whatsoever.

## How Much Makes a Context?

In some cases, adding a few words to a word or phrase doesn't make the meaning clear ("over the rainbow," "through the woods," or "the bear ate the porridge," e.g.). Sometimes it does, but usually it doesn't. An important question in our discussion of context, then, is how much context does it take to have a meeting of the minds, so to speak, and get the meaning? This is an important question, and there is no single answer. Sometimes, it takes a little; sometimes, a lot. The underlying principle, however, is that *the more context you have, the more opportunity you give the speaker/writer to clarify and pinpoint the meaning.* If you really want to understand what someone has said and means, as we do with the Bible, the more you should consider everything he or she said in that situation or context, especially in a written narrative or dialogue where the meaning of certain things may come to light only gradually or even be intentionally delayed for impact.

Often when reading a biblical text, we think that reading a few verses before and a few verses after will give us sufficient context to know what the author means. Problem is, it just hasn't worked, and it doesn't work because of the nature of much of the content of the Bible. This doesn't mean that short sayings or verses are never understandable on their own—some (like proverbs) are intended as such. But it does mean that if we are serious about wanting to understand what God has said to us in the books of the Bible, we should take every available advantage of the context he has given to help us get the overall picture and the individual points.

We could look at more examples. What does the word "pound" mean, or the word "bear," or "font"? Again, it all depends. What about "peace" or "grace," or "grace and peace to you," as the apostle Paul is fond of saying. "Love" is a key word in the Bible. It's very important to John and to Paul, and to most of the authors of Bible books. What does it mean? What does the Bible mean when it tells us to love our neighbor as ourselves? A lawyer took advantage of the potential ambiguity of that phrase (especially the word "neighbor") and asked Jesus, "Who then is my neighbor?" (Luke 10:25-37), trying to justify himself. (Notice how a different twist on the meaning of something can be used as a tool to justify not really doing what God says. We talked about this earlier with the temptations of Jesus.) John tells us that Jesus said people would know his followers by the way they love each other (John 13). For the most part, I think we understand the meaning. Or does our understanding of "love" in today's culture affect not only how we understand it, but also how we apply it? What does it really mean to love something or someone? Is it a feeling that comes and goes, as in a romantic or dating relationship—like a flickering candle in the wind? What about the divorce rate in our world today? What does that say about love? Can you turn it on and off like a light-switch? What is love? I love ice-cream, but I can't eat it because it doesn't "love" me (I'm allergic to it). Hmm. Jesus even said we should love our enemies. How in the world do you do that? And what does that mean?

Context is the key. First, the context of the whole book you're reading (summit #1—from the last chapter). Second, the context and scope of the Bible as a whole (summit #2). Finally, the context of your life (summit #3): what does this mean to you as a person in your family, your church, your workplace, your relationships, etc. Before we can really know the answer to what a verse or set of verses in the Bible really means, we have to first read and understand the use of the word in the context of the book we are reading. That's the starting point. Otherwise, personal and subjective connotations begin to creep in—faster than you would think—and we quickly begin to get out of synch with the author and out of sorts with each other.

I like to think of a contextual approach to the Bible as a tri-summit method. Our goal is, in effect, to get to God. We want to hear God, to know God, to please God, to draw close to him through his communications to us in scripture. The three perspectives or summits I have described help us with this. God is at the top of all the summits (he's also in and throughout everything, but that's another topic). Though I believe you can, in most cases, go directly from an individual book of the Bible (summit #1) to the application of truth to our lives, which includes our participation in the church (summit #3), a wider knowledge of the books of the Bible gives us a broader historical and theological base to understand how the teachings of God (summit #2) should affect our lives. We might picture it something like this:

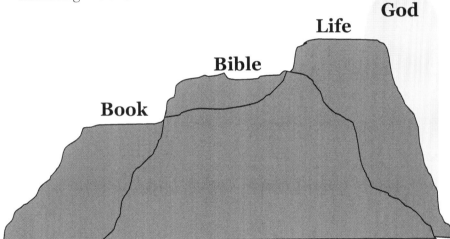

This is the tri-summit method of Bible reading, and these various perspectives combine to give us our integrated interpretive context.

To summarize: Words get their specific meanings from the words and sentences that surround them. Sentences get their specific meanings from the sentences and paragraphs around them. Paragraphs get their specific meanings from the paragraphs (and chapters) around them. The best way to understand a word or phrase—or a verse—from the Bible is, therefore, to see it in the context of all the words and phrases around it. This is the literary context.

"Context" means surroundings. We'll look more closely at how to do this—how to read words and sentences within their book-level contexts—in the pages to come. Again, the bottom line: The smaller the context, the wider the set of possible meanings becomes—which is why breaking the Bible up into small pieces is a little like shattering a mosaic. It gives us inkblotitis.

# Historical and Literary Contexts

The literary and historical contexts work together to create the (book-level) context of a Bible book. The historical context is the actual surroundings (to use our defining term) that caused the book to be written. Though the authors are sometimes unnamed and so technically anonymous, the books that made their way into the Bible were written by devoted followers of God in order to communicate teachings and convictions about God to a group or groups of people. They are, therefore, not works of fiction in the modern sense (stories describing imaginary people and events), but concern real ideas and teachings about God delivered to a set of people at a particular point and time in history. The contents of the books thus deal with particular persons, beliefs, events, and actions within the community to which the books were written. (Paul's letters are sometimes called "occasional documents" to highlight the cutting-edge, real-life contexts of their production.) The books reflect the dynamic faith of the authors and of the audiences. The historical context refers to everything involved in the life of the author and the audience that surrounds and informs the writing and receiving of the book.

Scholars sometime refer to the historical context as the "setting" of the book—the "setting in life" from a popular German phrase (*Sitz im Leben*). What are the historical ingredients that merged together to create the book? This includes such basic things as the author, the audience, the reason for writing, and the content of the book as part of the actual historical exchange. Though it begins to delve into the literary context, these ideas are sometimes expressed with a serious of questions starting with the letter W:

**Who** wrote it? Whom was it written to?
**When** (and where) was it written?
**What** does it say?
**Why** was it written? What does the author hope to accomplish?

These are the types of things we often read in commentaries or other study guides when we want to learn something about the *background* of a Bible book.

Because the books of the Bible were directed to real people, dealing with real problems in life and questions of faith, the historical context is an important part of understanding the content and purposes of a book. Take a more modern example. In July of 2009, the Museum of American History acquired a letter from George Washington. Imagine for a minute that you know nothing about George Washington or the United States of America during the time of the Revolutionary War and the election of Washington as America's first president. The letter was written by David Stuart (who is David Stuart?) from the front lines of the Virginia legislature in Richmond on November 30, 1785 and concerns the fate of the union under the Articles of Confederation (the nation's first constitution). What was going on at that time to cause a man known as General Washington, who happened to be a retired general at the time, to come out of retirement to become the nation's first president in 1789 (the letter was written before he became president)? Without trying to answer these questions at the moment—you likely know some of the background already because it's a part of our nation's history—it's easy to see how the circumstances generated and then (in retrospect) help to explain the meaning of George Washington's letter. The more you know about the circumstances of a document—its historical context—the easier it is to understand its content and purposes.

One more, brief example that shows the potential impact of losing the literary and historical context: I suspect you've heard of the "wall of separation between church and state." The phrase has essentially become an inkblot, often interpreted to mean exactly the opposite of its original intention. Of course, it's not in the Constitution, but in a letter from Thomas Jefferson to the Danbury Baptist Association on January 1, 1802. Given the historical context of the document, which in general includes Jefferson's writings and actions regarding the federal government's role in the religious affairs of the country, the phrase reflects Jefferson's adamant opposition to the government imposing any sort of national religion or meddling in the affairs of the states to encourage religion (which he hoped they would do and helped to initiate while serving in the Virginia legislature). Jefferson believed that the Constitution created "a [the actual quotation] wall of separation between church and state" that was to prevent the "state" (that is, the federal government) from interfering in establishing or interfering with the free practice of religion by the people and the states. Recently, however, the Supreme Court and various political groups have used Jefferson's statement for just the opposite. As W. Skousen puts it in *The 5000 Year Leap*:

> This obvious distortion of the original intent of Jefferson (when he used the metaphor of a "wall" separating church and state) becomes entirely apparent when the statements and actions of Jefferson are examined in their historical context.[2]

The historical context is critical for understanding accurately pieces of any document.

The same is true with biblical letters and other types of Bible books. The more we know about who wrote them, to whom, when, and what for, the more likely we are to understand the content clearly. Unfortunately, the historical surroundings are not always as clear and available as information about George Washington or Thomas Jefferson. In many cases, we have to "reconstruct" the ingredients of the historical context as best we can from the content of the book itself, and, at times, much of the circumstances is implied by the content of the book—just as you could infer some of the context of Washington's letter from its content, if we had no other sources. Fortunately, we have a large and ever-growing collection of information about life and history during the times the books of the Bible were written. Historical and archeological knowledge about the times and places of the Bible can be great aids in making sense of things that might otherwise make little or no sense. On the other hand, much of what we know about the settings of biblical books, especially the details of the particular historical contexts, comes from the documents themselves. This is one of the reasons I prefer to put

29

our focus on the literary context (the written words themselves) when it comes to our efforts to read and understand the Bible.

The *literary context* is the actual words and sentences themselves. It's the first word of a book or document to the last word of the book. For our purposes, the literary context is the first word of the book of Genesis to the last word of the book of Genesis. It's the first word of the book of Matthew to the last word of the book of Matthew. Each book constitutes its own literary context.

(Listen closely to what I'm about to say. It's very important.) Sometimes, when people talk about the context, they are referring to a chapter or to a paragraph, a set of verses before and after a particular verse. This is not what I mean by "literary context." I'm talking about the book as a whole—the overall, big-picture of the book as a whole. Of course, there are smaller paragraph- or chapter-level contexts, and reading a verse in context certainly means seeing it as an integrated part of that context—its *immediate* context. Any intelligent reading requires that; otherwise, you don't really have communication at all, just words or even letters, if we take the logic far enough. The literary context of a verse certainly includes its immediate context, if we want to understand it properly. But—if I may be elementary for a moment—a letter is connected to other letters to make a word. Words are connected to other words to make sentences. Sentences . . . to sentences to form paragraphs. Paragraphs . . . to paragraphs to make a letter, or an essay, or a book. *Breaking apart any of those connections risks the ability of the context to control the meaning.* So, yes, the literary context includes the immediate context of a sentence or verse, but it also includes the rest of the book. That's the heart of what I'm trying to say. Separating the verses or paragraphs—the immediate contexts—into individual pictures is the start of inkblotitis. (Think shattered mosaic.) What we want to do is learn to see how the immediate contexts fit together as smaller, but integrated pictures into the landscape view of the book as a whole.

# Putting Together the Puzzles of Scripture

## A Celebrating Church

This is why the analogy or image of a puzzle works so well. A puzzle is literally a cut-up picture (that's why we call them "jigsaw" puzzles). And this is what we do to the Bible when we examine small sets of verses in isolation from the rest of the book. The verses, which are certainly helpful to find and mark important places in scripture, function much like the cuttings or perforations in a puzzle, allowing us to take apart Bible books into little and sometimes big piles of pieces. Were we to keep the pieces separated into their own containers—as we do with individual puzzles—pull them out and put them together from time to time—as we do with puzzles—and then use those put-together pictures to learn and know the will of God, then compare them to the put-together pictures of other books to deepen our understanding and experiences of the Spirit's revelation to us; then verses wouldn't be a problem. But that's not what we do.

We take all the verses and sections of the Bible apart and put them into one container, with no guide-picture on the top of the box. This is often what we mean when we talk about the Bible as a book: we mean a pile of verses. The model we use to assemble the pieces then becomes our own personal way of thinking about God and life. Sometimes we leave a few of the pieces together in the box, so it's easy to have a "meaningful" little picture already assembled (reflecting very fundamental or pet beliefs); but we then relate or connect that picture with other small pictures we've assembled elsewhere from the Bible (or from church or family or . . .).

I like to use a hands-on example of a puzzle when I talk about this to a group of people. I show them a single piece of a puzzle, pass it around the room, and ask everyone to "interpret" it. "What is this?" "What's it a picture of? What does it mean?" Of course, there are all sorts of different answers. It's very much like a Rorschach inkblot. Take the following pieces of a puzzle, for example. What is it? How much detail can you provide?

First of all, notice that it's actually several pieces of a larger puzzle (think of reading 3 or 4 verses of scripture). Put together, the pieces are obviously a bouquet of yellow flowers, with green foliage, in a clear vase. There's some sort of grayish, brick veneer behind it, with a smoother gray wall or background above it. That's about it. Not a lot to go on, except that it's a pretty set of yellow flowers. But what does it mean?

Let's look at another example from the same puzzle:

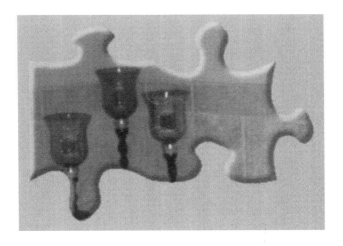

Here we have a couple more pieces put together, appearing to be a set of three decorative items, possibly candles, against the same background as the flowers. They are of different heights or are sitting on bases of different heights. Again, not much to go on, but let's surmise that they are some sort of decorative or ritualistic candles.

Now suppose we consider this a sacred image, one around which we were to help build and shape our lives? Suppose a certain group of people began to use this piece of the picture, isolated from other pieces and the picture as a whole, to develop some of its core values as a community? I can imagine the picture as a symbol of the Trinity and thus as a tool for divine presence and worship. (Perhaps the different heights represent the different roles of the Trinity.) If this picture were used by a faith-based community as a fundamental element of its thinking and action, then we could imagine a worship-centered church, perhaps in a traditional or liturgical fashion. On the other hand, if we focus on the flowers, then we might imagine a people who value beauty or perhaps celebration of critical events—maybe weddings or funerals. Can you begin to see how various styles of churches could grow based on separate, isolated components of scripture? Here's a big question: could denominationalism have its roots in inkblotitis, that is, in the sacred use of isolated, dislodged Bible verses?

Now let's look at the picture as a whole. And here's the critical point: what is the meaning of the same pieces of the puzzle that we looked at above now as they are connected to the rest of the picture?

When we look at the whole, assembled picture, it's quite easy to see the place of each element as part of a "bubble bath for two." The emphasis or meaning of the picture as a whole is the celebration and anticipation of a romantic encounter (given the two glasses; otherwise, it might just be a soothing bubble-bath after a hard day of work). Our emphasis on celebration was somewhat accurate—though of quite a different sort—while the association of the candles with the Trinity was completely off base, and the core or main thought of the puzzle was missing entirely from our interpretation of the individual pieces when we examined them in isolation from the picture as a whole.

This is what I'm suggesting we need to do with the Bible. We need to put together the books, one by one, into their own separate pictures, and then see or interpret the individual verses as parts of those pictures. We then need to relate the picture of each book to the pictures of other books to grow our overall understanding of the Bible. This is true biblical theology. We'll look into some specific guidelines and tools to help us put together the puzzles of scripture in the next chapter. The point I hope you won't miss here is how the context of a verse or set of verses is like putting together a jigsaw puzzle. The context is the put-together picture, *and that picture rules the way we understand the individual parts.* To say that "context rules" is to say that by necessity the whole—the picture—controls the meaning of its parts. When you take a picture of someone you love, you don't look at it as a picture of a nose, for example. You take in, think about and cherish the whole person.

## Connecting the Pieces: Shapes and Structure

Talking about how a piece of a puzzle fits into the puzzle as a whole concerns the design or structure of the puzzle. It's not random. You can't put any piece next to any other piece and have them create an intelligible picture. They fit together in a certain order and design, and they have points of connection that allow us to fit or put them together that way. The same is true of communication in general and a written document in particular: there is an intentional design that connects the words and sentences, and facilitates communication as a natural part of language and culture. It's inherent in verbal (oral and written) communication. Words are spelled with letters in a certain order. Scramble the letters, and you have a word scramble game (an anagram). Sentences also have design and order, as do paragraphs and stories. You can't start in the middle of a story, jump to the beginning, flip to the end, pick up in the middle again and hope to get the proper sense of things—even less, if you jump from one book or story to another. (Or course, there are sophisticated literary techniques that at times make use of non-standard flow and plot, but that's a different issue.)

I refer to this natural connectability of the parts of a written document with the word "structure." All communication has built-in structure that is inherent and understood to some extent on both sides of a conversation (even if it's not perceived). Various verbal (and non-verbal), grammatical, and conventional indicators or markers help to define the structure and sometimes make it explicit when we speak or write, and they can be different depending on the type of medium (like pauses, punctuation marks, spaces, hard returns, paragraph indentions, chapter headings, etc.). This is where punctuation marks, parts of speech, and rules of grammar come into play when reading and interpreting a document, and this is why it's important for us to have well-trained scholars who work in the original languages of the Bible to translate and help explain some of the subtleties of the original languages. Structure is important and at times can be technical and complex.

As we seek to understand complex questions or hard to understand portions of scripture, there are times when we need to dig deeper into the Greek or Hebrew structure in order to perceive the intended meaning. But that doesn't mean you have to become a scholar to understand the Bible. We'll let the scholars be the scholars and help us when we need it, but learning to read the Bible in light of its book-level pictures will require us to think about how the verses and chapters fit together—how they function and flow as part of the book-level picture. Or, to put it more simply, how they fit together, and this involves structure.

Once scholars have done the challenging and vital service of giving us English translations of the Bible, the larger, big-picture connections of the structure are often obvious and accessible. Of course, there will always be questions of language and grammar, but I believe there are many relatively easy-to-see points of structure that everyone can use to put together the bigger picture of a Bible book. On a small scale, how a sentence connects to or relates to the preceding and following sentences, for example, sometimes becomes an important question, if we want to hear it in context. From a broader perspective, how a section of scripture relates to the section that follows is, at least at first, more important for getting a sense of the bigger picture. Both of these are types of structures. Think of this—of structure—as the parts of a puzzle piece that connect it to another piece (the distinctive curves and circular endpoints). When you have a group of verses put-together into a larger section, then how does that section connect to another section? This is what I mean by structure. It doesn't have to be overly technical or complicated, but it is an integral part of visualizing the picture as a whole. To put it simply: how does it connect?

## Everything Has a Beginning, Middle, and End

When it comes to reading a story, essay, or document of almost any type, everything has a beginning, a middle, and an end. Something as simple as asking ourselves what part of this document functions as the beginning or introduction, what part is the middle or body, and what forms the conclusion can go a long way toward getting a sense of the big picture. How does it start? How does it end? Why does it start this way? Why does it end this way? How does the author/story get us from the beginning to the ending? If a medical doctor didn't know the difference between a person's head and her feet, none of us would put ourselves under his care. (The Hippocratic Oath would be in grave danger, to continue the absurd illustration.) Similarly, perceiving how a section of text functions within the scope of the whole book helps to show how the words and ideas are being used within that section, and for what overall purpose. It's like snapping one section of a puzzle into another. You get a clearer and more complete view. Without it: Inkblotitis. And to continue our analogy, finding the introduction, body, and conclusion is a little like finding the straight edges when you go to put together a puzzle. It gives you a framework for the rest. This is one of the basic practices or habits of Bible reading ("rules for reading") that I'll suggest in the next chapter. For now, I want to show you how identifying parts of the structure—like the introduction—clarifies and applies our topic (context rules).

Every document has a beginning. Usually that beginning functions as an introduction to the material that follows. Of course, there is more than one type of introduction. Sometimes, the introduction simply starts the first point or episode of a story—it gets the ball rolling, so to speak.[3] Often, however, introductions act as a sort of summary-highlighting of some of the key ideas or themes that the author will develop in the pages to come.

The introduction—sometimes called the Prologue—of the Gospel of John provides a good example. Like an overture to a great opera or musical, John 1:1-18 artistically and powerfully encapsulates many of the dominant themes of the book. In this sense, the book is very deductive—that is, John tells us at the beginning what he wants to communicate to us in his Gospel, and his claims are extraordinary: "In the beginning was the Word, and the Word was with God, and the Word was God. . . ." He then uses the rest of the book to show or prove what he has said in the beginning: that Jesus is the Word of God made human; that through him we come to see and know God; that he is the light of the world, the expression of truth and grace; and that by believing in him, we can be born anew and receive (eternal) life: "But to all who received him, who believe in his name, he gave the power to become children of God, . . . born not of blood or of the will of the flesh or of the will of man, but of God" (1:12). In a sense, John shows us what his picture will look like in the beginning of his book. (Introductions sometimes function like miniature versions of the picture on the top of the box.)

Knowing this simple principle about the introduction and reading the book with the intention of putting it all together gives us immediate and clear insight into the purpose and message of John's Gospel. That's very important, isn't it? From the beginning, we can be sure that the book is about finding life through faith in Jesus Christ, who is the very expression (that is, "Word") of God. John confirms this interpretation at the end of the book (a typical function of conclusions) when he says, ". . . . But these are written so that you may come to believe that Jesus is the Messiah, the Son of God, and that through believing you may have life in his name" (20:31). When we read the Bible this way, we are learning to allow the context to rule over what we take away, as we should. And, since the context comes from God as part of the revealed message, isn't this equivalent to letting God's Spirit lead?

We'll look more in the next chapter at some specific keys or clues as to how the parts of a Bible book fit together. For now, let's look at one more example.

## Recurring Words and Themes

Another technique for putting together the puzzles of scripture (illustrating the idea that context rules) is the discovery of recurring words and themes. Just as important ideas and topics (sometimes called motifs) are sometimes introduced in the beginning of a biblical document, so those same themes recur and are developed at various points along the way. Continuing our example from John, the themes of the identity and nature of Jesus, light, life, and faith are clearly key ideas and are introduced in the Prologue (as we saw). You can find these words, then, scattered throughout the book, and on several striking occasions, they come together in repetitious, powerfully explanatory, fashion.

John 3:11-21 is a good example. This passage comes right after Jesus has talked with Nicodemus (a Pharisee who came to Jesus "at night"—is there a hint of the opposite of light?) about the need to be born again ("from above") in order to enter the kingdom of God (recall being born of God as a theme from the introduction quoted above). The text then underscores the "from above" or heavenly perspective of Jesus, who prophesies that he must be lifted up (referring to his own death), "that whoever believes in him may have eternal life." Here we see the connection with the two key themes of faith ("believes") and life. Then we find what is perhaps the most quoted verse of scripture: "For God so loved the world that he gave his only Son, so that everyone who believes in him may not perish but may have eternal life" (3:16). Now check out the repetition of our theme words and ideas (the identity and purpose of Jesus, faith/belief, life, light) in the following verses:

Indeed, God did not send the Son into the world to condemn the world, but in order that the world might be saved through him. Those who believe in him are not condemned; but those who do not believe are condemned already, because they have not believed in the name of the only Son of God. And this is the judgment, that the light has come into the world, and people loved darkness rather than light because their deeds were evil. For all who do evil hate the light and do not come to the light, so that their deeds may not be exposed. But those who do what is true come to the light, so that it may be clearly seen that their deeds have been done in God (3:17-21).

When we read this passage with an eye on the words and ideas that were introduced to us in the beginning of the book, the convergence and the connections of the themes become obvious. (John uses such summarizing paragraphs often: 3:31-36; 5:19-29, for example). This is an example of putting together the pieces of a Bible book, and these kind of "literary" observations, then, help us build the overall picture of the book and allow us to see how the parts fit together into a single, though multi-dimensional, picture. We can then know that we understand what we are reading within the context of John's overall message, meaning that context—and may I say, Spirit—rules.

## The Question

I've spoken often in the course of this book about a question that can help us know if we are understanding a passage of scripture within its own book-level context. How do we know that context rules in our own reading of scripture, which is the only way to be sure (that is, by letting the context rule) that we are getting what God intended to communicate to us? Answer: Ask (and try to answer) the question. So helpful is this question that I've anointed it "The Question." And here it is: How does this verse or set of verses fit and function within the overall context or picture of this book? Inkblotitis is the reading and use of verses of the Bible outside of their original contexts and purposes caused by using verses in small, disconnected sections. We often say we shouldn't do this, which amounts to a sort of lip-service, because after we say a thing or two about the book, we think we've put our verses into context. To see otherwise, all you have to do is try to answer The Question.

Take your favorite verse or group of verses, for example, and ask yourself how these verses help to communicate the primary messages of the book from which they came. What is the primary message or messages of that book? (*Do we want to know the major points from the books of God?*) What role or function, then, do these verses fill, in communicating those messages? Where do they fit in the overall picture of the book? Do you know? If not, then you don't know for sure if you're understanding the verses with the meaning the author intended. You've cut them loose, so to speak. You may be understanding them correctly, but you may not be. This is why The Question is so useful for us: it forces us to step back and consider the bigger purpose and meaning of a Bible book. It's a literary way of zooming out. It's like standing far enough away from a mosaic to see the intended image; or, for the over-forty crowd, like holding something far enough away from your eyes to be able to read it. John 3:16 provides a great example. The things we touched on above barely begin to show us the amazing picture from God within which this verse fits. Allowing the context to reveal that picture to us is not merely an educational or grammatical exercise. It is an intensely exciting and life-changing experience.

"Context rules" means that the context governs and controls the specific meaning of a word, sentence, paragraph, or even a chapter. When it comes to reading the Bible, it means that God spoke in certain times and places, with certain messages, within well-defined written contexts: books of the Bible. "Context rules" means that the God-inspired, book-level context controls the meaning of a verse or set of verses. This is where good Bible reading starts—it starts when God spoke. The Spirit revealed face of God comes slowly into focus. It continues as we listen: "Jesus answered, 'Very truly, I tell you, no one can enter the kingdom of God without being born of water and Spirit. What is born of flesh is flesh, and what is born of the Spirit is spirit. . . .'" (John 3:5-6).

In the next chapter . . . *Thou shalt create no inkblot!*

## The Ten Rules of Good Bible Reading

1. Read the whole book, preferably several times.
2. View the verses in book-level focus.
3. Discover the shape of the text.
4. Highlight recurring words and ideas.
5. Appreciate the differences of genre.
6. Tune in to the historical setting.
7. Use commentaries and other study tools with discretion.
8. Digest your experiences in the word.
9. Live what you've learned.
10. Do it again.

## Notes

1. See http://www.flickr.com/photos/atwatervillage/3293185353/in/photostream for a good picture with a more context-revealing focus.
2. W. Cleon Skousen, *The 5000 Year Leap: The 28 Great Ideas that Changed the World* (National Center for Constitutional Studies, 2006) 88-89.
3. Even such seemingly immediate or non-existent introductions where the story just seems to start usually have a degree of inductive orientation of the reader that may or may not be made explicit later. In some cases, the introduction isn't the first thing you read.

# Chapter 9

# Ten Rules of Good Bible Reading

Who should read the Bible? Who can understand it? Only a few specially trained and prepared church leaders? Preachers? Pastors? Priests? Scholars? Or to consider the question from another angle, for whom were the books of the Bible written?

Beginning in 1752, local diggers began finding them—old documents of all sorts, written on papyrus (ancient paper-like material made from the papyrus plant). The first was a library of an Epicurean philosopher, uncovered in Herculaneum, an old Roman town that had been buried by the eruption of Mount Vesuvius in 79 AD. Twenty-Six years later, native diggers found a group of 40 or 50 rolls in Egypt (probably in the Fayum, part of the ancient site of Crocodilopolis). Many of the subsequent finds also came from Egypt where the arid climate had preserved the documents. The Serapeum papyri were discovered in 1820, followed by a great mass of private documents in 1877.

The first major find of Greek papyri by archaeologists came at the hands of the British archaeologist Sir W. M. Flinders Petrie at Gurob in the Fayum (an oasis/basin region to the west of the Nile) in 1889. In 1897, about 120 miles south of Cairo, Bernard P. Grenfell and Arthur S. Hunt made an extraordinary discovery in an ancient rubbish heap at Behnesa. In the site known as Oxyrhynchus (now considered one of the most important archaeological sites in history), they found piles of old Roman office records that were in the process of being thrown out and burned. The fires smoldered but somehow went out, and the documents had been buried and preserved in the sand, some in the very baskets in which they were carried out to be burned—baskets full of first-hand witness to the life and times of these ancient people. For a century now, researchers have been finding and gathering the Oxyrhynchus Papyri. Similar discoveries continued, such that the number of published papyri is now staggering.[1]

People used to think that the New Testament was written in some sort of out-of-this-world God-language that some called "Holy Ghost Greek," the language and style of most of the books being so dramatically different from classical Greek literature. The late 18$^{th}$ and 19$^{th}$ century discoveries of thousands of ancient papyrus documents—letters, bills and receipts, records, leases, wills, legal documents, among other things[2]—buried in trash piles under the sands of Egypt opened the door for exciting new insights into New Testament writings. The work of Adolf Deissmann on the nonliterary letters of New Testament times helped to distill the findings into one of the most significant implications about the New Testament.[3] Beyond Tischendorf's discovery of codex Sinaiticus ("the treasure in the trash") in combined importance, these documents showed us that in large measure the language of the New Testament was the language of the people—the common people of the day. It was written in common—*koine*—Greek.[4] The New Testament was written by commoners for commoners.

For the most part, the language and style of the New Testament is that of everyday people, like you and me—some educated, some not. In 1863, even before the discovery of the papyri, with a sort of prophetic insight, Anglican Bishop Joseph B. Lightfoot anticipated these ideas:

> You are not to suppose that the word (some N.T. word which had its only classical authority in Herodotus) had fallen out of use in the interval, only that ilk had not been used in books which remain to us; probably it had been part of the common speech all along. I will go further and say that if we could only recover letters that ordinary people wrote to each other without any thought of being literary, we should have the greatest possible help for the understanding of the language of the New Testament generally.[5]

Though this statement has proven to be an exaggeration, as there are certainly "literary" features in the New Testament, the main thought is very important for us. Just as some of the first translators of the

Bible into English believed that the written word of God should be available to everyone, so reading/hearing and understanding the Bible is for everyone . . . because it always has been.

The Bible is a book of the people. It was written *by* ordinary people *for* ordinary people, but that doesn't mean its contents are ordinary. On the contrary, this is part of the marvel of divine inspiration. The books of God are indeed "out of this world" in meaning, purpose, and efficacy—Holy Spirit-breathed—but the words, literary shapes, and communication styles embrace and embody the normal, everyday ways of regular folks, living abnormal lives because they had come to know the Lord Jesus. How else could they have spoken to the people of that time? Like the incarnation of the Christ, the word became page and speaks among us: the books of God made present the Spirit of God to those who heard them originally and continue to mediate that same word of God to us today.[6]

Who should read the Bible? You and I—whoever has "ears to hear," as Jesus liked to say.

As we've seen, though, distance—time and culture—is not always friendly to this truth and our efforts. If the Bible is for everyone, but if it's sometimes hard to understand and we've ripped it apart into thousands of inkblots, how do we read it so as to give the verses and the chapters a fresh and a fair hearing? How do we read the Bible to get God's points? I've spent a great deal of time trying to convince you that we need to change the way we read the Bible. That's why I've written this book. But if that's the case, if reading and using random verses (which often function) as spiritual inkblots really is a problem in Christianity, if there is a better way, what is it? We're now switching to that positive goal.

How do I read the Bible so as not to turn verses into inkblots? How do I read to hear the voice of God, as distinguished from all the other voices in my world and in my head—voices just waiting for a chance to capture and redirect breezes from heaven into their own self-invigorating images and currents of influence? The answer is simple: by reading (and experiencing) the books of God—prayerfully, carefully, and completely—from beginning to end.

# Rules 1-3 of Good Bible Reading

These are not really *rules* so much as they are principles and guidelines and tools. I use the word "rule" mainly to suggest the importance of these sorts of things and to complete our double use of the word from the last chapter. In the last chapter ("Context Rules"), we used the word "rule" as a verb; we now shift to a list of important considerations ("rules") for how we read. Though I have no desire to tell everyone how they have to read their Bibles, I strongly desire to help people understand the written word of God and to participate in a revival of Bible reading—of hearing the voice of the supreme Rule-Maker through scripture. To that end, I'll continue to use the word "rule" as we talk about some important dos and don'ts of good Bible reading.

## The First Thing: Check Your Motives

Before launching into a list of things to do when it comes to reading our Bibles, there's something we must consider. It makes a big difference in what we get out of the Bible. It's a very important application of the earlier chapter called "The Ways We Read the Bible," and it's a precondition for effective Bible reading. To put it simply: check your motives. To say it more positively: seek God honestly and fervently in scripture. This is the foundation—the first principle of good Bible reading. Like building a house on sand, without this, the other recommendations don't matter much.

Don't misunderstand. That doesn't mean you shouldn't read if your motives aren't always completely clear or perfectly pure—none of us are. Read regardless. Examining our motives is, however, an ongoing necessity and should help to clear away some of the weighty control of old habits and thinking when it comes to our approach to the Bible. Then, above our perception of our motives and impediments, by all means start with God, start with prayer. How better to seek the mind and heart of God than by asking him to help? If God didn't want to help us, he wouldn't have done so much to offer himself to us and give us his written word. So before we open God's books and begin to read, let's turn our hearts toward him, honestly, sincerely, reverently, fervently, excitedly, expectantly, and prayerfully. This is the first thing.

More on this shortly. But first, a heads up.

When it comes to the rules of good Bible reading, starting especially with Rule #3, the discussion may at times begin to sound more technical and academic. For those who want it, this can serve as a starting point to go beyond the things in this book. For others, please don't let this scare or discourage you. If something doesn't make much sense, then don't worry about it. Just keep reading (and you may want to come back to it later). Many of the things I'm about to say are just different ways (more specific, in-depth, and sometimes "scholarly") of expressing and applying the principles we're discussing. Some things will likely seem odd or even difficult simply because they're different from what you're used to. Again, keep reading and don't let that bother you. *You do not have to become a scholar to seek God in scripture*—only a listener and learner (isn't that what a disciple is?). Remember, the rules are just tools (except maybe the first two)—good tools, I believe—but just tools to help you read and understand the Bible in context. But—and this is an important "but"—you don't need any of my rules to do that, and there are other tools. What you need is a heart that seeks after God in his word. I never want to come across as "preaching a method" over the Person who is the Word of God.

This brings us back to the first principle of good Bible reading: our hearts. If seeking God is your goal, your real motivation for reading the Bible (not to prove a point or reinforce something you already think and believe), then I believe God will deliver. He always does. He will be with you, guide you, and draw near to you as you seek him. This is why God has given so much to make his word available to us. This is why he poured forth his Spirit in days gone by through the nation of Israel, and the writers and prophets of the Old Testament. This is why he sent his Son to reveal to us the Word of God in living color (to borrow an old television phrase). This is why he inspired the writers of the New Testament and delivered these messages of truth, justice, forgiveness, and love in various times and places. This is why he preserved the texts of scripture against all odds and why he motivated men and women to bleed and burn and die so we could read it in our languages today. Never doubt God's resolve to find and know you. And never, ever, doubt that God wants *you* to know *him*, that he awaits you, and will draw near to you with love and strength beyond all barriers.

So please don't let tools and rules and technical discussion ever discourage you. God wants you, and you want him. That's what matters. When you read the Bible, ask God to show you himself—time and experience in the word then promises sights (and insights) more vivid and beautiful than anything you've ever seen.

Okay, here we go. Rule #1 . . .

## Rule #1: Read the whole book, preferably several times.

The first practice or *to-do* of good Bible reading is to read the whole book—not the whole Bible (we'll do that over time), but the book you are reading, like Genesis or Matthew or Ephesians. This is the only way to prevent and to treat inkblotitis. It's the only way to position ourselves to hear what God has said and to know that we are getting his main points, and then to seek to apply them to our lives in a way that makes us like Jesus Christ.

God is a big God. In fact, that's what makes him God. But make no mistake; God is also God of the little things, of the details, as Jesus taught us: he knows when every bird falls to the ground, he clothes the lilies of the fields better than kings of the earth, and he knows the number of hairs on each of our heads (which isn't saying much in my case). But the sparrow only knows things about the sparrow. Taking care of sparrow things consumes her day—only seeing beyond her nest and duties to the extent that such needs are programmed within her. In contrast, one of the main things that makes God the creator and Lord of the universe is that he sees (and authors) the big picture—the biggest picture of all—and he knows how all the details fit together to create that picture. *The more we see the big picture, then, the more we are like God. This is a huge point because so much of our stress, turmoil, and even failures grow out of our focus on the small and the momentary.*

The books of the Bible were written to make several major points—to teach several important lessons about God and his will—to the people to whom they were written (and by extension to us). Sometimes you can sum them up in a single, powerful, life-altering statement. (And what is that point? Do you know what God would have you know from the book of Matthew? Mark? What about Revelation?) History—real circumstances, real people, real ink—gave them birth. They were (and are) inspired by God to help real people, struggling with the same kind of questions as we do today. Now here's the 64-gazillion dollar, soul-searching, life-altering, spirit-quaking question: when we read the Bible . . . (Let's make it more personal.) When *I* read the Bible, do I come away knowing and

51

seeking to apply the most important points made in each book? Do I get the messages that God intended to communicate to us? . . . the Spirit-inspired ideas that the authors intended for the original readers to hear and be changed by? When I read, do I see the big-picture and shape my life in conformity with that picture? Or do I get lost in the details of individual passages or verses or distractions?

The nature of the books of the Bible—the reality that God inspired them within historical contexts and motivated their authors to write with words and sentences and paragraphs and books to a living group of people to help them deal with real life circumstances—suggests that they communicate a limited number of teachings and make a limited number of points. Does that make sense? Let me say it again. Each book of the Bible contains a finite or limited set of thoughts about God (each represents only a partial view of God). *It's important to realize that not every valid and important spiritual truth is revealed in every chapter or every book.* No one would claim such a thing, yet we read as if they do (this is what a mystical approach to Bible reading implies). The books seek to deal with a limited number of focused questions and issues—not anything that our minds might leap to or conjure up . . . This demands that they have one or more dominant, over-arching purposes. This is the reality of Bible books (and human thought in general).

And do I know—do you know—what those messages from God are? The more we see and get the big-picture of each book of the Bible, the more we can know that we are seeing and thinking like God. The more we do not see the big picture—the primary points and purposes of each book—the less we can be sure we are hearing from God (instead of protecting ourselves). The less we see the big picture, the more each verse becomes an inkblot: the more we do not see the main points of Bible books, the more the enemy can use the very words of scripture to distract and deceive us. The more we are distracted, the greater the chances of one day looking around and simply not knowing where we are—of being lost.

There is nothing more important when it comes to reading the Bible than this: *read the whole book so you can get the whole picture.* Because of our fast-paced lifestyles, limited schedules and memories—things like that—I suggest that reading the whole book in order to get the big picture probably means (in actuality) reading it multiple times and perhaps in more than one version (we'll talk about what version to use next). For now, Rule #1 of good Bible reading is to throw away the verses and immerse yourself in the words and setting of the book before you. In short, read the book. We do this, using our puzzle analogy, so we can get a look at the overall, put-together picture.

**Rule #1 in short: Read the book.**

# The Version Question

Rule #1 (read the whole book, preferably several times) immediately raises the question of version: what translation or version of the Bible should I use? This is a good question, and the answer involves a little knowledge about the nature and types of Bible translations.

There are two main types of Bible translations,[7] along with a third that's a combination of translation and commentary. The first is called a *literal translation*. A literal translation attempts to keep as much of the original wording (translated consistently), word order (syntax), and verb tenses as possible. It's sometimes called a word-for-word translation. The goal is to make the English version look as much like the original as possible and still make sense in English. Several of the older, classic translations, like the King James and the American Standard Versions, lean more toward the literal side. Preference for literal translations comes from a respect for the inspiration of the text, recognition that the original (that is, inspired) version of Bible books was not in English, and a desire to leave matters of interpretation in the hands of the readers (not the translators). The biggest advantages of a literal version, in my opinion, are (1) help in identifying key words and ideas, since Hebrew and Greek words are usually translated by the same English words; and (2) help in finding structural patterns (more on this below) for those who want to delve into the text, but who don't read Greek or Hebrew. The obvious weakness of a literal translation is readability—it sometimes makes for awkward and almost unintelligible English.

The second type is called an *idiomatic*, functional or *dynamic equivalent translation*. The goal here is to express the meaning of the original in the clearest way possible in the receptor or target language (the language being translated into). In other words, to put it into the idioms (the way we say it) of those who will be reading it. This is sometimes called a thought-for-thought or sense-for-sense translation. Many modern versions lean more toward dynamic or functional equivalence, translating at the sentence or thought level and expressing the meaning in the clearest and most readable English style.

Preference for this type of translation comes from the purpose of translating as an effort to communicate the meaning and intent of the original language to a modern English reader. The obvious advantage of this style of translation is readability and the potential to reproduce some of the rhetorical and artistic characteristics of the original, which is difficult in a literal version. Its weaknesses are (1) perhaps a heightened dependency on the translators to understand accurately what they are translating (which is really a basic tenet of any good translation, though admittedly more challenging with biblical material) and (2) the potential loss of purposeful repetition and redundancy, as these were common components of ancient languages (of oral cultures) but conflict with elements of good English style.

A third type of English version is called a *free translation* or *paraphrase*. In a free translation, the author takes liberties that go beyond the actual content of the original, in an effort to interpret and clarify the meaning. These versions are, therefore, a mixture of translation and commentary, and are technically not translations, but something more. That's why they're called paraphrases, and they're usually done by just one or a few scholars. Examples include *The Living Bible* (Ken Taylor), *The New Testament in Modern English* (J. B. Phillips), and *The Message* (Eugene Peterson). I recommend saving these versions until after you've done your own work in the text (see Rule #8 below).

Reading level is another characteristic of Bible translations—that is, what grade or skill level it requires to read and understand. Some versions target a very young or less skilled reader, like the *New International Readers Bible* and *New Century Bible* ($3^{rd}$ grade), while others (*New Revised Standard Version, New American Standard Version, King James Version*) require an $11^{th}$ or $12^{th}$ grade reading level. (An internet search of "Bible versions reading level" will give complete lists of reading levels.) This obviously makes a difference in what version a person should choose.

In summary, we have two major types of English translations to pick from: (1) literal or formal equivalence (made to look like the original) and (2) idiomatic or functional equivalence (made to function or communicate like the original). Because languages are dynamic and complex, neither of these methods of translating is possible in a perfect/ideal sense. In reality, all translations have a degree of both, but there are clear differences between translations that focus on one approach or the other.[8] Since every version is a little different and translation is sometimes more of an art than a science, we can say that English versions of the Bible fall on a spectrum or scale of literal versus free. The following chart shows the general idea (the chart isn't meant to be precise, but merely to give you a vantage point on this difference):

| Literal | | Mixed/Balanced | | | | | Free |
|---|---|---|---|---|---|---|---|
| ASV/NASB | KJV/NKJV | NRSV | NIV/TNIV | NET | ICB/NCV | TEV/GNT GW | TM |
| ESV | RSV | HCSV NAB | | JB/NJB | NEB/REB | NLT NIrV JBP CEV | LB |

| | | | |
|---|---|---|---|
| KJV | King James Version (1611/1769) | NKJV | New King James Version (1982) |
| ASV | American Standard Version (1901) | NASB | New American Standard Bible (1971/1995) |
| RSV | Revised Standard Version (1952) | NRSV | New Revised Standard Version (1989) |
| JBP | J. B. Phillips, The New Testament in Modern English (1958/1972) | | |
| NEB | New English Bible (1970) | REB | Revised English Bible (1989) |
| NAB | New American Bible (1970, ongoing) | | |
| LB | The Living Bible (1971) | | |
| TEV | Today's English Version (1976) | GNT | Good News Translation (1992) |
| NIV | New International Version (1984) | TNIV | Today's New International Version (2001/2005) |
| ICB | International Children's Bible (1986) | NCV | New Century Version (1991) |
| JB | Jerusalem Bible (1966) | NJB | New Jerusalem Bible (1985) |
| CEV | Contemporary English Version (1995) | | |
| GW | God's Word (1995) | | |
| NIrV | New International Reader's Version (1996) | | |
| NLT | New Living Translation (1996/2004) | | |
| TM | The Message (1993-2002) | | |
| ESV | English Standard Version (2001) | | |
| HCSV | Holman Christian Standard Version (2004) | | |
| NET | New English Translation Bible (online translation) (2005) | | |

"So what version should I use?" I'd like to make two general suggestions. The first is that, depending on your immediate purposes according to the rules of good Bible reading, you use both types: a dynamic equivalent translation for reading with an eye on the big picture (like when you want to read the book as a whole) and a literal translation when you want to focus on specific words and structure (more about this in upcoming rules)—thus, a *zoom out* and a *zoom in* version. Of course, the specific version is up to you, but, for a literal version, the NASB is a traditional standard. For a recent literal version, the English Standard Version (ESV) is quickly becoming a favorite of some serious Bible students. Any of the freer translations (but not the paraphrases) could serve as a fun-to-read, big-picture version—the New Living Translation (NLT) is the "pew-," or in our case, "chair-Bible" of the church I attend. I've chosen to use the New Revised Standard Version (NRSV) for most of the scripture citations in this book, though I'm partial to the New International Version (NIV) for my own English reading. My second recommendation is that, if you plan to use only one or one primary version, you choose something in the middle of the literal-free scale, like the NRSV, the NIV/TNIV, or the REB. These middle-of-the-road, dynamic equivalent versions can be both readable and useful for some detailed work as well.

# Rule #2: Understand the verses in relation to the book as a whole.

Like the first, the second rule of good Bible reading is rather broad and basic; nevertheless, it's tremendously important. In fact, if you had to boil this book down to one primary, most-important point—the one thing that above all others would make the most difference in your Bible reading and in your life—if you remember one thing, it's this: read and understand each verse of the Bible, not as an isolated, independent, and individual thought, but as it relates to the book as a whole—that is, within its book-level context. Put briefly: *Book-level focus the verses.* Or even more briefly: *Zoom out.* This is the difference between trying to interpret a single piece of a disassembled puzzle and inserting that piece into the puzzle. Like our amazingly complex physical bodies, each verse may have a special purpose, but the verses all connect and work together to give us life and health.

We need to learn to read and understand the individual verses of scripture as part of their book-level contexts. We need to insert them rather than disconnect them. I've tried to say this numerous ways, perhaps to the point of redundancy and boredom—ad nauseam, some might say. But I have done so because *learning to read the Bible in context is the crucial point on which the whole discussion and approach to Bible reading hangs.* This is the bulls-eye of how to get God's point when we read the Bible. We've said it for years; we just don't do it, and we don't know how to do it. Reading in context gives birth to The Question: how does this verse or group of verses fit into the overall picture of the book? Like looking at a picture over the fireplace, we want to see the individual elements of the document as contributing to the picture as a whole, not as isolated messages, with distinct or unrelated meanings. It's one thing to say that and something else to do it.

The ability to interpret a verse of scripture as it relates to the book as a whole—within its book-level context—is not altogether unlike what we all learn to do when we work with maps online. It's easy to find almost anywhere in the world—a city, a zip code, a street, even a house. And then when we want a bigger view, that's easy, too: just zoom out. We can then see where in the world our particular place is, where it fits on a bigger map. Zoom in . . . zoom out.

This idea of zooming in and out is vital to our ability to hear God's word in context. Problem is that most of us have no framework for zooming. We don't know what the big picture looks like. Our lack of Bible knowledge—a form of biblical illiteracy—is the culture in which inkblotitis is born and spreads. What would it be like if you could find a street or city map, but it wasn't contextualized in a bigger-picture map? What if every city had no reference point within the state? Even if you found where you were, you wouldn't know where you are or how far from anywhere else. That's absurd, isn't it? Lost we would be—absolutely and perpetually. Yet this is what we do with verses of the Bible. Learning to zoom out and then back in to interpret verses of scripture is the secret, then, to solving our issues with contextless Bible quoting and reading. In other words—and this is the heart of Rule #1 and #2—*don't zoom in until you have zoomed out* (except, of course, as you read). The ability to zoom out is one of the most important new habits that we need to develop in our personal Bible study. This is why we started with Rule #1: we start by zooming out so that we have a framework and a context within which to focus the meaning of the chapters and verses (Rule #2).

Reading in context is so fundamental and so basic that, as I've said, it's usually assumed—everyone will say it and agree to it and then move on—and yet it's the most grossly violated principle of listening to God in scripture. Reading in context is a fundamental principle of language and literature. What's different about what I'm proposing—and it's radically different in its overall effect—is that we need to go beyond a cursory connection of a verse or group of verses with a sentence or two before and after (the immediate context) and then think we're reading "in context." This is like zooming out only slightly (a click or two). Our context is bigger than that. The context is the book as a whole. It provides the surroundings and control over the meaning of the verses.

The most critical principle for learning to read in context is, therefore, to get a sense, a view, of the bigger picture, to take several steps back and see each verse and each chapter of the Bible in the context/picture of the book as a whole. To read, not just "in context," but "within its book-level context." A small change in wording—a radical change in result. To zoom out, all the way—this is, in my opinion, the lifeline of a Spirit-filled and Spirit-led approach to Bible reading.

If this is so important, why don't we do it? Why haven't we been taught to do it? In a word: Inkblotitis. It's basically what we talked about in the first half of the book, and especially in the chapters "Why It's Hard to Understand the Bible" and "Diagnosis: Inkblotitis." Major changes in history, culture, language, motivation, and religious beliefs make out-of-context reading (inkblotitis) easier and more convenient. (And it fits our culture—like eating spiritual French fries.) Spiritual forces fan the flames, and inkblotitis has won the day. Inkblotitis is Christianity's unrecognized, deadly disease—even among pastors and spiritual leaders—which is why we're taking the time to look together at these principles of good Bible reading. Reading and understanding verses within their book-level contexts isn't always easy, as you know; though fundamental and critical, Rule #2 is easier said than done. I don't say that to discourage you—that's the opposite of my goal—but to encourage you to use all the rules of good Bible reading to change the way you read and build habits that will make this sort of reading automatic. Once you get used to it, it's not that difficult. We just have to learn to think "zoom out": zoomed-out Bible reading (ZOBR).

So in summary: When it comes to the best way for us to read the Bible, we start with two over-arching, fundamental principles (in this case, imperatives): (1) read the whole book . . . in order to see the big picture and (2) see (that is, interpret) the parts (the verses) as part of that picture—in relation to the whole. In other words, view the verses in book-level focus. Or, from a negative perspective and to underscore its significance in relation to our subject as a whole: *thou shalt create no inkblot.* Combining Rules 1 and 2: see the picture, get the point. Zoom out, then zoom in. On this, hang all the rules and exhortations (all the tools, books, commentaries, study guides, degrees, etc.) of good Bible reading.

**Rule #2 in short: View the verses in book-level focus.**

# Rule #3: Discover the structure or "shape" of the text.

In literature, words form sentences, which then form groups of sentences or paragraphs, which then form larger blocks of thought, like chapters and sections. A writer puts together the words according to rules of language and grammar. He or she then organizes or arranges (puts together) the sentences, paragraphs, and larger units according to the intentions and purposes of the document. In other words, written documents use order and design at various levels to accomplish their purposes. In *English Comp 101*, we learn how to plan a document by constructing a purpose or thesis statement and then an outline to organize and guide our thought. We do this because design—structure and structures—is inherent in written and spoken discourse. Like blueprints in architecture, flow-charts in computer programming, schematics in electronics, corporate vision and mission statements in business, effective writing requires intelligent design.

Now, let's replace the word "structure" with the word "shape." We don't usually use the word "shape" in this context, do we? We use phrases like "sentence structure" (remember diagraming sentences?) or "organizational structure" (outline) to construct and analyze a piece of writing. By a slight shift of perspective, however, I think the word "shape" can help us (it doesn't seem as academic or technical sounding).[9] For our purposes, I'm using the word "shape" to get our minds around the ideas of structure and literary design without sounding like we have to become grammarians or literary critics. Like building blocks in a youngster's playroom creations, the paragraphs and sections of a document go together to produce its overall design and effect.

Bible books—like all intelligible written documents—have shapes and use shapes (literary structure and organizational principles) to communicate their divine messages. Learning to see the overall shape of a text and how smaller shapes (units of material) fit together to produce complex yet integrated messages is a powerful tool for seeing the intended purposes of a book and thus preparing ourselves to connect with the heart of God in his first conversations with his people.

Before we look closer at some techniques for discovering the design of a book, I'd like to illustrate the point that books of the Bible have inherent design by pointing to a couple of examples: one from ancient letter-writing and another from ancient speech-making (classical Greek rhetoric). These common, classical shapes have clearly affected the design of Paul's letters.

## The Shape of Paul's Letters

As we saw in the beginning of the chapter, people used to think that the New Testament was written in some sort of special language of the Holy Spirit, since it was different from what we knew about other writings of the time. The discovery of the non-literary papyri changed all that. Now we know that the Bible was written in the common language and forms of the day. From a long history of the study of the papyrus documents and other letters of the time, valuable insights into the nature and designs of ancient Greek letters have emerged. A whole branch of New Testament scholarship (that I call Epistolary Criticism) has grown up around these findings.

Gleaned from the study of ancient letter-writing, various practices and conventions of the time illuminate the structure and shapes of New Testament letters, and in particular the letters of Paul. Combining these insights with Paul's own habits produces a fairly consistent picture of the shape of Paul's letters. From reading the letters themselves, it's easy to observe that the core or body usually has two major sections: an informational or theological first half and a more ethical or application-centered second half (the letters often, then, have two halves). Adding the openings and closings begins to reveal a shape. Though all of Paul's letters vary in structure and purpose (some do not contain all the elements, while others repeat several of them), a combined review produces the following theoretical shape:

63

Prescript (Address and Greeting)
Thanksgiving
Information (Disclosure)
Transitional Prayer
Request (Petition)
Exhortations
Transitional Prayer
Closing

The specifics are not important here (we'll talk about these more when we look into the shapes of the various parts). What I want you to see now is that—as we would expect—Paul's letters have an overall structure and design.

Similar to what we see in Paul's letters, ancient rhetoricians taught the importance of "arrangement" in the make-up of an effective speech. Next to Invention (the process of discovering or "inventing" the material/content necessary for a speech), Arrangement was, in fact, the second major division in classical Greek rhetorical theory. After gathering everything necessary to write the speech, the orator was to structure the material with utmost care into the most effect means for achieving the rhetorical ends. As Quintilian (approximately 35–100 AD), Roman author of a 12-volume textbook on rhetoric, put it, without arrangement, the results of invention would merely form a "useless," "confused heap."[10] Though no one speech would likely contain all the potential divisions or parts, an ideal speech might be arranged like this:

Introduction (*exordium*) or Proem (*prooimion*)
Narrative (*narratio*) with or without a . . .
    Proposition (*prothesis*),
    Partition (*partitio*) or Division (*divisio*),
Proof (*pistis, probatio*),
    Refutation (*refutatio, confutatio*),
Conclusion (*conclusio, peroratio*) or Epilogue (*epilogos*)

Although the names of the sections might not readily show it, there is considerable overlap between the arrangement taught in the ancient rhetorical handbooks and the usual structure of Paul's letters. Some of the overlap is doubtless due to the basic nature of effective communication (there are some things you just have to do/say to be understood)—that is, to common sense. Since most writings of biblical times were intended to be read to a listening audience and thus to be heard, the affinities with how to make a good speech seem natural enough. When we consider that Paul was an educated man of his time and that his hometown of Tarsus was a center of rhetorical training, it's likely that a real overlap existed between Paul's habits of letter-writing and the ancient principles of making and arranging a good speech.

The important point for us is to begin to realize that, like all written documents, Bible books have structure—natural, sometimes sophisticated, sometimes simple, intentional structure. The structure is their shape.

## Putting Together the Puzzles of Scripture

Using the words "shape" and how a text is "put together" to refer to the ideas of organization and structure quickly reminds us of our puzzle analogy, and I believe the concept of a puzzle and of putting together a puzzle has a lot of potential for helping us with our quest for understanding a Bible book. I use it, then, to help explain several of the principles of good Bible reading. Looking back on the first two rules, the connections are easy.

First, reading the whole book, possibly several times (Rule #1) is an effort to get some sense of what the finished product looks like. Unfortunately, Bible books don't come with their pieces placed neatly into a single, separate box, with a picture of the finished product on the outside (at least not for most of us). On the contrary, we've broken them up into lots of pieces, mixed with pieces from other Bible books (and various other ideas and influences). The only pictures we have are those in our heads and in books; those we have constructed from years of teachings, inside and outside of churches; individual verses and sets of verses that remind us of deeply entrenched and sacred things when we hear them. And we each have our own very complex sets of pictures. As we talked about earlier, this is part of the cause and effect of inkblotitis. *The disintegration of the Bible into thousands of verses, reassembled in our personal psyches according to a myriad of beliefs and feelings is equivalent to mixing up all the pieces of Bible books (puzzles) and throwing away the boxes. The first rule of good Bible reading lays claim to the idea that each book has its own unique picture—a divinely inspired snapshot of planet-earth reality and a vision of how life can and ought to be under the reign of God.* Reading the whole book—even more, learning the whole book—is how we come to know what the finished product is supposed to look like. It's how we put the picture back on the box and into the soul of our spiritual imaginations.

Rule #2 (interpret the verses as they fit in the overall picture, zoom out before you zoom in) depends on Rule #1 and makes a profound difference on our ability to really know what a verse is about. Here the puzzle analogy is particularly effective. Without repeating the earlier illustration, let me just remind you that you can pass many puzzle pieces around a room and get all sorts of opinions about their meaning, different views of what they are a picture. Put the puzzle together, however. Point to a single piece within the picture as a whole, and almost everyone in the room agrees on its meaning—its place or function—within the overall picture. See the picture, get the point. The piece doesn't stand on its own. Alone, it's an inkblot; inserted and connected, it has purpose and meaning.

Now, back to the concept of "shapes." As you know, puzzle pieces have shape—all sorts of strange and wonderful shapes. One piece is constructed so as to connect to or fit into another piece. The shapes create the connectivity. We could also say that the pieces and the overall picture have structure, but that's not the way we think or talk about puzzles. I'm borrowing the word "shape," then, to keep our puzzle analogy active and to keep us from feeling like we're back in *English* or *Greek 101*. Once we've put together various sections of the puzzle from pieces that look alike (theme, color, etc.), we then have bigger shapes (sections), with all sorts of potential connections to the other shapes (sections). This is very similar to what I'm suggesting we can do when it comes to reading books of the Bible. Each verse is, in a sense, its own shape. These shapes connect with other verses to form larger units, which then fit together to create the overall shape or structure of the book as a whole. You've probably seen outlines of Bible books, frequently found at the beginning of a commentary or study guide. This is similar to what I'm talking about, only what we're doing is more dynamic—more important and more fun.

Starting with the overall shape (structure or outline) of the text (there is a sense in which we are working backwards from the whole to the meaning of the parts), Rule #3 for good Bible reading calls for us to begin to learn to see the curves, contours, and resulting shapes of Bible passages, and to focus on how they fit together to produce the combined picture. We start with the overall arrangement of the book: we are learning to discover the design of the text. To be more concrete, let me give you some specific ways of starting that discovery. These are sub-divisions—the four steps—of Rule #3. The first: start with the beginning and the end. The second: explore the design of what's between—the core or heart of the document. The third: zoom in on the connections. And the fourth: figure out the purpose of the sections.

# Step 1 (of Rule #3):
# Find the Introduction and the Conclusion.

*Discover the shape of the text . . . by finding the Introduction and Conclusion.* Almost all extended forms of communication have beginnings and endings that function as Introductions and Conclusions (I capitalize these at times to emphasize their importance as integral parts of various genres). This is certainly true in written literature and in books of the Bible. Finding and analyzing the Introduction and Conclusion of a book thus becomes a tremendous tool for ascertaining the main points and possibly some direction as to how the messages apply to our lives.

## Introductions

My family fusses at me sometimes when we go to watch a movie 'cause I often make observations about how the story is constructed. "Shhh! Can't we just watch the movie?" they moan. What they don't get is that noticing the design doesn't detract from the experience for me; it helps me appreciate the artistry of the writers and editors. (I guess noticing it and talking about it while they're trying to enjoy the show are two different things, though. I shouldn't ruin their experience!) I'm attentively attuned to how a show starts; like, for example, when the camera zooms in on a beautiful lady pouring a half-empty drink down the drain and wiping off the glasses before we know anything about anything, teasing us with immediate questions of who and why and what happened. Modern cinematographic introductions can be excitingly complex or sweetly simple. The point is that writers have to create an experience that the audience can understand—we have to get the point in some fashion, at some time—or the story won't be a story at all. The Introduction prepares us for that experience.

Though most independent pieces of literature—in this case, books of the Bible—have introductions of some sort, they vary greatly in style and content. Some are deductive: they tell you the main ideas right up front. Others—usually narrative or story form—are inductive: they make you wait or force you to figure it out on your own. The common element is that all Introductions get the audience (the reader, the listener, the watcher) ready for what is to follow. In this sense, Introductions are preparatory. Exactly what members of the audience need to be ready for and how the author gets them there depends on the particular goals of the experience (from the viewpoints of the writer and the audience). Sometimes an audience needs to get ready thematically—that is, there are important subjects to be presented and discussed, and the writer wants you to know what they are. Other times, an audience needs to be prepared psychologically and emotionally—that is, you may need to be conditioned to receive what is about to be said: you might not agree with it or think it important. Usually, it's a degree of both. So, in a sense, the audience needs to be prepared both intellectually and emotionally.

As we noticed in the Gospel of John, a common form of Introduction contains a sort of listing of the conclusions or main points of a text. Paul does this frequently in his letters in the opening section called the "Thanksgiving." (Did you know that Paul's Thanksgiving Prayers were Introductions? More on this later.) For example, the Thanksgiving of Ephesians explicitly lists the subjects about to be covered: "I pray . . . that you may know [1] what is the hope to which he has called you, [2] what are the riches of his glorious inheritance among the saints, and [3] what is the immeasurable greatness of his power for us who believe . . ." (1:17-19). As I mentioned earlier, I refer to these—the hope of his calling, the riches of his inheritance, and the greatness of his power—as the triadic themes of Ephesians. (Do you know the primary points and purposes of the book of Ephesians? This introductory listing of themes can help you pinpoint and grasp them.)

Rather than a listing of themes, an Introduction can simply be the first part of a story. More often than not, however, it provides the part that gives you the appropriate background information, preparing you for and bringing you up to the beginning of the "real" story. This type of Introduction will often—though not always—contain key thematic elements to be developed as part of the story, or it will surface underlying values on which critical points or decisions turn. These preparatory features can sometimes be subtle and even implicit. On rare occasions, the Introduction will contain neither themes nor background information, but simply be the first episode of a series of things to come. In such cases, the real "Introduction" comes later or is scattered piecemeal throughout the text or story. Sometimes, we have to be "caught up" or given background information later (this is called exposition).

For our purposes, after you have read an entire Bible book (preferably several times), finding and focusing on the Introduction often gives considerable insight into what the book is all about. It makes sense, doesn't it? The writer is going to introduce what's important to him, and isn't that what we want to know?

## Conclusions

Similar things can be said about Conclusions. Almost every written document has some kind of ending or conclusion that makes the point(s) of the text in a summarizing, dramatic or practical way. The Conclusion puts on the finishing touches, so to speak. Conclusions do this by reminding, extolling, highlighting and amplifying, or applying the key ideas of a text. Their purpose is to remind, to summarize, to motivate, to wrap things up and bring them to a close. Whereas Introductions are preparatory, Conclusions are by nature concluding or finalizing.

Like Introductions, Conclusions contain both intellectual and emotional features. Summation and recapitulation are common. In other words, whereas Introductions tell us what we're about to hear, Conclusions sum up what we just heard. As the last chance for the writer to make his or her case, moreover, Conclusions often contain a heightened sense of passion and rhetorical flare. The language becomes more grandiose and at times emotional. As an important part of persuasion, Classical Greek rhetoricians taught that the

Conclusion of a speech was the place where free rein was to be given to the emotions in a final attempt to persuade the audience.

For example, think about the image of the soldier at the end of Ephesians (6:10-17), receiving the armor of God, piece by piece, to be used to stand against the deceptive schemes of the real enemy. What a powerful image! With that image, Paul graphically exhorts us to stand, and to do so with the empowering pieces of the armor of God. The passion of the scene is fairly obvious, though perhaps not always presented as passionately in sermons or Bible studies. As a conclusion, moreover, we often forget the summarizing aspect. In other words, the pieces of armor artistically remind us (in shortened form) of the things the author has discussed in the previous parts of the book. Did you catch that? The shield of faith . . . the shoes of peace . . ., etc., relate to and encapsulate important themes of Ephesians. Or, for another biblical example, think of the power and impact of the Conclusions of the Gospels—the world-altering story of the resurrection of Jesus and the sending out of the disciples with the good news.

Like Introductions, Conclusions vary in style and content. They often summarize and bring together some of the most important points, but they do so with colorful variety: they may apply the key ideas to life, look to the potential difference such things will make, or give one last plea to the audience to do what has been asked. The potential is limitless. But there is a commonality. By nature, the purpose of a Conclusion is to end the communication, to wrap things up, and in some way bring the point or message home. In some ways, then, the Conclusion can be seen as the most important part—the climax. It's the writer's last chance to make his or her case, to motivate the readers to action, and to accomplish the purposes of the text. How important for us, then, are Conclusions in books of the Bible?

## The Corner Pieces: Ruth as an Example

Going back to our puzzle analogy . . . When you first start to work on a puzzle, what do you do? After dumping out the pieces and examining the picture on the box (not necessarily in that order), most people look for the corner pieces and the straight edges. They have distinctive shapes that make them easier to find and routine places in the design of the puzzle, characteristics that get us started and guide us in connecting the other pieces. Introductions and Conclusions of Bible books can have a similar function. In fact, I'd like to brand them "the corner pieces." The corner pieces literally surround and establish the boundaries of a puzzle. So do Introductions and Conclusions in a literary sense.

The Old Testament book of Ruth provides a good example of an Introduction that tells the first part of a story, but at a much faster pace than what follows (typical of introductory and summary material) and in such a way as to evoke intent-relevant values in the original audience.

> In the days when the judges ruled, there was a famine in the land, and a certain man of Bethlehem in Judah went to live in the country of Moab, he and his wife and two sons. The name of the man was Elimelech and the name of his wife Naomi, and the names of his two sons were Mahlon and Chilion; they were Ephrathites from Bethlehem in Judah. They went into the country of Moab and remained there. But Elimelech, the husband of Naomi, died, and she was left with her two sons. These took Moabite wives; the name of the one was Orpah and the name of the other Ruth. When they had lived there about ten years, both Mahlon and Chilion also died, so that the woman was left without her two sons and her husband (Ruth 1:1-5).

Knowing the story that follows, this is a fascinating and artful Introduction. Its conciseness and matter-of-fact directness supplies some of its potency. Its indirectness provides the rest.

I'll highlight a few things. First, notice that in summary fashion, the Introduction prepares us for the story that follows by giving background to Naomi and Ruth's return from Moab and the events that follow. But that's not all: the author packs the brief Introduction with informative and value-laden descriptors of the people and places that mark the beginning of the story. The names and places provide immediate information about the family, not least of which is an association with the heartland and value-system of Judaism. The first sentence succinctly summarizes a critical action: during the time of the Judges (a turbulent and difficult time in the history of Israel), in a time of famine, a man from Bethlehem (means "house of bread") of Judah took his family to live in the country of Moab. In Hebrew, the man's name, *Elimelech*, means "My God is King." Not just Jews, but more specifically "Ephrathites" (perhaps an old name for Bethlehem meaning "fruitful") from the "house-of-bread" town in Judah. A very Jewish man, then, whose name means "My God is King" takes his family from the heartland of Israel—from God's "fruitful" breadbasket, you might say—to live in Moab during a famine (think economic depression). Sounds sort of odd, doesn't it? Why would he do that? When you consider that the country of Moab was one of ancient Israel's bitterest enemies, symbolic of everything dark and evil,[11] where worship of other gods and forbidden practices flourished, the oddity quickly blossoms into suspicion and apprehension. How could a good Jew make such a bad decision? And what will be the result?

The answer comes swiftly. Elimelech dies. "Uh huh," I can hear an orthodox Jew of that day saying, with a degree of "I told you so." Then, as if to be sure the audience gets the point, the author repeats the pattern. Naomi's sons marry Moabite women—an action strictly forbidden to Jews of that time. "Oh no," a cultured hearer reacts: "I can't bear to look." And, as if to confirm the foreboding expectation, the story doesn't disappoint: both sons die! Thus, Naomi (whose name means "sweet") is left without her husband and her sons—just about the worst position possible for a woman of that day (notice that she became just "the woman" [1:5] when that happened, in a sense losing her identity). It's no wonder that she later replaces her name with the Hebrew word for "bitter" ("Don't call me *Naomi*, call me *Mara* . . . I went away full, but the Lord has brought me back empty" [1:20-21]).

Though the Introduction succinctly and skillfully prepares the readers for the story to follow with direct and informative background information, I believe the writer uses some masterful indirection in the structure and craft of these verses. Notice that the tragedies portrayed in the text are never described as the results of the previous actions. They are simply juxtaposed. The causal connection must come from the listener or the reader. In other words, the text never says that the reason Elimelech died was *because* he chose to leave God's house of bread in a time of famine to seek provision for his family in the land of Moab. . . . that he acted without faith, that he was disloyal, in other words. It doesn't even say that Moab is bad. The author leaves it to the audience. For an informed or targeted reader—a good Jew of the day—the implications flow so easily, however, that the events implicitly pull the underlying values into the story, like slivers of metal firmly attached to a powerful ideological magnet. And in case one misses it, the writer does it again. The sons marry Moabites. They die. The combined effect is to evoke some basic Jewish values and their associated subjects—trust (after all, "My God is king"), obedience, loyalty and faithfulness, food and provisions, health (the name of Ruth's son *Machlon* may have meant illness or weakness) and sustenance, family and future, etc. The book of Ruth is most fundamentally a story about loyalty and love. How artfully the author introduces that subject to us! And in such a way that he leaves himself the right to question or even challenge our initial judgments. The skill is extraordinary.

As is not uncommon in narrative literature, the Conclusion to the book of Ruth is a little fluid and hard to isolate. Technically, one could argue that 4:18-22 constitutes the Conclusion:

> Now these are the descendants of Perez: Perez became the father of Hezron, Hezron of Ram, Ram of Amminadab, Amminadab of Nahshon, Nahshon of Salmon, Salmon of Boaz, Boaz of Obed, Obed of Jesse, and Jesse of David (Ruth 4:18-22).

The ending certainly depends on and highlights the importance of David (who was also an Ephrathite) and his lineage. It probably also implies his renown to the original audience.[12] The previous paragraph clearly connects to the ending, however, and should probably be seen as part of the Conclusion:

> So Boaz took Ruth and she became his wife. When they came together, the Lord made her conceive, and she bore a son. Then the women said to Naomi, "Blessed be the Lord, who has not left you this day without next-of-kin; and may his name be renowned in Israel! He shall be to you a restorer of life and a nourisher of your old age; for your daughter-in-law who loves you, who is more to you than seven sons, has borne him." Then Naomi took the child and laid him in her bosom, and became his nurse. The women of the neighborhood gave him a name, saying, "A son has been born to Naomi." They named him Obed; he became the father of Jesse, the father of David (Ruth 4:13-17).

The ending thus extols the faithfulness of the Lord as seen in the character and actions of Boaz and Ruth.

In stark contrast to the beginning, the book of Ruth ends with an amazing blessing upon Naomi and her family: there could be no greater honor than to be the mother and father of King David—the greatest king in the history of Israel. There could be little worse than to be a Jewish widow with no sons in the land of Moab, as the story began. The question or movement of the story, then, must take us from the broken devastation upon Naomi and her family in the opening to the extreme blessings of the closing: from the horror of the Introduction to the honor of the Conclusion. How did they get from there to here? . . . from the shadow, stench, and misfortune of Moab to the throne-room of God's people and the bloodline of her king? This is indeed a fascinating question and points a stethoscope to the heart of our story. A careful study of the book displays a profound and perhaps even challenging answer—or at least a whole new set of questions (which is one of the most unexpected yet powerful features of the Bible—it doesn't always give us easy answers). One thing we can be sure of, the implication of the Conclusion to the book of Ruth, and indeed the crux of the story, is that somehow God's divine presence—his providence, his oversight, his faithfulness and love—went with Naomi, even when—as we learn in the course of the story—Naomi rails against him (1:20-21). And . . . don't miss this . . . *even in Moab.*

Sometimes biblical literature challenges our assumptions and traditions to the point of making us start over and rethink why we think what we think and why we are what we are. Otherwise, we might become lazy or legalistic or lost to the things that really matter. (If I may get ahead of myself and offer a brief commentary on the purposes of Ruth . . .) Perhaps it wasn't being on the geographic soil of Moab or even females from there that was the root of the problem. Perhaps it ran deeper than that. Perhaps love and faithfulness transcend borders and boundaries. Perhaps it has something more to do with the spiritual and moral heartbeat of a person than the blood that flows in her veins. After all, Moabite blood flows in David—the book of Ruth says—and, as we learn from Matthew (1:1-16), in the Christ. Can anything good come out of Moab? . . . or Nazareth? Ruth did. So did her great grandson David. So did Jesus.

## The Three-Piece Shape

My purpose is not to present an in-depth discussion of the book of Ruth, but simply to show you how much of a leg-up you can get by checking out the beginning and the ending of a book (after you've read the whole thing, of course). It won't tell you everything the book has to offer, but it certainly helps to provide guiding parameters as to what the rest of the text is all about. In some cases, the beginning highlights the key themes and shows how they are introduced. The ending reveals how they are summed up and driven home. Like looking for the corner pieces when you begin to put together a puzzle, I highly recommend that you check out the beginning and the end when you study a Bible book.

Upon finding the Introduction and Conclusion of a Bible book, you have actually uncovered the most basic literary structure of the text: a three-part shape or picture consisting of the Introduction, Body/Core, and Conclusion. Continuing our puzzle analogy, this is the three-piece, ABC shape of a Bible book. I honestly believe that if a person has read all the way through a book of the Bible (preferably several times) and isolated the Introduction and Conclusion, he or she will be miles ahead of the typical, inkblot use of extracted verses toward a proper understanding of the messages of that book. Sure, it's just a beginning. It's sort of elementary. But it gives us a real God-inspired framework from which to work.

We give our children very simple five-piece or ten-piece puzzles to stimulate them when they're young. Though more complicated than those jigsaw puzzles, of course, finding the three-piece shape of a Bible book is a major step toward our goal of seeing the bigger picture and being able to hear all of the verses within their own book-level context. This is our first step as Bible students: find the corner pieces. This will isolate the Middle, and voila, you have the B-M-E (Beginning, Middle, End), ABC, 1-2-3-part shape. From that shape, other divinely inspired jewels will begin to emerge, sparkling in the sunlight of your growing vision.

## Step 2 (of Rule #3):
## Divide the Middle into its major sections.

Having isolated the Introduction and Conclusion, we're presented with the core of the document, the part that lies between the opening and the closing—the Middle, if you will. This is our basic three-part structure:

| Introduction | Middle/Body | Conclusion |
|---|---|---|

I refer to the middle section in different ways, most often with the words "body," "core," "central section," or just "Middle." These three sections make up the most basic shape of a text. The words "Introduction" and "Conclusion" remind of how these sections fit or function in the overall picture. The word "Middle" doesn't say much about its function, however; so, we need to break it down more.

Usually, but not always, the Middle is considerably longer than the Introduction and Conclusion. This is because the Middle is often a collection of parts or sections, with varying degrees of length and complexity. It might help to think of these sections as different images or themes within a puzzle (a picture in a picture), made up of many individual pieces that fit together to create the larger shape. Each of the sections is made up of individual pieces—similar to a single puzzle-piece. These are the verses. Separated into individual pieces—looking and acting much like inkblots—these are what we often use to stimulate and construct our spirituality. But there is a better way.

Once we've found the Introduction and the Conclusion, we can begin to look closer at the arrangement of the central or core section of a book, which will then help us see the overall shape and strategy. Our next step then: *Discover the shape of the text . . . by dividing the Middle into major sections.* This gives us a sense of how the major sections of a book create its overall shape.

What we want to do now is to go exploring. We need to spend enough time reading and thinking about the material carefully to begin to see how the Middle is organized. Forget about the chapter and verse divisions! We're interested in what we can discover for ourselves about how the inspired writer arranged what he had to say. We're interested in the major pauses and movements, so we can properly hear the primary points. Does it have more than one part, topic, or theme? Most do. If it's a short book, the main section may only have one or two parts. Longer books have more. How is it divided? What are the sections? Where do certain subjects begin to be discussed? Where does something new start? How does the writer get (transition) from one section or subject to another? These are the kind of things that help us *explore the core*. Once we see the most basic three-piece shape of the book, our goal is to produce an outline or division of the book into its main parts. By dividing the Middle into its parts, we're using the ebb and flow of the text to uncover the primary shape of the book.

My daughter-in-law got a 2000-piece puzzle for Christmas from her father. It's become a tradition in her family for her and her father (and sometimes her two sisters and others) to put together a large puzzle that one of them gives the other at Christmas. Alicia, my daughter-in-law, and my son were married this past July, and they happened to be staying with us during the Christmas season. This was Alicia's first Christmas away from her father and her family. A little tough, but . . . no problem: Alicia's father sent her a gigantic, 2000-piece puzzle for Christmas. Alicia's sisters and her father opened a similar size puzzle back home. It was a race. Who could put their 2000-piece puzzle together faster? They sent cell-phone snapshots of each other's progress. It took a week or so, with intrusions of normal life getting in the way of chronic puzzling, and—you would know it—it ended in a tie. They finished the same night.

Needless to say, a puzzle of that size has all sorts of images and parts that go together to make up the overall picture. This one was a picture of a brightly lit Times Square in New York City. There were buildings and cars and lights and signs and . . . As they put it together, they worked on various sections scattered about on a large coffee table in our living room, as different images began to take shape. Similarities in color and theme helped to find the right pieces and make the connections. A day or two after they finished, my son, Paul, put the puzzle away. You don't want to dismantle something that took that much work too fast; so, he carefully measured the size of the box and divided the puzzle into pieces just small enough to fit into the box. The result: A 2000-piece puzzle became an eight or ten piece (sectional) puzzle. It will be relatively easy to reassemble those much larger pieces and put them back together, if and when they ever want to.

This is similar to what we can do once we've read and studied a Bible book. We don't have to start from scratch each time, and—this is the real point—just as a puzzle might have several images that make up the one, composite picture, so Bible books have sections of material, and those sections contain unique images and serve varying purposes. Our goal (Step 2) is to begin to see how the Middle of the book is divided into basic sections or units of thought—not chapters or verses, necessarily, but paragraphs and groups of paragraphs. When we're done, we should be able to come up with a tentative outline of the book. In other words, we're looking for the major divisions to go with the Introduction and Conclusion that we've already found. The result might look something like this:

| Introduction | Section 1 | Section 2 | Section 3 | Conclusion |
|---|---|---|---|---|

Now we have a five- or six- or ten-piece puzzle, depending on the number of sections in the Middle. The specific content of each individual verse is not important at this point. Ultimately, we want to see how all the pieces fit—to understand each verse—but before we start looking too intently at the individual trees, we need to get a more nuanced, wide angle look at the forest as a whole. This is why we go exploring.

Exploring means reading, thinking, looking at how it's built—praying as you go. If you're not dedicated to understanding the books of the Bible, then this may begin to sound a little excessive or threatening and is perhaps where one could legitimately begin to distinguish between "reading" and "studying" the Bible. To a certain extent, this is true and will become more so as we delve deeper into the how-tos of good Bible reading. At this point, however, I would suggest that what I'm saying is still pretty basic and not that hard; and if you're motivated to hear the word of God, then a little scurrying about and looking around the wonders of the forest of a Bible book is certainly not too much to ask. It's as if we're exploring a forest to map out where it starts and stops, and how to find our way around without getting lost—or perhaps eaten by some unanticipated, dangerous beast.

The number of pieces makes a lot of difference in how hard it is to put together a puzzle. It's certainly easier to put together a 10-piece puzzle than a 2000-piece one. The same is true when reading and studying Bible books. The longer the book, the more sections and the more potential relationships between the sections. I will readily admit that reading books like Matthew, Luke and Acts require considerable more time and effort than the shorter books. But in theory, the approach is the same. The project is the same, just bigger, with differences that come from the type of book (genre).

An example from the gospel of Matthew illustrates the point. Matthew is one of the longest books of the New Testament, with 28 total chapters. Once you've read the whole thing (which is somewhat of a challenge of itself for many of us, with our schedules) and isolated the Introduction and Conclusion, how do you go about mapping out something that big? This is a legitimate question. I believe the answer is simply, *you explore longer*. The process is the same; the territory is just larger. For example, have you ever noticed that there are several major speeches (discourses) by Jesus in Matthew, starting with the Sermon on the Mount (chapters 5-7)? There are other discourses in chapters 10, 13, 18, 23-25, with narrative and dialogue sections between. Hmm. These look like they might be major sections within the Middle of the book. Of course, there are challenges and complexities, but when you notice things like this, you're beginning to think in big pictures; and when you see the picture, you can get the point—God's point.

## Step 3 (of Rule #3):
## Look at how the sections are connected.

Once you've found the Introduction and the Conclusion, and explored the Middle enough to divide it into major sections, another helpful task/step is to zoom in a bit and pay attention to how the sections connect with each other. In literary terms, we call these "transitions." Sometimes they are as short as a single word; other times, they constitute whole sections of material. Step 3, then, is *Discover the shape of the text . . . by looking at how the sections are connected;* or, *Zoom in on the transitions.* Adding transitions to our two-dimensional model looks like this:

| Introduction | Section 1 | Section 2 | Transition | Section 3 | Conclusion |
| T | | T | | | T |

What is a transition? Just what you would think—a movement from one thing to another—and maybe more. In a document, transitions bridge or segue from one section or line of thought to another. In a puzzle, "transitions" are the protruding knobs and the receiving slots or holes that provide the connectivity; the bumps and valleys of Legos, to use another image. Likewise, in written documents, transitions provide the connectivity and often reveal the logical relationship between a sentence or paragraph and another. They signify that one thing is ending and another, beginning, and sometimes give us important clues about the literary function of the preceding and/or following material. Put briefly, transitions help the reader know how to hear and respond to the text. In some ways, they are like signposts, guiding us along our literary way; and mile markers, revealing the relationship between where we've been and where we're going. In short, they connect and direct. For our Step-3 purposes, beyond the experience of reading, transitions help us find and confirm the divisions of the text, and provide insight into the relationships of the various parts and sections.

Like most things in writing and speaking, there is almost endless variety in how a transition can be effected. Theoretically, you can have no transition at all. A writer might do this for effect, or something else might take the place of the transition and serve to guide the audience (a chapter heading, for example). More often, however, transitions occur at the sentence, paragraph, and section levels. Within a sentence or between sentences, a single word sometimes identifies the movement: "It's raining outside, *so* you should take an umbrella." The simple word "so" provides the logical and grammatical movement between two potentially unrelated statements. On one bright day, I could say, "You should take an umbrella" because it's very sunny. On another dark day, I might say, "It's raining outside." And those two things would have no inherent relationship. The word "so" makes a simple and obvious connection when we put them together.

Sometimes just a word or two will reveal movement between paragraphs. Other times writers use whole sentences to move from one paragraph to another, sometimes at the end of the first paragraph or the beginning of the second, or both (and remember, biblical literature didn't have paragraphs as we think of them). "Therefore, since we are surrounded by such a great cloud of witnesses, let us lay aside every weight and the sin that clings so closely, and let us run with perseverance the race that is before us, looking to Jesus . . ." (Hebrews 12:1) comes to mind. The first phrase, starting with the word "therefore," points backwards to the preceding discussion of those witnesses, while the enjoinder to run with freedom and perseverance looks forward to the following examples and exhortations. In Bible books, the authors sometimes transition from one theme or subject to another by using a transition word (like "so" or "therefore," "but" or "because") and then use a key word on both sides of the transition, as a sort of linking or hook word.

Finally, whole paragraphs and even sections of material can sometimes have a transitional function. Such larger transitions typically divide and connect major sections of a work, characteristically bringing to a close, summarizing, and transitioning from a larger block of material and introducing the section to come. In this way, they have characteristics of both Conclusions and Introductions, and that is, in effect, what transitions are—closing and opening, ending and beginning—with the added benefit of revealing the relationship between the sections. Paul does this in several of his letters. We'll talk more about this later, but take, for example, Ephesians 3:14-21, which contains some very well known (often punched out) verses:

> For this reason I bow my knees before the Father, from whom every family in heaven and on earth takes its name. I pray that, according to the riches of his glory, he may grant that you may be strengthened in your inner being with power through his Spirit, and that Christ may dwell in your hearts through faith, as you are being rooted and grounded in love. I pray that you may have the power to comprehend, with all the saints, what is the breadth and length and height and depth, and to know the love of Christ that surpasses knowledge, so that you may be filled with all the fullness of God. Now to him who by the power at work within us is able to accomplish abundantly far more than all we can ask or imagine, to him be glory in the church and in Christ Jesus to all generations, forever and ever. Amen.

The language here is beautiful and inspiring. It's no wonder we're tempted to tear it out and turn it into an ornate inkblot.

Ephesians 3:14-21 is actually a marvelous example of a section of material serving as a transition. It certainly sounds like a conclusion, doesn't it? as the prayer report concludes with a powerful doxology, praising God. It even ends with "Amen." The passage is chock-full, moreover, of abbreviated (that is, summarized) key themes. Among them: Unity and love in Christ, the recipients' need for the strength and power of God, their need to understand ("with all the saints") some critically important ideas about the depth of Christ's love and the nature of the church, to be encouraged by the limitless potential of God at work in them, and more. A careful study of the preceding sections of Ephesians displays a multitude of thematic and verbal links. As a transition, moreover, several of these ideas prepare directly for the primary exhortation of the letter that follows in Ephesians 4:1-6 (since there is only one body in Christ, they must do everything possible to maintain the Spirit-created unity in that body, which is the church). Likewise, the ethical material of the remainder of the letter builds on the language and ideas summarized in this transitional prayer. Like the lever of a fulcrum between the two parts of this letter, Ephesians 3:14-21 brilliantly concludes the first half and prepares the reader/listener for what's to come.

This is the function of transitions: moving from one sentence or section to another. And they're not isolated verses. They connect what's before with what follows (which raises a real question about what we're getting if we pull out a transition and highlight it without what comes before and after). This is why we need to check them out a little more closely as we're exploring the center of a book. After we've read a Bible book (preferably several times), identified the Introduction and Conclusion, and gotten a feel for the major divisions of the Middle; zooming in on the transitions will definitely help us in our quest to become intimately acquainted with the shape of the text and the Spirit of its author.

## Warning!
### Technical Advisory
The next Step contains technical material that may be inappropriate for some readers.

**Proceed with caution.**

If you find yourself "in over your head" or "bored to tears," skip to *Putting Together the Shapes* and *Rule #3 in Review* at the end of the section.

☺

## Step 4 (of Rule #3):
## Determine the purpose of the sections.

What's different about the words "Introduction," "Conclusion," and "Transition," compared to "Middle" and "Section" ("One of these things is not like the other . . .")? The names "Introduction," "Transition," and "Conclusion" reveal something about the nature and purpose of the material in that section. When we find those sections, we assume and discover something about their role in the book. "Middle" and "Section," on the other hand, tell us little about the nature of the material. What sort is it? Is it narrative? Dialogue? A quotation or citation? Is it autobiographical? Direct or indirect discourse? A summarizing report or a detailed description? Does it develop a theme, refute an argument, or exhort the listeners toward a common goal? Is it addressed to the reader or to someone in the story? These questions concern the type and function of the material, which is a basic part of coming to understand the literary context of a document.

By examining the major sections that we've isolated in Steps 1-3, we now want to determine their purposes. What role do these sections play in the overall construction? When we answer that question, we can give more meaningful names or descriptions that imply something of their purposes as well. This is extremely important for coming to understand how verses of scripture *function* within the overall makeup of a document. This is Step 4 (of Rule #3): *Discover the shape of the text by . . . determining the purpose of the sections.*

At this point, I must admit, we're getting deeper into some serious Bible reading, which we can legitimately call "Bible study," if you're willing to go the distance. And if you've come this far, why stop now? It's not that difficult. It's not something that only scholars can do. It just requires a little different mindset from what we're used to when we read and study our Bibles.

## The Purpose of Sub-Shapes

Putting together a puzzle of any significant size and complexity usually means putting pieces together in sections, as various images and color patterns begin to emerge and take shape. These are pictures within a picture—the smaller images that come together to make up the big picture. Each sub-picture is also made up of an assortment of individual pieces. These pieces are like verses of scripture. Grouped together into sentences and paragraphs, they form sub-pictures or -sections within the overall picture of the book. Though the analogy begins to break down at this point, determining the purpose of a section of scripture is like coming to see the size and shape of a sub-picture in a puzzle and especially in perceiving how that section fits in and contributes to the composite picture as a whole. We do this intuitively when we look at the completed puzzle—or the picture on the box.

A better analogy for our purposes here might be that of the human body. Of all the amazing parts of the human body, none have any real meaning or purpose cut off from or out of the body. Together, each part has its own purpose or function. The heart pumps blood. The eyes see sights. The feet . . . (you get the point). And yet the purposes are integrated. After reading an early draft of some of this material, a good friend of mine who is an engineer sent me an e-mail. In it, he said,

> In electronics, a well-trained technician knows when to zoom in and when to zoom out when analyzing a circuit. Looking only at the voltages and currents of a single component would yield only minimal benefit. Typically, the experienced tech will study the block diagram first (to get the big picture), then the individual circuits and then finally the individual components. Doing so otherwise, would most probably waste time and the results could be misleading. I suspect the same to be true with Bible study.

I suspect he's right.

Similarly, passages of text have roles or functions within their larger contexts. They are not all introductions (but some are). They are not all conclusions. They are not all transitions or narratives or explanations or teaching or . . . But, as in a puzzle or a human body or an electrical gadget, they all connect together to create the literary organism or—the word we've become used to—context. If we can determine the function of the major sections within a Bible book, we will have a clear lens through which to see and understand the intended meaning of the text. To put it another way, we won't pull out a verse that was a quotation of some secondary character and put it in the mouth of God, to use an extreme example. Or, more subtly, we won't take verses used primarily as an illustration, analogy, or supportive material of various types as if they were *the* most important teaching of the book. For example, puzzle-building is not the point of this book, as you know.

As our brains naturally merge the many images of a picture into a composite whole when we look at it—though we can, of course, zoom in on any particular part we like—we understand the purpose of sections of written material naturally to a certain extent as we read: if the writer is competent, the language and structure does its job and carries us along. We don't necessarily know what to call all the various literary techniques that are enacted upon us. That's okay. It doesn't matter if we know all the technical terms—I don't. You don't need a M.D. to know that a heart is not an ear. You're ability to read the text gives you what you need to think about the nature and purpose of the material.

But . . . (there's always a "but," isn't there?) the literary function of written material can be a complex subject. Ancient Greek rhetoricians taught highly detailed and skilled methods of argumentation, arrangement, and style as a part of effective speech-making. There are, moreover, many different types of materials and potential purposes within a written document. Rather than try to classify them with complicated-sounding names and characteristics, I'd like to give some examples of literary forms commonly used in Bible times (think sub-pictures and sub-shapes, zooming out from the verse level). In addition to common-sense considerations of structure that help us navigate a text—like what part functions as introduction and what part functions as conclusion—literary conventions from Bible times significantly increase our ability to decipher an author's primary reason(s) for writing a document. These "forms" or shapes were common ways of structuring and using certain types of material in Bible days, similar to our paragraphs (or a few paragraphs). More than that, they were conventional ways of expressing various types of information and requests. They can, therefore, be a clue to the nature and function of a section of material. We'll focus on New Testament letters, especially the letters of Paul as a way of getting our minds around this idea of purpose and function.

## Clues for Reading Paul's Letters: The Straight Edges

When the Bible was written, most literary documents (except for private or mundane letters, receipts, etc.) were written to be heard. Long before the invention of the printing press, it was, in fact, an oral culture. This using–the-ears-instead-of-the-eyes setting where written material was to be delivered, read, and at times performed naturally impacted writing and the way writers put together documents. H. Parunak refers to this impact as "oral typesetting."[13]

Generally speaking, there is a far greater tendency toward circular or concentric structure as opposed to purely linear, as well as a tendency to standardize ways of expressing certain kinds of information and themes. Since they didn't have single and double spacing, carriage returns, paragraph indentations, italics and bold and underlining, colored ink, and all the formatting options we've gotten used to, something else had to guide the reader and the listener. The structure and formatting thus tended to be built into the language of written discourse. This becomes more evident when you look at our oldest copies of New Testament documents: all capital letters with no spaces between the words. Words were sometimes split between one line and the next. When it comes to writing letters during New Testament times, then, there were several common, built-in ways of guiding the reader and the listener; these were the *conventions* or *standard practices of letter writing* (and speech-making). Since they had to do with putting together the parts of a letter, scholars sometimes call these "formulaic conventions" of letter writing; that is, they use common structures, themes, and even words.

Does this remind you of anything that's standard with most puzzles? We've already noted the corner pieces. Straight edges are the other standard shapes.

Although not nearly as many, we still have some conventions of letter-writing today, don't we? Though quite different because of typing, print, and now electronic formats—the conventions evolve as the medium changes—you wouldn't want to send a very casual, sloppy cover letter to a high-powered company, if you have any real aspirations of landing the job. While instant messaging, texting, tweeting, instagramming, and other forms of communication are quickly defining a new sort of "literary" world, standardizations remain, and there are still standard ways to structure formal letters. More simply, think of how we start all letters. We say "Dear so-and-so." That became the standard. And we sign them with some adverbial expression like "Sincerely yours . . ." Letters (and speeches) of Paul's day had many and more extensive kinds of standardizations. Moreover, as an oral culture, writers often used the same words and phrases to alert the audience to distinctive types of material. Scholars refer to these as "New Testament" or "Pauline letter forms."

For our purposes, let's think of these conventions of letter writing as *special paragraph markers and shapers*. Like pre-assembled components that can be plugged into a motherboard to accomplish a particular task, these pre-fabricated shapes or sections, assembled into a letter or speech, alert us to the purposes of those sections. Some of them have clear patterns and are deeply ingrained in the letter-writing culture of the time; others appear to be more like common themes of letters of the day. Just as they might have functioned in first century settings to alert and condition the audience to a proper understanding of the content, because of the work of Bible scholars (like John L. White[14]) and students through the years, we can use these as clues to the shape and function of sections. They're like the "straight edges" of our textual puzzles.

# The Opening

## Prescript

Paul's letters begin with two basic units: the Prescript and the Thanksgiving. The Prescript contains two components: the Address and the Greeting. The opening Address conforms to the most common letter-writing pattern of the day: A (sender) to B (recipient). For example:

"Paul . . . to the Church of God that is in Corinth . . ."

"Paul . . . to Philemon . . ."

Simple enough.

Following the Address, all the Pauline letters except 1 and 2 Timothy and Titus have a similar opening Greeting or Salutation: "Grace to you and peace from God our Father and the Lord Jesus Christ." Paul's use of the phrase "Grace to you and peace . . ." as an initial greeting appears to be a theological modification of both the standard Greek and Jewish practice. In contrast to the consistency of the greeting itself, however, the epithets and phrases Paul uses to describe himself and his addressees change in accordance with the situation and purposes of the letter. This is significant because these subtle changes in the modifying phrases often reflect the major concerns and themes of the letter.

"Paul, called to be an apostle of Christ Jesus by the will of God . . . to the Church of God that is in Corinth, to those who are sanctified in Christ Jesus, called to be saints . . ."

"Paul, a prisoner of Christ Jesus . . . to Philemon our dear friend and co-worker . . ."

In other words, Paul naturally and intentionally alters the way he describes himself and his audience, as we might expect. How exciting! *These descriptions give us our first clues to the purposes of the letters.* (For example, you might guess that the book of 1 Corinthians would include something regarding who Paul is, his right and authority as an apostle, and you would be right.) We might say that these brief opening sections *function* to connect the writer and the audience (any letter opening should do that) and to introduce some key values and ideas that will undergird or somehow be involved in the letter.

## Thanksgivings (Introductions)

After identifying the audience with a customary address and greeting, Paul begins all of his letters (except Galatians, 1 Timothy, and Titus) with an expression of thanksgiving to God for the recipients of the letter: "I thank my God . . ." or "We always give thanks to God for all of you . . ." This phrase introduces a section of material that's become known as the (Pauline) Thanksgiving.[15] The expression of thanks is followed by details of Paul's appreciative memories of his encounters with the listeners and prayerful requests on their behalf. As a regular part of Paul's letters, the Thanksgiving has its own unique shape and function.

Although the modifying elements of the Prescript and perhaps the Salutation set the tone for significant ideas and motifs within the letters of Paul, by far the more significant literary feature of the opening is the Thanksgiving. A brief expression of thanks to the god(s) has been seen as a typical formulaic feature of ancient Greek letters, often in combination with the health wish and commonly written as a prayer of obeisance or entreaty. In Paul's letters, formulaic (structured the same way) expression of thanksgiving for some aspect of the recipients' faith, followed by intercessory prayer, appear to reflect these conventions, combining the supplication and remembrance formulas of the Hellenistic letter opening and thanksgiving to form a discrete unit of material. *The key concept for our purposes is the realization that these Thanksgiving passages in Paul's letters function as Introductions.* While maintaining the intimacy characteristic of friendly letters of the day and focusing the situation of the letter, the

Thanksgiving introduces the major ideas, motifs, and themes of the letter. On occasion (2 Corinthians 1:3-7; Ephesians 1:3-14), Jewish Blessing (*berachah*) passages serve similar introductory purposes.

1 Corinthians 1:4-9 is a good example of one of Paul's Thanksgiving sections.

> I give thanks to my God always for you because of the grace of God that in every way has been given you in Christ Jesus, for in every way you have been enriched in him, in speech and knowledge of every kind—just as the testimony of Christ has been strengthened among you—so that you are not lacking in any spiritual gift as you wait for the revealing of our Lord Jesus Christ. He will also strengthen you to the end, so that you may be blameless on the day of our Lord Jesus Christ. God is faithful; by him you were called into the fellowship of his Son, Jesus Christ our Lord.

We'll look more closely at the introductory function of a Thanksgiving in our analysis of Philemon, but for now, two quick things: First, observe the common features of Paul's Thanksgivings in this example ("I give thanks," followed by some aspect of the recipients' faith, prayer or blessings, etc.) Once you begin to notice the common design of these sections—their conventional nature—then the phrase "I give thanks to God always for you . . ." will jump out at you at the beginning of a letter and serve as an easy-to-find special paragraph marker to help identify the shape of an important block of material (in this case, the Introduction). It's like knowing how many clicks to zoom in or out.

Second, knowing that these paragraphs serve as literary (or auditory/oral) introductions, you're off to a great start in reading the book so as to see and understand its major messages. To back up this idea—if you've ever read the book of 1 Corinthians, would you say that "being enriched in speech and knowledge of every kind . . . so that you are not lacking in any spiritual gift" has anything to do with the content of that letter? Bingo! It's at the very center of Paul's reason for writing. And he introduces it to us in the Thanksgiving.

93

> **Advisory:**
> For those of you who want to take this to the next level, see Appendix 2 for a digest of the typical elements and function of Thanksgivings, Disclosures, and other common letter-writing conventions & standardizations of New Testament times.

## Disclosures (Narrative or Background Information)

Occurring in some form in each of the major sections of the body, informational formulas or phrases of disclosure were an important convention in ancient Greek letters. The phrases "I . . ." or "We want you to know . . ." or "I don't want you not to know . . ." (translated "be ignorant" or "unaware") occur frequently in Paul's letters as a way of introducing important informational sections. As a conventional form/shape, the disclosure has four basic and one optional element: (1) "I want," (2) identification of the person addressed: "you," (3) a verb of knowing in the infinitive: "to know," (4) person(s) being addressed: "brothers," "beloved" (this is the optional element), and (5) the information, usually introduced by "that."[16] Although the fullest expression occurs often in Paul, other versions of the form were common in the papyri and have also been detected in Paul's letters.

Besides helping to demarcate the opening and closing of the body of the letter, disclosures function as transitions to major subjects within the body of the letter. Stereotyped in form, *Disclosures call attention to these transitions to important subjects and thus provide a sort of heading or topic sentence that states briefly the content of the paragraph*—analogous to a newspaper headline or subtitle.[17] Often in papyrus letters and the letters of Paul, however, the disclosure does not stand on its own, but introduces information that explains the occasion, need, or rationale for a request to be made of the audience (another important form). Disclosures function, then, as background for requests, and the combination produces a background-request letter structure.

In Philippians 1:12, Paul says, "I want you to know, beloved, that what has happened to me has actually helped to spread the gospel . . ." The following verses then explain how the gospel has spread through Paul's imprisonment and emphasize that Paul is able to rejoice in spite of his circumstances—major themes in the book of Philippians. Examples are everywhere in Paul: "For I want you to know how much I am struggling for you, and for those in Laodicea, and for all who have not seen me face to face" (Colossians 2:1). Sometimes the disclosure statement is put in the negative, as in 1 Thessalonians 4:13: "But we do not want you to be uninformed, brothers and sisters, about those who have died . . ." Seeing these phrases as introductions to important (background) information—topic sentences—helps us understand the role of these paragraphs in the overall shape and purposes of the letter.

## Petitions or Requests

Another common stereotyped shape in ancient Greek letters and the letters of Paul is the Petition or Request form.[18] As a means of making formal request, sentences beginning with "I appeal to you (brothers)" or "I ask you (brothers)" highlight a very significant section of material that often represents the main reason for the letter. The three basic and necessary (always present either explicitly or implicitly) elements are (1) the background, (2) the petition verb, and (3) the desired action; (4) the address and (5) the courtesy phrase appear frequently as optional elaborations: "I ask you, therefore, brothers . . ." All types of requests were put into this form.

In the letters of Paul, such standardized requests occur frequently. *These formal requests—especially the first one in the letter[19]—usually reflect the situation that produced the letter (the epistolary setting) and thereby show the primary purpose or goal of the letter-writer*, especially in combination with the Thanksgiving (and in some cases, a Disclosure). The Petition thus contains the actual concern or request of the letter. Observing the literary and historical (epistolary) value of the Petition as an introduction to a key section of material in Paul's letters (another sort of topic sentence) certainly helps us understand the function of these sections and underscore their significance as special paragraph makers. They are, in other words, a sort of ancient way of bolding or highlighting a request.

1 Corinthians 1:10 is a clear example. To illustrate, let me first ask a question: if you've read 1 Corinthians, what does the big picture look like? What sort of problem or issue lies at the heart of the book? Something like ego and conflict over the importance of spiritual gifts come to mind? With that issue in focus, see if you think the first Petition, coming immediately after the end of the opening Thanksgiving passage, has anything to do with the main purpose of the letter:

> Now I appeal to you, brothers and sisters, by the name of our Lord Jesus Christ, that all of you be in agreement and that there be no divisions among you, but that you be united in the same mind and the same purpose.

Romans 12:1-2 is a famous example: "I appeal to you, brothers and sisters, by the mercies of God, to present your bodies as a living sacrifice, holy and acceptable to God, which is your spiritual worship. . . ." Like Thanksgivings and Disclosures, the initial sentence introduces a paragraph or section of material that serves a particular purpose in the overall shape of the document (a desire for the audience to respond and act).

## Prayers and Prayer-Requests

In keeping with their spiritual purposes, Paul's letters contain a heavy concentration of prayer, both by the apostle for the recipients and in reference to their prayers. Actual prayers, reports of prayer, exhortations to and requests for prayer punctuate Paul's letters.[20] Most important for our purposes is the awareness that the prayers serve more than spiritual or pastoral purposes within the contexts of the letters. Paul certainly believed in prayer and modeled it for his audiences as he sought to present them guiltless at the coming of the Lord; but, as with Thanksgivings, prayers and reports of prayer have significant literary purposes. In other words, Paul uses prayers for more than praying—he uses them as effective rhetorical tools.

In a general sense, *prayers and prayer reports in Paul's letters serve to summarize and apply key ideas*. Isn't it natural that the content of his prayers would relate to and reflect his concern for the readers? Of course. He talks to God about the things that matter most. We might say that prayers pinpoint as they punctuate the letters—they pinpoint key subjects and values. They occur at strategic points, moreover—usually the beginning, middle or important transitional points, and end—and thus help to define the shape and movement of the text. As Thanksgivings use prayer reports to introduce key ideas, so prayers and prayer reports often highlight major themes within concluding and transitional units. Prayers thus help to focus the situation behind the letter and to summarize the specific points and exhortations of the letter as introductions, conclusions, and/or transitions.

1 Thessalonians (3:11-13; 5:23-25) and Romans (15:5-6; 15:13) contain the longest examples of actual prayers. For example,

> Now may our God and Father himself and our Lord Jesus direct our way to you. And may the Lord make you increase and abound in love for one another and for all, just as we abound in love for you. And may he so strengthen your hearts in holiness that you may be blameless before our God and Father at the coming of our Lord Jesus with all his saints (1 Thessalonians 3:11-13).

These verses wonderfully illustrate the summarizing and transitional purposes of an embedded prayer. The previous material focused on Paul's deep love and concern for the Thessalonians and his great frustration at not being able to visit them again, having heard that they were suffering persecution for their faith. When he couldn't stand it any longer, he decided to be left alone in Athens and sent Timothy his apprentice to see how they were doing. Timothy had just come back from that trip with the good news of their faith and love when Paul wrote the letter. The next section (4:1-8) is a strong Petition ("Finally, brothers and sisters, we ask and urge you in the Lord Jesus . . .") for them to hold on to the foundational teachings Paul had given them in his initial visit, about how they were to live and please God, to grow and be sanctified—for them to "do so more and more." In 4:9-12, Paul uses another Petition form to encourage them to love each other as they were doing: "But we urge you, beloved, to do so more and more . . ." The prayer of 3:11-13 skillfully brings the first part of the letter to a close and leads effectively into the vital exhortations to follow. Finally, notice how the prayer in 4:23-24 briefly brings the message of protection and spiritual growth to a resounding conclusion: "May the God of peace himself sanctify you entirely; and may your spirit and soul and body be kept sound and blameless at the coming of the Lord Jesus Christ. The one who calls you is faithful, and he will do this." Powerful and comforting words for those living out their faith in the midst of suffering for that faith.

In addition to his prayers and prayer reports, Paul sometimes asks for prayer from the recipients of the letter. Such requests are not casual and are not separated from the context and concerns of the letter, but are intimately connected with the reasons for writing. In fact, they sometimes come as a deliberate climax, completing the circle of prayer that Paul began in the early part of the letter. He engages his readers in lifting him up to the Father, as he does them. At the close of Ephesians, Paul says, "Pray also for me, so that when I speak, a message may be given to me to make known with boldness the mystery of the gospel, for which I am an ambassador in chains. Pray that I may declare it boldly, as I must speak" (Ephesians 6:19-

20). Paul is in prison for preaching the mystery of the gospel of God, especially to Gentiles. The Gentile readers have become potentially angry and discouraged because of what has happened to Paul (3:1-13). Yet Paul assures them that God is in control and that they can be encouraged and live lives committed to the nature and purposes of the church. If they pray for him to speak boldly, how can they be angry and discouraged when he does it well? The impact goes beyond literary genius.

## The Closing

As with the openings, the closing conventions of the Pauline letters reflect the letter-writing practices of the time, though they exhibit more variety in the components used.[21] Paul's letters usually close with a grace-benediction ("Grace . . . be with you"), which appears to be a christianized replacement for the customary secular expressions of final greeting and which, standing at the final place in every letter, functions "to bring the letter to a definite conclusion."[22] Prior to the closing, several optional letter-writing items occur, in this order: (1) peace wish, (2) request for prayer, (3) secondary greetings, (4) holy kiss, (5) autographed greeting (various positions).[23] The peace wish stands out from the context and thus functions as a transition from the body to the closing elements. Requests for prayer typically occur within the closing elements of the letter and bring to climax the intercessory circle of the letter in direct association with the particular needs of the situation. Secondary greetings give some indications of the intended readership of the letter and serve as an emotional bridge between the parties on both sides of the epistolary setting, thus fulfilling one of the basic functions of ancient letters. On several occasions, Paul exhorts his readers to greet each other with a "holy kiss," which appears to be a concrete community enactment of the greetings of the letter. Five of Paul's letters close with a personal, autographed greeting, which, in line with the practice of the day, authenticates the contents of the letter with respect to the author.

## Putting Together the Shapes

There are other types of paragraphs, special markers and themes (see Appendix 2 for digests of additional letter forms). We could talk about *autobiographical sections*: when Paul talks about himself, he typically uses self-descriptions as paradigms or examples to illustrate the point he's making. Like when he said, "Follow me, as I follow Christ" (1 Corinthians 11:1) to summarize his example of putting the needs of others above his own preferences for the good of the church. We could talk about *collections of ethical instructions* (sometimes called "parenesis") and how Paul doesn't just pick a random Christian thing to encourage them to do—but what they need most in relation to the concerns and purposes of the letter. We could deal with *visit talk*, a common theme in ancient letters and in Paul, where Paul uses his (coming) *apostolic presence* to reinforce his friendship with the recipients and as motivation for his requests. Or how about *expressions of confidence?* Did you know that when Paul says something like "I know that you will do even more than I ask" (Philemon 1:21), he was using a commonly occurring expression to underscore the intention and impact of the letter?

To summarize: Scholarly information regarding letters and speeches of the day can help us when we study various books of the Bible (given how much we've learned from the papyrus discoveries, for example). In short, let cultural conventions be your guide. My purpose, though, is not to train you to be a literary critic or exegetical expert. My purpose is to help you see that groups of verses, paragraphs, and sections of material have their own purposes or roles within the overall structure of a document—their own shapes, if you will—which, like sections of a puzzle, connect together to form the overall shape and picture of the text. When you discover the purposes of the sections, you can then see their relationships and gain clear insight into the broader context of the document. *You can then point to any single verse and see how it fits into the picture as a whole, and this is the key. It's the key to understanding what God intended and the key to community based on that understanding.*

This is what we want to do when we read and interpret Bible verses: point to the verse as if you were pointing to a piece in a put-together puzzle, then immediately zoom out. The book is our field of vision or angle of view, to borrow a term from photography. This is the only way to be sure we see everything in relational (focused) perspective. When you do this, you drastically improve your ability to read and understand the verses as they were intended, as part of God's first conversations with his people, in context and targeted to specific spiritual purposes Like a dandelion after a generous dose of weed-killer, inkblotitis withers and dies in an environment saturated with God's wide-angle, book-level pictures.

## Another Common Shape: Circles

Most of the special paragraph markers we've seen in the letters of Paul don't occur in other books of the Bible. Why? Because they are not letters, but different types of documents. Like its own little library, the Bible is really a collection of different types of documents (see Rule #5 below on appreciating the . . . genre). Similar types will use similar devices and strategies for organizing and developing the material. Knowing all the possible types of sub-genres is not practical, if it's even possible, however. That's not our purpose. I went through some of the specific types of paragraphs in Paul's letters primarily to illustrate one way to go about dissecting the middle sections of a Bible book and to give you some tools for reading Paul's letters. We're interested in how the sections of material relate to the other sections (= function) to create an organic whole. We'll look more closely at how this works with narrative material in our "How To" chapter on Mark's Gospel a little later. The intention here is to get you thinking about how verses and groups of verses fit together and function within their book-level contexts. Remember, we're still talking about Rule #3, *discovering the shape of the text*.

That being said, I would, however, like to talk about one other specific way that biblical writers arranged their material—another shape. This one is a circle. Have you ever been reading along in the Bible and found yourself thinking, "I just read that" or "He just said that," almost as if the writer forgot what he just wrote? More than likely the repetition is intentional as part of a circular structuring device—remember John F. Kennedy's famous quote, "Ask not what your country can do for you; ask what you can do for your country" or Byron's "Pleasure's a sin, and sometimes sin's a pleasure"? When you find such repetition in scripture, you may have found the center and emphatic piece of a circular structure. Similarly, have you ever wondered why a subject seemed to be discussed in one location and then again a little later, with maybe a block of material between? For example, the apostle Paul talks about spiritual gifts in 1 Corinthians 12, then again in 1 Corinthians 14. Why the gap? Between the two comes the famous chapter on love (13). The break is intentional. Like the meat of a sandwich, the material about love is inserted into the middle of the highly inflammatory discussion of spiritual gifts. See the connection? The structure is part of the rhetorical strategy.

Biblical scholars refer to this circular structuring as *chiastic* (from the Greek letter *chi*, shaped like an X) or *concentric*, and the result, a *chiasm* (or inverted parallelism).[24] With possible roots in the nature and practice of storytelling or poetry in oral cultures, ancient writers/speakers often arranged their material in circles (this sort of structure can actually be found in many types of music, drama, and literature). That is, instead of a straightforward, linear A, B, C, D out-line—the way we structure things—they often used a more circular or concentric pattern, like A, B, C, D, C, B, A, sometimes repeating the center element (ABCCBA), sometimes not (ABCBA). A simple ABA or ABBA pattern was very common: A—a key idea or (grammatically similar) phrase, B—a second idea or phrase, B'—repeat and/or develop point B, and A'—then return to A. We can diagram it like this:

| A  | My first idea          | A tree fell loudly in the woods, |
|----|------------------------|----------------------------------|
| B  | My second idea         | But no one heard it.             |
| B' | My second idea again   | If no one heard it,              |
| A' | My first idea again    | Did it really fall loudly?       |

The in and out, crisscross pattern gives it the appearance of an X, and thus the term "chiastic."[25] We'll think of it as a circle since the structure revolves around a center point, moving toward the center and then away from it, with parallel elements encircling the middle. Whether such circular structuring evolved as a mnemonic for speakers and storytellers or as a part of poetry and poetic prose, biblical writers often arranged their material in circles, at the sentence, paragraph, and sometimes even book levels.

So how's this helpful? Structuring things in a circle doesn't mean that the logic is circular (that's different altogether) or that each point is simply repeated verbatim. On the contrary, the repetition is as nuanced and dynamic as any other literary device. As in Hebrew poetry, the repetition develops and carries forward the thought with the linear movement of the text, creating an unfolding balance. Though it's easily lost in English translations, observing this circular movement not only helps us know where sections start and stop, but also provides insight to important questions of thematic relationship and interpretation.

Three major things we can use: (1) Bible sentences, sections, and even whole books sometimes use circular structuring, (2) each repeated or parallel element relates to and helps to develop its structural counterpart, and (3) the center point is often the most important or critical (sometimes contrasting) idea, especially in longer patterns. In other words, the center is the fulcrum or the key. When the center element itself is repeated (ABCCBA), the emphasis is immediate and clear (by being said twice in a short span of text). This is why you sometimes run across things in the Bible where the writer sounds like he just started repeating himself. In a sense, he did.

Short, phrase and sentence level circles are common in Bible literature. (a) By faith (b) we walk (a') not by sight (1 Corinthians 5:7). Mark 10:31: (a) But many who are first (b) will be last; (b') and the last (a') will be first. The habit goes way back historically; Genesis 9:6 is a good example:

A  Whoever sheds
B      the blood
C         of man
C'         by man shall
B'     his blood
A'  be shed

Paul frequently used simple circles to formulate sentences: "Indeed, man was not made from woman, but woman from man" (1 Corinthians 11:8); "For the flesh lusts against the Spirit and the Spirit against the flesh" (Galatians 5:17). These brief expressions are often parts of bigger circles, moreover, that constitute paragraphs and sections. Galatians 5:13-6:2 clearly displays a circular pattern (the highlighted words show some of the repetitions, thematic parallels and contrasts):

A    For you were called to freedom, only not the freedom for an opportunity to the flesh, but through love serve one another
> For the law is fulfilled in one word: you are to love your neighbor as yourself

But if you bite and devour one another, watch yourselves lest you be destroyed by one another

B    But I say, walk by the Spirit and the lusts of the flesh you will not complete
> For the flesh lusts against the Spirit and the Spirit against the flesh
>
> For these are contrary one to another

But if you are led by the Spirit, you are not under law

C    **But the works of the flesh** are manifest, which are sexual immorality, impurity, reckless living, idolatry, witchcraft, hatred, strife, jealousy, angers, selfish rivalries, divisions, factions, envies, drunkenness, orgies, and the like

D    I am warning you, just as I said before, that the ones who practice such things will not inherit the kingdom of God

C'    **But the fruit of the Spirit** is love, joy, peace, patience, kindness, goodness, faith, humility, self-control

B'    Against such things there is no law
> But the ones who are of Christ have crucified the flesh with the passions and lusts

If we live by the Spirit, by the Spirit let us also conduct ourselves

A'    Let us not become conceited, making one another angry, envying one another
> Brothers, if a man is caught [overtaken] in some sin, you who are spiritual restore this one in the spirit of gentleness, considering yourself, lest you also be tempted

Bear one another's burdens and so fulfill the law of Christ

The pattern emphasizes the central item, as does the language itself: "I am warning you, just as I said before . . ."

The Gospel of Mark uses many intriguing circular patterns. Joanna Dewey made a strong case for the following structure of the stories in Mark 2:1-3:6:[26]

A    2:1-12      The Healing of the Paralytic
B    2:13-17     The Call of Levi/Eating with Sinners
C    2:18-22     Sayings on Fasting and on the Old and the New
B'   2:23-27     Plucking Grain on the Sabbath
A'   3:1-6       The Healing on the Sabbath

Chapter 4:1-34 is also a good example:[27]

A    4:1-2       Introduction: Jesus Teaching in Parables
B    4:2-9       Parable of the Sower/Seed
C    4:10-13     Understanding Parables
D    4:14-20     Interpretation of the Sower
C'   4:21-25     Understanding Parables
B'   4:26-32     Parables of Growing and Mustard Seed
A'   4:33-34     Conclusion: Jesus Teaching in Parables

These are just examples of the idea that biblical material has built-in structure—shapes—and sometimes those shapes are circular. I'll give you an example of a whole book (though admittedly a short one) with a circular shape in our "How To" chapter on Philemon.

I have found that the easiest way to identify concentric patterns when you're reading the Bible is to start from the center and move out. In other words, when you read something that seems to be repetitious, look on both sides of the repetition and see if a similar subject or expression occurs. If so, then move out again, checking both sides (another example of zooming out). Often you'll come to a clearly defined starting point and the result will be an intricate artistic circle.

# Rule #3 in Review

Rule #3 of good Bible study is to discover the shape of the text. We do this in four steps. Discover the shape of the text by . . .

(1) finding the Introduction and the Conclusion,
(2) dividing the Middle into major sections,
(3) looking at how the sections connect, and
(4) determining the role or purpose of the sections

The Introduction and Conclusion often give quick insight into the major themes and purposes of a book, to what was important to the writer; and if the writer of the book was inspired by God, then to what was and is important to God. That's why Introductions are important, not because of sophisticated-sounding rules or guidelines, but because in the Bible they introduce us to the heart and face of God, book by book. Conclusions impress God's messages upon our minds and hearts so that we might be remade, renewed, and inspired by the daylight of his absolute power, mercy, love, and grace. One starts up; the other drives home. We're not exploring the Bible for the sake of exploring or sounding educated. We're exploring because the paths and the destinations contain the richest treasures of earth, given to us by the breath of God.

Isolating the opening and closing sections yields a basic three-piece shape. The Introduction and Conclusion work like corner pieces in our puzzle analogy. As we explore the Middle, we begin to uncover other shapes that go together to make up the overall design and strategy of the book. Zooming in on the connections (transitions) between the sections clarifies that design by highlighting the relationships between the sections.

Though we can investigate without any directions or clues, the conventional, stereotyped forms of Bible times reveal some standardized (plug-and-play) shapes that help to show what roles various paragraphs and sections play. These letter-writing and speech-making forms, and any other recognizable sub-genres—special paragraph markers—function like straight edges (giving clear indication of where and how something fits) as we put together the puzzles of scripture.

*The key is not anyone else's directions,* however, *but your own exploration.* Once you've spent time plowing through the fertile fields of a biblical text, not only do you get deep into the content, but you're also learning to see how the parts fit together and function in relationship to one another and to the picture as a whole. This is the literary context. Not a verse or a chapter or two, but the whole book. By the time you get to Step 4 of Rule #3, you're doing some fairly serious Bible study, and I commend you. You're learning to be not just a Bible reader, but a skilled reader. And did you notice that we're not reading commentaries or other books besides the Bible itself? Like digging up hidden treasure, we're uncovering Holy-Spirit-inspired intentions within the book-level context.

And it's not hard. Don't be bothered by the technical stuff. And you don't have to do it exactly the way I've described. Essentially, it just means get into the text. That's what you have to do. Explore the book. Read it, several times. Observe the sections. Read them again. Look at how they fit together. Zoom in—zoom out. And then—and this is the pot of gold at the end of the rainbow—you've put yourself into position to hear the voice of God. . . . to get God's point. . . . to see his big picture and understand the smaller parts (the verses), not as personalized inkblots, but as they truly are, the word of God.

In archaeology, the work is painstaking and sometimes seems unrewarding. Until the discovery. Then it's all worth it. The Bible can be like that sometimes. There's so much that has been buried under years of tradition, denominational doctrines, books and commentaries, sermons, and all sorts of out-of-focus readings and discussions. Rule #3 of good Bible reading puts the Holy Spirit back in the driver's seat, as you buckle up for a Sunday (or Monday or Tuesday . . .) drive, an excursion into unexplored territories, filled with life-changing discoveries, as you investigate the design and intent of a book of God—checked out from the library of God. There are few things you can do in life that will equip you for life as much as this.

**Rule #3 in short: Get into shapes.**

## Chapters 9 and 10: Ten Rules of Good Bible Reading

## Chapter Resources

Aune, David E. *The New Testament in Its Literary Environment.* Philadelphia: Westminster, 1987.

Bjerkelund, Carl J. *Parakalô: Form, Funktion und Sinn der parakalô-Sätze in den paulinischen Briefen.* Oslo: Universitatsforlaget, 1967.

Blume, Frederick E. "The Value of the Papyri for New Testament Study." http://www.wlsessays.net/files/BlumeValue.pdf.

Charlesworth, James H. ed. *The Old Testament Pseudepigrapha.* Vol. 1: *Apocalyptic Literature and Testaments.* New York: Doubleday & Company, 1983.

*1 (Ethiopic Apocalypse of) Enoch.* Translated by E. Isaac.

*2 (Syriac Apocalypse of) Baruch.* Translated by A. F. J. Klijn.

Cicero. *De Inventione.* Translated by H. M. Hubbell. LCL. Cambridge: Harvard University, 1949; reprint ed., 1960. In the volume with *De Optimo Genere Oratorum* and *Topica.*

*De Oratore.* In Cicero 3 and 4:1-185. 2 vols. LCL. Cambridge: Harvard University, 1942; reprint eds., 1967/1968. Book 3 is in the volume with *De Facto, Paradoxa Stoicorum,* and *De Partitione Oratoria.*

*De Partitione Oratoria.* In Cicero 4:306-421. Translated by H. Rackham. LCL. Cambridge: Harvard University, 1942; reprint ed., 1968. In the volume with *De Oratore, De Fato,* and *Paradoxa Stoicorum.*

*Orator.* In Cicero 5:297-509. Translated by H. M. Hubbell. LCL. Cambridge: Harvard University, 1939; reprint ed., 1971. In the volume with *Brutus.*

Daniell, David. *The Bible in English: Its History and Influence.* London: Yale University, 2003.

Deissmann, Adolf. *New Light on the New Testament: From Records of the Graeco-Roman Period.* Translated by L. R. M. Strachan. Edinburgh: T. & T. Clark, 1907.

Dewey, Joanna. *Markan Public Debate: Literary Technique, Concentric Structure, and Theology in Mark 2:1-3:6.* SBLDS 48. Chico, CA: Scholars, 1980.

Fay, Greg. "Introduction to Incomprehension: The Literary Structure of Mark 4:1-34." *CBQ* 51 (1989) 65-81.

Funk, Robert W. "The Apostolic *Parousia*: Form and Significance." In *Christian History and Interpretation: Studies Presented to John Knox*, pp. 249-68. Edited by W. R. Farmer, C. F. D. Moule, and R. R. Niebuhr. Cambridge: Cambridge University, 1967.

"The Apostolic Presence: Paul." In *Parables and Presence: Forms of the New Testament Tradition*, pp. 81-110. Philadelphia: Fortress, 1982.

Gamble, Harry. *The Textual History of the Letter to the Romans: A Study in Textual and Literary Criticism.* Grand Rapids: Eerdmans, 1977.

Long, Lynne. "Scriptures in the Vernacular Up to 1800." In *A History of Biblical Interpretation: The Medieval through the Reformation Periods*, pp. 450-81. Edited by Alan J. Hauser and Duane F. Watson. Grand Rapids: Eerdmans, 2009.

Lund, N. W. *Chiasmus in the New Testament.* Chapel Hill: University of North Carolina, 1942.

Lyons, George. *Pauline Autobiography: Toward a New Understanding.* SBLDS 73. Atlanta: Scholars, 1985.

Malherbe, Abraham J. *Ancient Epistolary Theorists.* SBLSBS 19. Atlanta: Scholars, 1988.

Mullins, Terence Y. "Ascription as a Literary Form." *NTS* 19 (1972-73) 194-205.

"Benediction as a NT Form." *AUSS* 15 (1977) 59-64.

111

"Disclosure: A Literary Form in the New Testament." *NovT* 7 (1964) 44-50.

"Formulas in New Testament Epistles." *JBL* 91 (1972) 380-90.

"Greeting as a New Testament Form." *JBL* 87 (1968) 418-26.

"Petition as a Literary Form." *NovT* 5 (1962) 46-54.

"*Topos* as a New Testament Form." *JBL* 99 (1980) 541-47.

"Visit Talk in New Testament Letters." *CBQ* 35 (1973) 350-58.

Olson, Stanley N. "Epistolary Uses of Expressions of Self-Confidence." *JBL* 103 (1984) 585-97.

"Pauline Expressions of Confidence in His Addressees." *CBQ* 47 (1985) 282-95.

Parunak, H. van Dyke. "Oral Typesetting: Some Uses of Biblical Structure." *Bib* 62 (1981) 153-68.

Quintilian, *Institutio Oratoria.* 4 vols. Translated by H. E. Butler. LCL. Cambridge: Harvard University, 1920-22; reprint eds., 1980, 1977, 1966, 1979.

Sanders, Jack T. "The Transition from Opening Epistolary Thanksgiving to Body in the Letters of the Pauline Corpus." *JBL* 81 (1962) 348-62.

Shelley, Bruce L. *Church History in Plain Language.* Updated 2d ed. Nashville: Thomas Nelson, 1995.

Schubert, Paul. *Form and Function of the Pauline Thanksgivings.* Berlin: Töpelmann, 1939.

Stowers, Stanley K. *Letter Writing in Greco-Roman Antiquity.* Philadelphia: Westminster, 1986.

Thompson, Mark D. "Biblical Interpretation in the Works of Martin Luther." In *A History of Biblical Interpretation: The Medieval through the*

*Reformation Periods*, pp. 299-318. Edited by Alan J. Hauser and Duane F. Watson. Grand Rapids: Eerdmans, 2009.

Wengert, Timothy. "Biblical Interpretation in the Works of Philip Melanchthon." In *A History of Biblical Interpretation: The Medieval through the Reformation Periods*, pp. 319-340. Edited by Alan J. Hauser and Duane F. Watson. Grand Rapids: Eerdmans, 2009.

White, John L. "Ancient Greek Letters." In *Greco-Roman Literature and the New Testament: Selected Forms and Genres*, pp. 85-105. Edited by D. E. Aune. SBLSBS 21. Atlanta: Scholars, 1988.

*The Form and Function of the Body of the Greek Letter: A Study of the Letter-Body in the Non-Literary Papyri and in Paul the Apostle.* 2d ed. SBLDS 2. Missoula, MT: Scholars, 1972.

"The Greek Documentary Letter Tradition Third Century B.C.E. to Third Century C.E." *Semeia* 22 (1982) 89-106.

"Introductory Formulae in the Body of the Pauline Letter." *JBL* 90 (1971) 91-97.

*Light from Ancient Letters.* Philadelphia: Fortress, 1986.

"New Testament Epistolary Literature in the Framework of Ancient Epistolography." *ANRW* 2.25.2 (1984) 1730-56.

"Saint Paul and the Apostolic Letter Tradition." *CBQ* 45 (1983) 433-44.

"The Structural Analysis of Philemon: A Point of Departure in the Formal Analysis of the Pauline Letter." *SBLSP* (1971) 1-47.

*Studies in Ancient Letter Writing* (Edited). Semeia 22. Chico, CA: Scholars, 1982.

Wiles, Gordon P. *Paul's Intercessory Prayers: The Significance of the Intercessory Prayer Passages in the Letters of St Paul.* SNTSMS 24. New York: Cambridge University, 1974.

113

## Notes

1. Discussions of the discovery of the ancient non-literary papyri are plentiful; see, e.g., Blume's ("Value of the Papyri") nice summary of these events (from whom I got some of my brief list).
2. Some of these are extremely important fragments of biblical texts like p52, our oldest piece of a Bible text, containing portions of John 18:31-33 and 37-38.
3. See Deissmann, *New Light*, 14-16 for a brief history of their discovery, and White, *Light from Ancient Letters*, 193 for a background description of the origin of these papyrus letters.
4. Daniell (*The Bible in English*, 138) refers to it as "rough everyday Greek."
5. As quoted in the Prolegomena of Moulton's *Grammar of New Testament Greek*, 1906.
6. Commenting on William Tyndale's translation of the Bible into the common language of the people of his day, Daniell (*The Bible in English*, 138) makes a similar comment: "God became man, low experiences and all."
7. The linguistic challenge of word-for-word versus sense-for-sense translation goes back a long time, being clearly understood by Jerome in his work on the Latin Vulgate. In his famous letter to Pammachius in 395 AD, Jerome observed that he was content to use a sense-for-sense rather than a word-for-word strategy, except where the syntax itself contained a mystery (see Long, "Scriptures in the Vernacular," 452-53; citing D. Robinson, *Western Translation Theory* [2nd ed.; Manchester: St. Jerome, 2002] 25).
8. The NET (New English Translation), a relatively recent, online version, claims to have solved the tension between formal and functional equivalence by using a more literal or formal equivalent translation in the notes and a more functionally or dynamically equivalent translation in the text itself. See http://bible.org/ and http://net.bible.org/bible.php for the text itself.
9. Though the word has been used at times to translate the Latin *dispositio* (usually rendered "arrangement"), which is the second of five canons of classical rhetoric; cf., e.g., Wengert, "Biblical Interpretation," 322.
10. Quint. 7.PR.1-2; Cic. Inv. 1.14.19; Or. 15.50. For "the occasion chosen for saying anything is at least as important a consideration as what is actually said" (Quint. 11.1.7).

11. In Bible times, Moab was a highly organized territory/state on the east side of the Dead Sea and along the south few miles of the Jordan River. Moabites were the descendants of Lot (Abraham's nephew) from an incestuous relationship with his oldest daughter (Genesis 19:37). In those days, Israel and Moab were constantly warring with each other. When Israel was migrating to Canaan, Moab refused to allow her to travel along "the King's Highway" which crossed the plateau (Judges 11:17). Because of their unfriendliness, Moabites were to be excluded from Israel (Deuteronomy 23:36; Nehemiah 13:1). Balak, a king of Moab, distressed by Israel's success, asked the prophet Balaam to curse them (Numbers 22-24; Joshua 24:9). As Israel prepared to cross the Jordan river, they camped in the "plains of Moab" (Numbers 22:1; Joshua 3:1) and were seduced by Moabite and Midianite women to participate in idolatrous practices (Numbers 25; Hosea 9:10). In the days of the Judges, the time period of the book of Ruth, Moab invaded Israelite lands as far as Jericho and oppressed Israel for 18 years (Judges 3:12-30). Moab was thus a fitting symbol for everything anti-Jewish and would appear, from a Jewish perspective of that time, to be the last place a good Jew would go to find help in times of trouble.

12. Unless, perhaps, it was written to "justify" a piece of David's heritage.

13. Parunak, "Oral Typesetting," 153-68.

14. For example: White, *Form and Function*; "Epistolary Literature," 1730-56; *Light from Ancient Letters*.

15. The classic study of the Pauline Thanksgiving is Paul Schubert's *Form and Function of the Pauline Thanksgivings*.

16. Mullins described the form in "Disclosure: A Literary Form in the New Testament," 44-50; see also Sanders, "Transition" 348-62.

17. Sanders, "Transition," 354.

18. The petition form was analyzed extensively by Bjerkelund in his (German) monograph *Parakalô* and summarized effectively by Mullins, "Petition," 46-54.

19. Bjerkelund repeatedly seeks to demonstrate in his book that the first petition of a letter contains the actual epistolary concern of the apostle.

20. In his classic study of prayers in the letters of Paul (*Paul's Intercessory Prayers*), Wiles analyzed all the various types of prayers, along with requests and exhortations about prayer. Admitting the difficulties of demarcation and interpretation, Wiles considers his selected passages under four functional classes: (1) intercessory wish-prayers, (2) interces-

115

sory prayer-reports, (3) parenetic references to intercessory prayer (requests for and exhortations to such prayer), and (4) didactic and speculative references to prayers.

21. Gamble (*Textual History*, 56-83) provided a good examination of the closing elements of the Pauline letters in his study of the history of the text of Romans.
22. Gamble, *Textual History*, 67.
23. Aune, *New Testament*, 186.
24. The classic study is Lund's *Chiasmus in the New Testament*. Many good sources exist on concentric/chiastic structuring in Bible books. A recent online example is Robert Bailey's "The Structure of Paul's Letters" (4th ed., http://www.inthebeginning.org/stucture/index.html, 2009).
25. The root of the word means to mark with an X.
26 Dewey. *Markan Public Debate.*
27. Fay, "Introduction to Incomprehension," 65-81.

# Chapter 10

# Ten Rules of Good Bible Reading

Walking downstairs—my desk is in the basement—and across the room this morning, I picked up a couple of pieces of paper lying on the floor, which is certainly not unusual for my papers, but these were in the *middle* of the floor. That was a little unusual. As I picked up the paper, I remembered that my daughter had a group of teenagers from her (Christian) theatre group over last night for a Bible study. When I picked up the paper, it was an outline of the first, orientation-style lesson of a Bible Study series that the kids were using. My eyes quickly scanned the page and paused on the all-caps in the middle of the page: "RANDOM PROVERB!" It went on to cite the proverb (20:24) they were reading that night. The word "random" caught my attention, fittingly: **R**andom **A**ccess (here-a-verse, there-a-verse) **B**ible **R**eading is deeply embedded into our culture. At least, this was a proverb. But even proverbs deserve a fair hearing, in case the context has something to add. In most books of the Bible, the context not only has something to add, but it's the divinely inspired wineskin (holder, shaper, controller, and protector) of the messages of God.

So how do we give them a fair hearing? How do we read the Bible so as to drink deeply from the new wine of God's Spirit in Jesus Christ? How do I read the Bible so as to create no inkblot?

Instead of a random proverb or verse, what if we came away from our Bible studies with a sort of "devotional" or "spiritual digest of a Bible book"? (See Rule #8 below.) What if when we were done we could summarize the primary purposes and messages of a Bible book? What if we could give the book a title that would help us remember its life-changing impact? What if we knew its key themes and teachings, and could see how it was shaped and put together by the author? What if we could summarize its thought about God and his kingdom, and thus understand what it says to us about how we should live within that kingdom? These are the kinds of things that good Bible reading gives to us. They are a "fair hearing."

We continue our look at a better way with Rules 4-10.

# Rules 4-10 of Good Bible Reading

## Rule #4: Highlight recurring words and ideas.

I encourage highlighting—mentally and perhaps literally. I like to make several photocopies of the Bible book I'm reading for personal study. I don't want to start marking up my main copy until I know a little better what to highlight. (Once you've read through a book several times, you begin to see what words and ideas stand out and are repeated throughout the text.) Then I get a set of different colored markers and highlighters. Starting with the Introduction, I begin highlighting (coloring) words that I know are repeated and seem significant. For example, I might highlight the word "faith" with green and the word "love" with blue. I then go through the whole book highlighting and coloring all the repetitions of those words and sometimes similar expressions. Does that make sense? I'm like a kid with crayons, but I'm coloring with a purpose.

This is pretty straightforward. But let's look at an example. Here's a simple one from 1 Thessalonians. In Paul's first letter to the Thessalonians, he begins the Thanksgiving (think Introduction) like this:

> We always give thanks to God for all of you and mention you in our prayers, constantly remembering before God and Father your <u>work</u> of faith and <u>labor</u> of love and <u>steadfastness</u> of hope in our Lord Jesus Christ. For we know . . . . (1:3).

For those reading this in black and white, to see the full effect, you'll need to get out your color highlighters and mark as follows:

faith = green
love = blue
hope = yellow

Then continue that pattern in the citation of 1 Thessalonians 4:8-11 on the next page.

Paul talks about faith, hope, and love often in his letters. So it's possible—especially coming as the first line of the Introduction—that these might simply be very broad, fundamental values of his theology and not specifically related to the historical context and needs of the letter. On the other hand, if you're coloring the text, when you get to the section of teaching (4:13-5:11) about the Lord's coming and those who have died (possibly due to persecution—why Paul was worried about them), we find the section introduced with the word "hope" (and in a Disclosure/topic sentence, no less): "But we do not want you to be uninformed, brothers and sisters, about those who have died, so that you may not grieve as others do who have no hope." Then all three words are repeated at the close of the section:

> But since we belong to the day, let us be sober, and put on the breastplate of faith and love, and for a helmet the hope of salvation. For God has destined us not for wrath but for obtaining salvation through our Lord Jesus Christ . . . Therefore encourage one another and build up each other, as indeed you are doing (4:8-11).

As this comes immediately before the closing of the letter, I'm inclined to think that the repetition of all three words serves as a type of bookend (*inclusio*) with their use in the opening (possibly involved in some circular structuring). And the point is that I might not have noticed this if I hadn't colored the words. Not only can highlighting recurring words and ideas help to pinpoint key themes, therefore, but it also helps to show how things are put together.

But what about version? I would be remiss if we didn't talk a minute about the question of version. The advantage I have in coloring the text is that I do it in Greek. That way I know the author really used the same word. Sometimes this is not clear in English, as one of the values of good English style is to vary the word choice. This was not the case in the Hebrew and Greek literature of the Bible, as repetition served different purposes, as we've seen. What this means is that when you go to highlight recurring words and ideas, you'll want to use as literal a translation as you can (that makes sense to you), since a principle of literal translations is to duplicate the structure and language of the original as much as possible. This is why I recommend having two versions of the Bible to use when you read and study: (1) a modern, idiomatic translation (one that tries to capture in English the essence of what's being said) and (2) a more literal version when you want to pay attention to the choice of words, specific word order, etc. A concordance (a reference book that lists all the occurrences of specific words) can be helpful here as well.

The impact of recurring words and ideas in a text is a natural—intuitive and sometimes subconscious—effect the writer produces on the reader simply by the deliberate choice and repetition of words. Observing that repetition can help us as readers to get a richer picture of the content and purposes of a book, however.

Since he gives us a key-idea summary of what his story is about at the beginning, the Gospel of John provides a great example of how color-coding the text can help to focus the messages. Let's take the very beginning:

> In the beginning was the Word, and the Word was with God, and the Word was God. He was in the beginning with God. All things came into being through him, and without him not one thing came into being. What has come into being in him was life, and the life was the light of all people. The light shines in the darkness, and the darkness did not overcome it. . . . (John 1:1-5).

---

Word = blue
life = green
light/darkness = yellow
the Word being (with) God = red letters

---

First, can you see how this opening sentence is an amazing introduction to the story John is about to tell? The very first affirmation—and it's made boldly, without reservation—is that Jesus (verse 14 makes the association of "the Word" with Jesus clear from the beginning) is creator God and the very expression ("Word") of God.

Light and life come from him. The story to follow tells about that light, how it shines in the darkness, and what it means for all people.

For starters, I colored the words "Word," "life," and "light" (and "darkness"). I then highlighted the sentence that underscores the identification of the Word as God. He is the divine source of all things, and in this case particularly of light and life. Are you interested in light and life? Then I assume John's story of Jesus is of interest to you—based on the use and repetition of this word. When you go through the rest of John's book and highlight these words, along with several other key terms (like "faith" or "belief") introduced in the opening passage (John 1:1-18), the importance and meaning of these ideas comes through loud and clear.

Many verses in John's book illustrate this. For now, check out 12:44-50. In the heat of battle when the religious leaders were doing all they could to squelch the response of the people to Jesus (like throwing them out of the synagogue), the text says:

> Then Jesus cried aloud: "Whoever believes in me believes not in me but in him who sent me. And whoever sees me sees him who sent me. I have come as light into the world, so that everyone who believes in me should not remain in darkness. I do not judge anyone who hears my words and does not keep them, for I came not to judge the world, but to save the world. The one who rejects me and does not receive my word has a judge; on the last day the word that I have spoken will serve as judge, for I have not spoken on my own but the Father who sent me has himself given me a commandment about what to say and what to speak. And I know that his commandment is eternal life" (John 12:44-50).

Amazing! And do you see how the repetition and convergence of key words and ideas help us catch the importance of these ideas? It's pretty obvious, isn't it? Did you notice the identification of Jesus with God the Father in both texts?

The impact of coloring the text can be tremendous. Don't let the relative brevity of our discussion of this rule fool you. Highlighting recurring words and ideas is a helpful tool of good Bible reading. I'm not spending much time on it because it's easy to understand and easy to do, not because it's less helpful. When you take the time to color a Bible book, highlighting recurring words and ideas, the veins of thought begin to emerge and broadcast the pulse of the text. Like different colored threads woven into a beautiful cloth, a divine tapestry of interconnected thought begins to stand out in the pages of scripture (as opposed to "jumping out" at us because of something we are thinking about or feeling at the moment), and we begin to enjoy the heartbeat of God.

And remember, as the heart pumps blood through the veins of our bodies, the pieces work together to create and support the whole. Once these veins/threads of thought stand out in the text (helped by our highlighting), we can then zoom out and consider how they help shape and join together the sections and points of the book as a whole. We do this so that we won't just put individual words and phrases under a microscope (another way to create potential inkblots), but so that we may look clearly into some life-giving features of the face and kingdom of God—revealed to us in the books of God.

**Rule #4 in short: Highlight key words.**

## Rule #5: Appreciate the differences of genre.

As we read and explore books of the Bible, it becomes obvious that the Bible contains different types of literature. This is because, like a small library, the Bible is a collection of writings from a span of 1,500 years. Containing such types as historical and theological narratives, legal and genealogical documentation, songs and poetry, proverbs and wisdom sayings, prophecy and oracles, parables and short stories, letters and speeches, among others; the Bible incorporates a wide variety of literary styles and types. We call these differences in type of literature "genre." The genre naturally affects the way you read a particular book or document—if you are familiar with the type, that is. You don't read an internet blog the same way you read a published autobiography. You don't read a romance novel the same as you do a medical text book. They're just different, and we make natural mental adjustments to get what we're supposed to from the different kinds of texts.

Because the Bible is full of different genres and sub-genres, and some of them are unfamiliar to us, it's important to appreciate the impact of the literary type on the shape and content of a book. This is why some books on how to read the Bible focus on these differences. At the book level, moreover, appreciating the genre is really another way of expressing Rule #1 ("Read the whole book . . ."), if we take the book-level genre seriously enough, since most will imply the need to read and work with the book as a whole. In their classic *How to Read the Bible for All Its Worth*, Gordon Fee and Douglas Stuart organize their presentation around the major types of Bible literature, and I highly recommend it as you seek to appreciate the differences of genre. This is also why I gave you information about some of the conventions of letter-writing in New Testament times (Thanksgivings, Disclosures, Petitions, etc.). These are pieces (sub-types) of the letter/speech genre. Any knowledge we can gain about the culture and particular characteristics of the way they thought and wrote back then is helpful and valid.

As you know by now, however, I believe that even though some of the types are foreign to us and require a little extra work (exploration and investigation), the majority of Bible genres are common and intuitive enough that if we focus on the book itself—reading and thinking and reading again—the more important questions of the purposes and meanings can be answered without a technical knowledge of the genre. We find comparable types to most biblical content in our reading and writing and viewing today. That's why, from a standpoint of genre, reading the Bible is not inherently different. On the other hand, differences in genre do at times make understanding a verse, a group of verses, or even a whole book more difficult. So, again, don't let the brevity of my discussion of genre mislead you into thinking that I don't think it's important. I wouldn't have included it as one of the rules of good Bible reading if that were the case.

## The Apocalyptic Genre

A notable exception to the idea that we can get the main points by simply reading and exploring the text itself is a genre of Bible days called apocalyptic. "Apocalyptic" is actually a Greek word brought over into English (= a transliteration) that in its verb form means to *reveal* or *disclose*. As a noun, the word (*apokalupsis*) means *revelation*. This is—as you are thinking—the genre of the book of Revelation. If you've ever tried to read the book of Revelation or listened to various prophetic and end time interpretations, you've been exposed to how unfamiliar this type of writing is to modern Americans and to the difficulties of understanding it brings.

True to its name, apocalyptic literature has to do with divine unveiling or revealing of important, hidden messages about the unfolding of history. The revelation is usually given through dreams and visions. The language is magnificent and highly symbolic. Numbers convey overarching themes of good vs. evil and various periods of time, as part of its use of symbolism. The purpose of apocalyptic literature was to help a group of people—God's people—endure the worst of times, when political or religious suffering challenged the very fabric of life and faith. As a way of communicating God's

125

ultimate control over history and the depth of his passion for his people (despite appearances to the contrary), the building blocks of apocalyptic thus became extremely imaginative, with fantastic, non-real images, like giant beasts and dragons and multi-headed creatures, with ultimate end time (eschatological) predictions and expressions.

The extreme language of the apocalyptic genre/style attempts to capture the importance of the events it describes and reflects the severity of the purpose. In other words, the style reflects the nature of the content because the messages often have to do with the most significant events in the unfolding of history. To illustrate, 1 Enoch (an apocalyptic book from before the time of Christ) attempts to describe one of Enoch's visions: "And in every respect it excelled (the other)—in glory and great honor—to the extent that it is impossible for me to recount to you concerning its glory and greatness" (14:16-17).[1] In other words, it's beyond words.

Apocalyptic literature appears to have roots in the Old Testament prophets like Isaiah and Ezekiel, as their messages and predictions of the coming day of the Lord used the strongest possible language to help people see the seriousness of sin and the consequences of rebellion.[2] Joel 2:30-31 provides a good example: "I will show portents in the heavens and on the earth, blood and fire and columns of smoke. The sun shall be turned to darkness, and the moon to blood, before the great and terrible day of the Lord comes."[3] Over time, the goals of communicating the severity of God's righteous judgment appear to have combined with the hardships of extreme religious and political pressures to produce a whole new way of communicating the control of God over history and his care for his people—the apocalyptic style or genre. (Remember, the bulk of the Jewish people were violently ripped away from their homeland by Nebuchadnezzar II and carried into Babylonian captivity in the seventh and sixth centuries BC). Part of the inherent purpose of apocalyptic literature was, therefore, to give people hope and courage in the face of great oppression and spiritual crises.

To help God's people endure the worst of times: apocalyptic is hope for a brighter future in the middle of intense suffering and despair during times of overt oppression and persecution.[4] Seeking to comfort the Jewish people after the destruction of Jerusalem, 2 Baruch (a Jewish apocalyptic work thought to have been written around AD 100) provides a nice statement of the purpose of his writing:

> But also hear the word of consolation. For I mourned with regard to Zion and asked grace from the Most High and said, "Will these things exist for us until the end? And will these things befall us always?" And the Mighty One did according to the multitude of his grace, and the Most High according to the magnitude of his mercy, and he revealed to me a word that I might be comforted, and showed me visions that I might not be again sorrowful, and made known to me the mysteries of the times, and showed me the coming of the periods.
>
> My brothers, therefore I have written to you that you may find consolation with regard to the multitude of tribulations. . . . (2 Baruch 81:1-82:1).[5]

The revelation is of God's coming judgment and salvation to those who put their faith and fortunes in his hand.[6] This is part of the reason that the language is not only highly symbolic, but also cryptic or esoteric—it was designed to communicate to those who were suffering (the righteous and elect of God) while hiding its "illegal" or "subversive" ideas from the leaders/governments responsible for the suffering. It was thus a way of communicating and concealing at the same time[7] (Jesus used the parables like this—they both revealed to those who were interested and concealed from those with selfish, impure, or political motives).[8]

Apocalyptic became a relatively common genre for the Jewish people for several hundred years, from roughly 200 BC to 200 AD and extending into Jewish and Christian literature for centuries. The latter part of the book of Daniel (beginning in chapter 7) is a good early example of an apocalyptic style. The text describes a series of visions, starting with a dream about the four winds of heaven and four great beasts that came up out of the sea: a lion with eagles' wings; a bear with tusks; a leopard with four heads and four wings; and a dreadful and terrifying beast, with ten horns and iron teeth. The numbers four and ten also illustrate the common, symbolic use of numbers in apocalyptic literature. Many of us are familiar with Daniel's famous vision of the four kingdoms—a statue with a head of gold, chest and arms of silver, middle and thighs of bronze, legs of iron, and feet of iron and clay. "And in the days of those kings the God of heaven will set up a kingdom that shall never be destroyed . . ." (Daniel 2:31-45).

The intertestamental (between the Old and New Testaments) book of 1 Enoch contains numerous examples of the ultimate and cosmic style of apocalyptic literature:

> The God of the universe, the Holy Great One, will come forth from his dwelling. . . . And great fear and trembling shall seize them unto the ends of the earth. Mountains and high places will fall down and be frightened. And high hills shall be made low; and they shall melt like a honeycomb before the flame. And earth shall be rent asunder; and all that is upon the earth shall perish (1:3-8).

Readers familiar with the book of Revelation will recognize similarities in Enoch's language about the end of heaven and earth:

> And I saw a deep pit with heavenly fire on its pillars; I saw inside them descending pillars of fire that were immeasurable (in respect to both) altitude and depth. And on top of that pit I saw a place without the heavenly firmament about it or earthly foundation under it or water. There was nothing on it—not even birds—but it was a desolate and terrible place. And I saw there the seven stars (which) were like great, burning mountains. (Then) the angel said (to me), "This place is the (ultimate) end of heaven and earth: it is the prison house for the stars and the powers of heaven" (18:11-14).

Jesus himself used the language of apocalyptic at times, illustrated by his description of the destruction of the temple in Mark:

> But in those days, after that suffering, the sun will be darkened, and the moon will not give its light, and the stars will be falling from heaven, and the powers in the heavens will be shaken. Then they will see the Son of Man coming in clouds with great power and glory. Then he will send out the angels, and gather his elect from the four winds, from the ends of the earth to the ends of heaven (Mark 13:24-27).

The Apocalypse of Enoch, The Apocalypse of Ezra, The Apocalypse of Zephaniah, The Apocalypse of Baruch, . . . of Sedrach, . . . of Abraham, . . . of Adam, . . . of Elijah: the first lines (= the names) of these documents reveal the popularity of this style of writing during those times.

## The Book of Revelation

This history lies behind the language and purposes of the book of Revelation: "The Apocalypse of Jesus Christ."

> Then I turned to see whose voice it was that spoke to me, and on turning I saw seven golden lampstands, and on the midst of the lampstands I saw one like the Son of Man, clothed with a long robe and with a golden sash across his chest. His head and his hair were white as white wool, white as snow; his eyes were like a flame of fire, his feet were like burnished bronze, refined as in a furnace, and his voice was like the sound of many waters. In his right hand he held seven stars, and from his mouth came a shape, two-edged sword, and his face was like the sun shining with full force. When I saw him, I fell at his feet as though dead. But he placed his right hand on me, saying, "Do not be afraid; I am the first and the last, and the living one. I was dead, and see, I

am alive forever and ever; and I have the keys of Death and Hades. Now write what you have seen . . ." (Revelation 1:12-19).[9]

My purpose here is not to give you detailed instruction about how to interpret the book of Revelation—that's a study for another day. My purpose is to help you see that the style and genre of apocalyptic is unique; it's different from common literary and cinematic styles of today. And here's an important point: *any creditable interpretation of the book of Revelation—its themes, symbols, prophecies, and purposes—must take into account*, therefore, *the inherent character and purposes of this type of writing, as well as the overall picture of the book as a whole.* As we've seen, one of the primary purposes of apocalyptic literature was to help the people of God endure the worst of times.

Complicating any interpretation of the book of Revelation is that we do not know exactly when it was written, as well as other ingredients of the historical context (more on the importance of the historical context in Rule #6). We do know that beginning with Nero (37-68 AD), imperial Rome released a torrent of intense persecution (64-68 AD) against the Christians of that day—Tertullian (160-220 AD) later referred to persecution of Christians as an "institution of Nero."[10] It's highly likely that both the apostle Peter and the apostle Paul—pillars of Jewish and Gentile Christianity—were martyred in Rome as part of that persecution (it's said that Peter was crucified upside down and Paul was beheaded). You've probably heard the adage—Nero fiddled while Rome burned, and then blamed it on the Christians. The *Annals* of Tacitus (56-117 AD) record some of the horrors:

> Therefore, first those were seized who admitted their faith, and then, using the information they provided, a vast multitude were convicted, not so much for the crime of burning the city, but for hatred of the human race. And perishing they were additionally made into sports: they were killed by dogs by having the hides of beasts attached to them, or they were nailed to crosses or set aflame, and, when the daylight passed

away, they were used as nighttime lamps. Nero gave his own gardens for this spectacle and performed a Circus game, in the habit of a charioteer mixing with the plebs or driving about the race-course (XV.44).

In case you didn't catch that, let me say it again: Nero had Christians rounded up, killed, impaled on poles, covered with wax and set on fire to light his nightly garden parties. He had some of our greatest leaders killed, and he sought to blame and destroy Christians everywhere. Does the language of apocalyptic begin to sound fitting?

These types of persecutions continued under the Flavian dynasty (69-96 AD) and other Roman emperors. Describing the persecution of Christians in his day, Tertullian wrote in his *Apology*: "If the Tiber floods the city, or if the Nile refuses to rise, or if the sky withholds its rain, if there is an earthquake, a famine, a pestilence, at once the cry is raised: 'Christians to the lion.'"[11] The emperor Domitian (81-96 AD) resurrected the imperial cult, which declared Caesar a god. Many biblical scholars believe that the book of Revelation was written during the latter part of Domitian's reign. As "Caesar worship" developed, Christians were given the opportunity to deny their faith and save themselves from criminal punishment. All they had to do was burn a pinch of incense and say, "Caesar is Lord," and they could go free. Some did. Many did not . . . because for them only "Jesus is Lord." Is it any wonder that many students of the book of Revelation believe that John refers to Rome when he describes "Babylon the great, mother of whores and of earth's abominations"—the woman who "was drunk with the blood of the saints and the blood of the witnesses to Jesus" (17:5). This is not to be the final outcome, however, Revelation proclaims:

> Then I heard a loud voice in heaven, proclaiming, "Now have come the salvation and the power and the kingdom of our God and the authority of his Messiah, for the accuser of our comrades has been thrown down, who accuses them day and night before our God. But they have conquered him by the

blood of the Lamb and the word of their testimony, for they did not cling to life even in the face of death. . . ." (12:10-12).

When we read the Bible to get God's point, genre makes a difference in how we are to read it. It certainly does in the case of apocalyptic literature and thus with the book of Revelation. As such writings sought to give courage and hope by the revelation of God's sovereign hand in the final outcomes of history through highly symbolic, cryptic, cosmic, catastrophic, and prophetic language to suffering people of God; any credible interpretation of Revelation must first answer the historical question of how the words and images spoke to the people of God for whom they were originally written— God's first conversation with his people. In other words, how did the verses and the book as a whole comfort and encourage the Christians of that day who were striving to hold on to their faith in the midst of terrible troubles? What if you were one of them and tomorrow might be asked to burn a pinch of incense and proclaim Caesar Lord? Or your father or brother or mother or wife . . . Is it worth it? For every individual verse or group of verses, we must also seek to answer The Question (how does it function within the book-level context) before we can assign it some modern connection to power and politics. Genre makes a difference and so does the historical setting, which is our next rule for good Bible reading.

**Rule #5 in short: Appreciate the genre.**

# Rule #6: Tune in—as much as possible—to the historical setting.

The reason I say "as much as possible" is because in some cases—as I suggested with the book of Revelation—we just don't know much about the specific historical setting. This is where secondary information, like church tradition, historical and archaeological information about the times and places, characteristics of genre, conventions of letter writing, etc. (these sorts of things) become more important. Most of our discussion to this point has focused on the literary context of a Bible book. This changes when we talk about the historical context, although the primary ingredients of the historical setting also come to us through the literary context—which is why I'm a big fan of reading the text first.

We've covered the meaning of the "historical context" previously (see Chapter 8), so I won't repeat that here. Let me remind you, however, that every document has a real-world context that causes it to be written and shapes its style and content. The historical context exists outside of and surrounds the written document, though it can be referenced and described within the document. Does that make sense? It involves the people who participated in the writing and the reading of the original document. We sometimes think of it as background information—the W questions: Who wrote it? To whom was it written? Where was it written? When was it written? Why was it written? The more we know about the background of a document, the better situated we are to understand it properly. The question "Why in the world was this book written?" gets at the core of the historical context.

When it comes to books of the Bible, sometimes we know a lot about the history that produced a book; sometimes, we know only a little. And each book is slightly different. The book of Revelation is a case in point where we know a few things about the specifics of its composition, but not other things. Like most books, there are internal clues that help to contextualize it. For instance, the author identifies himself as "John" and addresses the book to "the seven churches that are in Asia" (1:4). Again (in 1:9-11), the author states explicitly who he is and to whom he's writing:

> I, John, your brother who share with you in Jesus the perse-
> cution and the kingdom and the patient endurance, was on
> the island called Patmos because of the word of God and the
> testimony of Jesus. I was in the spirit on the Lord's day, and I
> heard behind me a loud voice like a trumpet saying, "Write in
> a book what you see and send it to the seven churches, to
> Ephesus, to Smyrna, to Pergamum, to Thyatira, to Sardis, to
> Philadelphia, and to Laodicea."

These kinds of statements provide us valuable background information to begin piecing together the historical context. From these, we know who wrote it (at least we know it was someone named "John"), we know where, and we know for whom it was written, generally. We don't know when, however, since the "to whom" is broad and we don't have any clear date references in the course of the book (but a lot of symbolic, apocalyptic stuff). As we read the book, moreover, the apocalyptic genre combines with clear indications of suffering and even martyrdom on the part of Christians to give us a broad picture of severe historical pressure and persecution (". . . who share with you in Jesus the persecution and the kingdom and the patient endurance"). These are the kinds of things involved in reconstructing the historical setting.

Some time ago, my father-in-law gave our family an old radio that belonged to his family when he was a boy. He kept it up and working through the years (he was an electronics repairman) and gave it to us as an historical and family keepsake. Just think, some of our relatives, perhaps curled up together on the floor by the fire on a cold wintry night, enjoyed evening shows and listened intently to major historical events—like news of World War II—on this radio. It now sits on a small table against the wall in our living room. From time to time, I turn it on and slowly turn the dial (that's the way they used to tune radios) to see what I can get.

Unlike the little radio I wear when I jog, this old radio has several bands and frequencies that I'm not used to (AM and FM was basically all I knew). This radio includes police radio frequencies, airline frequencies, amateur radio, and others. When I first plugged it in and turned it on—it takes a minute for the tubes to warm up—I didn't know what the knobs were for, so I went exploring. After turning the main knob for a while and enduring some jolting static, I changed the other control knob, which switched to another range of frequencies, to another band. As I turned the frequency turner again, I began to notice all sorts of languages—Spanish, French, something that sounded like Chinese. One was in English, but after listening for a while, I learned it was coming from China! I had heard of this before, but never experienced it. I was listening to short wave radio. I was actually tuned in to something that was happening on the other side of the world.

When we read Bible books, we do something similar. We tune in to something that was happening in the world far away—not just in miles, but also years. Though there is much static at times and some of the information has passed into the crevices of history, amazingly, the tubes and tuners still work. That is, footprints of the writer and his or her relationship with the readers are still there, evident in the Bible book. Sometimes the prints are many and deep; so, the circumstances are clear. Other times, they are light or even implied; so, we have to tune in more carefully and listen closer to see what we can glean from the clues and the echoes. Like looking into a mirror of history that we hold up next to the text, the circumstances and events that produced the books are reflected in the pages and can sometimes be inferred. It's like listening to one side of a telephone conversation, however, and that's why we need to take some time to think about the historical situation that lay behind the book we are reading. This glimpse into the past—especially the concrete statements included in the document—is an important part of the makeup of a Bible book. It surrounds and imprints the text. The historical setting is, therefore, a real part of the book-pictures we are putting together as we seek out the voice and messages of God.

135

If you know nothing about a Bible book that you're about to read, then it will probably be helpful to do a little background reading to learn something of where the book fits in the scope of Bible history. It would be quite a challenge to pick a book at random and read it with absolutely no knowledge of the Bible or the historical setting of the book. If you are new to the Bible, then, I recommend that you read a brief introduction to a book so that you won't be completely lost and have to start totally from scratch; though you could, because—and this is an important point for all of us—most of our specific information about the historical setting is primary information; that is, it comes from the book itself. This is where we get the best data about what was going on to produce the book we're reading. If you have very little Bible knowledge, even that information might not help much—'cause you might not know anything about the people and places the book mentions. So again, reading background material about a Bible book as a sort of historical introduction can be a helpful starting point for tuning in to the situation behind the book. (Here again Gordon Fee and Douglas Stuart's *How to Read the Bible Book by Book* is a good tool).

For the most part, however, the situation behind a Bible book is gleaned from the book itself. That is, we have to see what the book says before we can know anything about what was going on. This is where scholars and those who write the introductory materials about the book get their starting information (and from other scholars who through the years have helped us understand the history and culture of Bible times). Once you know enough about a book to begin reading it (and that can be nothing), the historical situation that surrounds the book is to be reconstructed—as much as possible—by piecing together the various clues from the book that indicate what the situation was like. What's the problem or need? Is there a problem? Who's involved? How does the writer try to solve the problem or meet the need? What's the overall goal and purpose of the book in relation to the situation? Our goal as we read is to perceive the problem or situation behind the document, then see how the contents fit together to deal with that situation. (Do you see how the historical context merges with the literary to produce the contours and content of the biblical material?) The specific situation can then be placed within the more general historical setting and culture of the time, taken from other Bible books and secondary sources, commentaries, whatever.

The historical context is an integral part of the shape and substance of a Bible book. Tuning into the situation is, therefore, a part of good Bible reading. I'll give you some specific examples of how we do this in the chapters to come. For now, the word is "tune in"— be observant, think about, deduce, reconstruct, envision—as much as possible the real world circumstances that gave birth to the text in front of you. If the document itself, the literary context, is the offspring; the historical context is the mother and father of the things we read in the pages of scripture—God acting in history and inspiring his word to us.

**Rule #6 in short: Tune in to the situation.**

## Rule #7: Use commentaries and other study tools with discretion.

Related to our discussion of how we learn about the historical context is Rule #7 for good Bible reading about books and commentaries on the Bible. It really applies to about any sort of secondary information on the Bible, and it's important enough that I've made it one of the ten rules of reading. Rule #7 is to use commentaries, books, and other study tools with discretion, which basically means don't get your information about the Bible from somewhere or someone else. Read it yourself.

I do not want to disparage or criticize those who take the time to learn and make the effort to teach us about the Bible, and help us understand its messages. What would we do without good teachers? Without pastors? Without scholars? The New Testament includes teaching as a fundamental gift of the Spirit within the church. If teaching about the Bible were of no use to us, my efforts in writing this book would be ironically wasted. The years have produced an enormous amount of good information and helpful materials on the Bible and books of the Bible (so much that we can't possibly read it all), and we can learn a lot from them. They have also produced a lot of unhelpful and even bad material. So how do we know which is which?

One of the main points of this book has been that in several real ways the Bible has become a kind of lost treasure, buried under multiple layers of cultural, historic, traditional, psychological, and spiritual barriers, separating us from the living word of God. It's as if the Bible were surrounded by a sort of deafening noise that drowns out the sounds of scripture. Inkblotitis is itself a form of separation between us and the word of God caused by the disintegration of scripture. Another form of separation between us and the word is—and this is our point—what someone else has said about what a verse or group of verses means. And then what someone else has said on top of the last person. And then someone else. Sermons, theology, commentary. "Glosses," the Reformers referred to it in their translations of scripture. The Bible is not only the most read book of all time, it's also the most written and talked about. . . . the most commented on. . . . the most theologized. . . . the basis for denominational teachings. . . . for our history. . . . for our beliefs. . . . for churches. . . . for our practices. . . . for our Sundays. . . . for our spiritual lives. . . . for our differences. . . . for fights. . . . for wars. . . . for just about anything you can think of. It's like there's this gigantic pile of tradition and history, dumped out over time (or dripped like ecclesiastical stalagmites), with epochs of theological dust and debris that's settled on top of the books themselves—sometimes moldy and even rotten.

For many of us, the Bible is what someone else says it is and is thus buried under layers of talk and tradition. This is why I say use commentaries and books about the Bible with discretion. Not that they are evil or bad for us. Books based on the Bible are in many cases the next best thing to the Bible itself. But that's just it: they are the *next* best thing. And sometimes they are not even that. As valuable as commentaries and books on the Bible are, they can be a devilish diversion that keeps us from exploring the amazing word of the Spirit of God for ourselves.

The point is that you should let nothing stand between you and the experience of God in scripture. Of course, we need help at times. Of course, we need to learn things about the background and history of Bible books. Of course, it's good to know about the orthodox teachings of the Christian faith. Of course, we should compare notes with fellow believers who are on the same quest to know and love God. And, of course, it's okay to read books and commentaries on the Bible. But—and this is tremendously important—when all is said and done, you need to spend time in the word of God, with God, not with someone else's thoughts and experiences in the word. How do you know that what some commentary or professor or pastor says about a section of scripture is what God says? Inkblotitis plays no favorites. I have read many commentaries that are not only one step removed from the text, but amount to little more than commentary on commentaries and years of Bible tradition.[12] Or they serve as platforms for subjective ideas and personal or corporate agendas (as many sermons do as well). They don't get anywhere close

139

to answering the fundamental questions of the text—things you and I know about—like how it fits together and what its primary messages are as part of God's sacred history. Like piles of spiritual soot—or perhaps sand, as in the discoveries of the papyri of Egypt—our theological discussions and opinions can bury the very thing that sparked our interest and caused us to start digging in the first place.

How do we remove the soot? Simple, we blow it away with the turn of a page.

So, yes, use any sort of Bible helper book you want—a little to get you started, and then more only after you've done your own work in the text. How else can you personally experience the renewing power of God's Holy Spirit than by journeying with him through the inspired pages of God's encounters with his people? How else can your developing-through-the-word faith be *your* faith? How else can you overcome your own challenges of inkblotitis? Much less, filtered through someone else's? Inkblotitis (and every form of evil) is healed from within through intimate encounter with the Spirit of the Lord God himself. Not pastor Chuck or professor Barry or any other human. If you read the Bible with the passion and care we've been talking about, not only are you likely to see and uncover long buried truths of God that most pastors or commentaries never get around to commenting on—if they even notice—but I believe you will be accepting and opening one of God's greatest gifts to humanity. But in this case, he's not giving it to humanity; he's giving it to *you*. Think of that. The God of all creation wants to come to your house, spend time with you, and give you his Holy Spirit. Let nothing keep you from that divine appointment.

**Rule #7 in short: Use commentaries with discretion.**

## Rule #8: Digest your experiences in the word.

When our bodies digest the food we've eaten, it becomes a part of us. When we digest the things we learn from scripture, our goal is that the teachings and messages of God become a part of us. Our goal in reading the Bible is to come to know God, to draw close to God, and to have those experiences renew and remake us. (We'll look more closely at the idea of applying the Bible to our lives in the next rule.) If we're honestly seeking God, then it's not just a mental exercise or part of a list of things we should do. Change happens as we accept the presence and influence of the Spirit, because he recreates us from the inside out—what we believe, what we think, what we feel, and how we act. It's all being affected as we hear the voice of God in scripture. Real life-change ("transformation" and "sanctification") is not easy, however, and sometimes takes careful attention (prayer, planning, and practice) because of the depths of our old beliefs and habits. Just because we learn something new, even though it affects the old, it doesn't replace it—at least not immediately. The new self and the old self battle on for years. (Again, we look at application next.) Before we're ready to take that step, to equip ourselves in our ongoing battles with evil, we need to digest the word.

Frequently, the Bible compares the word of God to food or bread. Jesus said, "I am the bread of life. Whoever comes to me will never be hungry, and whoever believes in me will never be thirsty" (6:35). He says it again a little later in the same chapter and compares himself to the manna that God used to feed the Israelites in the desert, saying, "This is the bread that comes down from heaven, so that one may eat of it and not die. I am the living bread that came down from heaven. Whoever eats of this bread will live forever . . ." (6:50-51). The association with faith, with coming to know and believing in Jesus, in the context is clear and connects this image of Jesus as the bread of life with the overarching themes of faith and life in John's Gospel. Another well-known example of the association of the word of God with food and nourishment is Jesus' classic response to Satan's temptation for Jesus to turn stones into bread. Quoting Deuteronomy 8:3, which also uses the image of God's

141

manna in the desert as a symbol of our need for God and his word, Jesus said, "One does not live by bread alone, but by every word that comes from the mouth of God" (Matthew 4:4). This was in fact the purpose and test of God's manna—to trust in God.

When I use the word "digest" here in our 8th rule of good Bible reading, I'm using it as a reminder that reading is not enough. Reading is the starting point. We need to read, to understand, to believe, to ingest, to breathe in, and to absorb the truths of God deeply into our minds and hearts. We do this as we think about what we're reading. We do this as we seek to understand the mind and actions of God. We do this as we meditate (a word we don't use much anymore) on the ideas of the text and as we grapple (another odd word) with our experiences in the word (remember Jacob wrestling with the angel?), knowing that it all points to Christ as the living Word with whom and through whom we know God. The first song in the Old Testament book of songs (Psalms) kept this idea before the ancient people of God: "Happy are those who do not follow the advice of the wicked . . . but their delight is in the law of the Lord, and on his law they meditate day and night" (Psalm 1:1-2).

So when I say we need to digest what we've read, this is what I mean. Like a soft rain on dry ground, the truth of God must begin to soak slowly into the hardened soil of our deeply broken selves, seeping past the cracks of our fundamental deception and misunderstandings, consistently penetrating into the underground rivers that flow forcefully with the distortions of our enslaving wounds of self-interest, to a place at the very core of our being; so that, with seeds of life and renewal, the Spirit of God might implant himself into the nucleus of our souls. Change begins at a deep place with God in the heart. Like a tiny seed breaking through the suppressing sod into the light of dawn, this happens in prayer and personal encounter with the Word, as we experience God in the Bible and in our lives.

Some people like to journal as they pray and spend time with God—a sort of devotional diary. This is one good way to crystallize and personalize some of the meanings of our encounters in the word, and if this fits your style, then I recommend it as a tool for digesting the word. Carrying on an ongoing conversation with God ("praying") as we seek to understand God's first conversations with his people should be at the top of our list of ways of digesting the will and word of God. Prayer-partners—what if we broadened that to book-partners and life-partners, as we approach God in scripture? And, as I'll recommend in the conclusion of this book as part of a plan for combating inkblotitis in the church, how about doing it in teams? Good ol' fashioned Bible study groups that we reframe as "book-groups"—Bible book clubs—whose goal is to help a group of people listen carefully and closely to God's original conversations with his people and then seek to digest and live the word as a small group community of God's people. Perhaps social networking sites dedicated to putting together the big-picture puzzles of Bible books? Of course, there are other ways to meditate on and digest the word of God. These are just examples.

The word "digest" has some other common meanings. In addition to "breaking down" and processing food, it also means to absorb something mentally—this provides the basis of our analogy between eating and reading. It can mean to organize something, to abridge, or summarize. We also use it as a noun to refer to a shortened or summary version of a work, or to a collection of such abridged or condensed versions. *Reader's Digest* comes to mind. I suspect that as part of our efforts to digest the things we learn as we read and study the Bible, we should probably write down some things—produce a condensation of the things we learn—as a way of helping us remember, think about, and refer back to the points and purposes of Bible books. The word "distill" also fits: we want to distill and summarize our experiences in the word. Once we've done that with several books, we'll have our own, growing, personal *digest* of our journeys in scripture. Remember the story I told you of my son carefully putting away the 2,000-piece puzzle, assembled in sections? Our notes will help us retain and use the results of our time in scripture.

To help you document your journeys in the Bible, I'd like to propose a series of questions. These are just samples—you can do it however you like. But these are the kinds of things I think would be beneficial to know and remember when you read and study a book of the Bible. Try to answer each question in a sentence or two, or with a short list. I'll give some samples in our look at Philemon and Mark in the following chapters.

**Rule #8 in short: Digest the word.**

## Building a Devotional Digest of Bible Books

### Title or Subtitle
Give the book a title (instead of its Bible name) that you believe captures the essence of its message and purpose.

### Purpose
What is the primary purpose of the book?
> What result or action did it seek from the original readers?
> What other actions did the book seek from the audience?

### Message
What is the major message of the book?
> What idea(s) or teaching does it convey?
> What are other key points or messages?

### Themes
What are the key words and themes of the book?
> Is there a verse or set of verses that seem to capture the essence or core of the book?

### Shape
How is the content shaped?
> What are the major sections?
> How do they fit together and function in relation to each other?

### Summary
Summarize the main ideas and primary purposes of the book in a short paragraph.

### Theology
What does the book teach us about God (the Father, the Son, and the Holy Spirit)?

### Kingdom
What does the book teach us about living for God in the kingdom of God.

### Life
List the ways that you believe the book should impact and change your life.

## Rule #9: Live what you learn.

Dependent on where you are in your spiritual journey and on your reasons for reading the Bible, the outcomes will be different. If you are new to the Bible and are in early stages of seeking God, then you may not be ready to embrace Rule #9, and that's okay. There's more than one legitimate reason for reading the Bible. You may just be curious, and that's a good place to start. If, on the other hand, you've checked your motives and you're at a place in your life where you're reading to encounter God and be changed by that experience, then you should not be satisfied with an academic exercise or with merely becoming acquainted with the history and thinking of the Bible. That would be like a hungry person nibbling on a potato chip, with a three-course, buffet-style meal spread before him.

If you read the Bible to get God's point, more than likely, you want to be changed by the same Spirit of God who spoke in times past through the books of the Bible. That Spirit speaks through those same books to us today; consequently, encounters with the text can transcend the literary and fully engage the spiritual—they become a means of divine grace to us today (like a sacrament). After all, the first step in any journey is to know the way you're headed.

Traditionally, talking about how teachings from scripture come to make a difference in the way we live is called *application*. How does this apply to us? How do I apply the values and teachings of the word to my life? Without application, reading the Bible is merely an academic, educational, or religious exercise—legitimate in its own right perhaps, but far beneath the goals of Christians who seek God through his word. This, then, is our 9th rule of good Bible reading. Don't just leave it in the bedroom or on the couch. Take it with you. Synchronize your actions with the heart and plans of God, with the pictures of the kingdom revealed in the text. Let the values of scripture become your values and permeate your plans. Let the word of God live within you, challenging you, guiding you, changing you. "Let the word of Christ dwell in you richly . . ," remembering that Jesus himself used the written word in his battles with the evil one.

To a certain extent, applying begins with digesting (our last rule), since that which becomes a part of us has already made a difference in what we are ("you are what you eat"). (I'll have more to say about this in a minute.) But it's not complete, if we stop there. For now, let's think about the cognitive process of applying the teachings and values of scripture to our lives. I'd like to offer a simple little model that you can use when you ask yourself how the teachings of a Bible book "apply to me." I call it *the triangle of application*.

Before tracing out the triangle, it's important to keep in mind that there are at least two major ways in which the values of God are taught or displayed in the Bible, corresponding to some extent to the difference between brain-actions (thoughts and emotions) and physical actions. Our physical actions are based on our brain actions (things we think, feel, and believe), resulting in things we value. Values are sometimes stated directly (or almost directly) in the Bible, like when it says, "God is love" or "Jesus is truth and life." These are fundamental characteristics of God and the kingdom. When God or people act, on the other hand, we have to deduce what values lie behind the actions. Why do you do what you do? Commands like "Don't steal" target actions based on values, and usually in ways that make the values behind the command fairly easy to see. On many other occasions in the Bible, moreover, we get specific, real-life instances of someone acting or being told to act in a certain way. The text may inform us of the values behind the actions or it may not. We sometimes call these examples—they are instances of someone or a group choosing to act based on a given principle or value. Now, back to the triangle of application.

There are some things in the pages of scripture that apply immediately and directly to us today—or anyone in any day. That's because they represent values and actions closely associated with basic values that transcend time and place. "Don't murder," "don't steal," and many other direct commands are so close to the values they reflect that the application is clear. We wouldn't debate about whether it's okay to murder someone today with a handgun because guns didn't exist in Bible times. The value behind the command is one of respect for human life, and, since the Bible teaches that

147

humans are made in the image of God, it gets back to the basic value for life itself and its Creator. The point is that there are numerous teachings in scripture, values and implied actions that transcend time and are easily applied to any person in any age. When you read and study a book of the Bible to get God's point and come to see the most important messages, many of the applications are obvious—they may not be easy to carry out, but they are obvious. More often than not the problem is not in *learning* what we should do, but actually *doing* it consistently.

Direct and straightforward applications represent the bottom or floor of our triangle of application (see below). These are commands and actions in the Bible that flow straight across from then to now (like "forgive one another as Christ has forgiven you," for example):

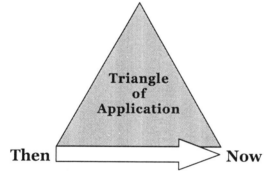

As we'll see in our look at the book of Philemon, however, there are many specific commands in the Bible that don't apply to us directly and are actually impossible for us to do in a literal sense. For example, Paul tells Philemon to receive Onesimus—a runaway slave who became a Christian—back, no longer as just a slave, but as a brother in Christ. We can't do that, can we? Onesimus doesn't belong to us. He didn't run away from us. In fact, he's dead. So there's no way we can literally obey this command. Of course, this is a silly example; the command was never issued directly to us. That doesn't mean it doesn't contain Holy Spirit-inspired meaning about how we are to live in the kingdom of God, however. Another example: in the book of Philippians, Paul urged Euodia and Syntyche, two women in that church, to start getting along with each other ("to be of the same mind"). We can't do that either; we're not them. In fact, most everything in the letters of Paul is addressed to someone else—Christians of that day dealing with problems in their churches and their lives—not to us. You see the point. There are many things inspired by God in the Bible that reflect the real-life situations of *those* people. They are pictures of how they were attempting to live out the will of God in their churches and their world, of how to follow and be like Christ. In many, if not most cases, we simply can't apply the text directly. But that doesn't mean it doesn't apply to us, that we can't apply it meaningfully and even easily.

Obviously, we can envision similar circumstances where the actions sought in these books apply quickly and easily to situations today. Though you may not have thought about it, when we do that, we are actually extracting the values behind the teachings and using them to address similar situations and issues today. When Paul tells Euodia and Syntyche to get along, it's relatively easy to see what God values and apply that in our lives today: division and fighting are not characteristic of the kingdom—friendship and love are. (You'll have to look closer and place this verse within the book-level context to see how it relates to the big-picture and themes of the book of Philippians, however. Since Philippians has a lot to do with the mind of Christ, the community of Christ, and being joyful in all kinds of circumstances, I suspect there's more than meets the eye if we turn the command into an inkblot.)

Extracting or deducing the values behind the specific instances and examples in the Bible is the upper part of our triangle of application. Once we see the values, we can then use them to govern our thinking and behavior today. We come to know the heart of God (or "the mind of Christ," as Paul calls it), see it in action in the book-level snapshots of the kingdom, then synchronize our own values and actions.

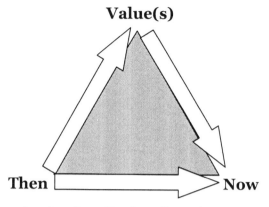

This is the triangle of application. Sometimes you can go straight from then to now. Other times you first have to understand the teachings and the values, and then apply those values to your own particular set of circumstances. This is often not difficult, once you understand the text—once you get God's point, in other words.

There are times, however, when it's not quite so easy. I don't want to mislead you. Sometimes it's debatable as to whether a particular action in the Bible should transcend the culture and flow straight across to us today. This is really a discussion for another day, but let me give an example where I think an application becomes fairly obvious, though some might chose to apply it more literally. At the end of several letters, Paul tells Christians to greet each other with a holy kiss (1 Thessalonians 5:26, 1 Corinthians 16:20, 2 Corinthians 13:12; Romans 16:16; cf. 1 Peter 5:14: "with a kiss of love"). Should we take that literally and greet each other with holy kisses today, as we seek to apply God's word to our lives? Some do. Many don't. Does the triangle of application help us in cases like this?

As with any verse of scripture, The first Question we should answer is how these verses fit and function within their own book-level contexts. These brief exhortations may very well transcend their literary contexts and carry the same (distinct) meaning regardless. Some verses are like that. But we don't know until we've read them in context. In each case, these exhortations are part of the closing greetings of the letters. Removing for now the possibility that they functioned as part of Paul's own greeting to the churches (to be passed around and shared by the church as a whole) and assuming the simple and natural meaning that Christians (everywhere) are encouraged to "greet each other with a holy kiss," then comes our question of applying this to our lives. Since in America (and some other countries), a kiss of greeting doesn't mean what it does in some other cultures, especially during ancient times, then applying the text literally would not create (instantiate, to use a computer programming term) the value behind the command and accomplish the desired result. Were I (to try) to kiss each Christian that I run into in my day-to-day encounters, it would create such an odd, off-putting result, that it would not only destroy my relationship with Christians, but it would also severely damage my personal ability to share the good news of Christ with non-Christians. The change of culture dramatically impacts the application of the value. In a culture where that would not be the case, where it would evoke and create the same value, a literal application (= duplication) might be possible and even preferable. But where it's not, the triangle of application reminds us of our goal.

As a Christian reader of the Bible, I want to know and live the heart of God—what he thinks, what he wants, what makes him smile. If we think about the values that lie behind the exhortation to greet one another with a holy kiss, we can then begin to see some options for how we can effectively apply it today. To do that, we should think for a minute about the word "holy." As Christians we are being commanded to greet each other in some way—in a "holy" way. Peter's "kiss of love" provides some insight, and I think we all get the idea to some extent. The word "holy" in Greek means sacred and different. The word "saints" comes from it—an identifying word for all Christians. The word "holy" has been used as a fundamental characteristic of God throughout the ages. It means he's completely unique, different from everything else. When applied to us, it doesn't imply the same degree of uniqueness, but it still carries that idea. There's no good English word to capture all this, I'm afraid, though I do like the word "special." Paul is, therefore, exhorting his audience to greet each other in a different way, in a special, even sacred, way—more than just a casual "hello," something that reflects the very special bond that we share as followers of Christ.

151

As I write this, I'm convicted that I don't live up to this exhortation of scripture the way I should. Paul is saying that my greeting to you as a fellow believer, as my brother or sister in Christ, is not the same as my ev'ryday greeting to everyone (if I even have one). There's something so special that we share because we have been incorporated into Christ, something that makes you and me different, that distinguishes us before God, and creates a fundamentally different and new relationship that calls for me to remember that, to act on that, and to remind you of that when I see you again. Easy to see why Peter called it a "kiss of love," isn't it? Now, Paul doesn't want us to act silly or absurd. He doesn't mean you have to do somersaults any time a Christian comes around the corner. But it does teach us that the relationships we share are extremely valuable. You have a new value to me because you are in Christ. I have a new value to you because you are in Christ. Christ makes us one. Our reconnecting with each other, seeing and greeting each other again (especially after personal and extended separation, like Paul from his churches), reflects and reminds us of that radically cool reality of God's kingdom. It's like reaffirming core values by the way we look at and talk to each other. "Greet each other in a very special way," we might say. But I think it's even more than that.

Do you see how thinking through and working with the teachings and values of the Bible help us in our efforts to apply it? After all, we really do want to live the word. Sometimes the application looks identical to the ones we read about in the text. Other times, we have to digest and then act on the basis of what we've learned and become. And just think, if you really are experiencing the thinking and speaking of God the Father, the Lord and Creator of all things, then your response will be one of faith, worship, and attraction—attraction to the most amazing, powerful, loving, healing, eternal source of all that is good and beautiful. And you'll want to be like him: "Be holy for I am holy." "Be different for I am different." "Be special, for I am special."

When the crucibles of life surround us with crushing blows of grief and pain, I want to be different. When the touch of simple joys and sprinkles of heartwarming meaning blow like gentle breezes into our routine moments, I want to be different. I want to soak in the breezes and hold up under the pressures. I want to be like my Father, whom I come to know through my Brother, the Lord Jesus. *I want to be like God.* When I read the book of God, I read it with the sincere prayer that God will hold me and mold me and change me to be like him (I bet you do, too); otherwise, I'm lost and lonely.

So when you read the Bible, read it with the prayer and the expectation that God will draw near to you as you draw near to him. He has promised that he will. But let me warn you. Two things will happen. Number one, you will be crushed: your old self, the part of you that's broken and failed because of sin. Not necessarily the first time you read or every time you read, but really and fundamentally. And the experience is certainly not pleasant. In fact, it's crushing. But it's a good thing. Like labor pains of birth, it's the beginning of change. Number two, you will be changed. You will be changed because your thinking is changed. Your mind is changed. Your heart is changed. You will be coming to know truth—distinguishing what's real and what's not. You will be changed because you see the truth in high-def. You encounter God, and that's where change begins. The effect continues as we seek to apply the values of God to our world, our lives, our thoughts and the actions they produce. Much of it will simply be the proper response of a believing heart in the presence of God. Other things aren't so easy. Our distorted thinking and bad habits run deep. Our ears of full of wax thicker than walls. That's why becoming more and more like God—sanctification—is a life-long process. We have to grow new spiritual muscles, and that takes time, work, exercise, discipline, training. It's all a part of spiritual growth, and it's a very important part of good Bible reading. New life comes from the Spirit of God. Isn't that why we read? This is why reading, applying, and experiencing the Bible is so powerful, such a wonderful gift from above, that it makes no sense not to open it. And once the books are opened, who knows what will become of you.

**Rule #9 in short: Live it.**

# Rule #10: Do it again.

There's no way to exhaust a Bible book in one read (or two or three). Because of the profound potential of every opportunity to hear from God and see his work in history, and some of the things that make understanding the Bible difficult, one could spend a lifetime unpacking most books of the Bible and never reach bottom. I suspect inspiration has something to do with that. So when you have spent some time reading and studying a Bible book, you should do it again, which brings us back around to where we started: Rule #1 for good Bible reading is to read the whole book—and don't miss the last part—*preferably several times.* After I've done some work in a book, I like to go back and read the whole thing again to see what I might have missed, to catch as much of the big-picture view that's been coming into focus through my exploring and digesting.

Our goal is to see God's purposes and teachings in each book of the Bible. We want to learn to put our emphasis where God puts his. . . . to major in the majors and not to miss the smaller things. As you read and learn to do your own work in a book of God, like putting together a great big jigsaw puzzle, the designs and meanings will begin to come together to form an overarching picture. Like a beautiful mosaic, the verse divisions (perforations) will begin to fade as you become a first-hand witness to God's original conversations with his people. This is the summit that we talked about earlier. Remember that? The acronym SABR: Summit Access Bible Reading? It's not until we've reached the summit that we have a clear view of how the rest of the landscape comes together in a wonderful panoramic of God and his kingdom. *The summit is the book-level view.* We reach the summit by reading the whole book—and then by reading it again.

Rule #10 of good Bible reading—do it again—applies to later times in your life as well. As you grow and change over time, you'll be different. When you come back to books that you've read and worked on before, you'll see things in a different light and they'll speak to issues in your life that you didn't have previously. The word will be the same, but you'll be different; so your reading and your applying will likely be different.

So do it again. Summit again. The view is just as beautiful the second time, and even more so.

Finally, there are many more books in the Bible, waiting to be read, explored, digested, and applied. When I say "do it again," I'm also talking about those books. Do what you did with one particular book—reading it to get God's points—with another book. Check out another book from God's sacred library. Then another. Do it again. And just think, as you do, you're experiencing more and more of the heart, mind, and history of God and his people in the world.

# Summit Access Bible Reading

Here's the point I've been waiting to make through all of this book (well, I've actually said it lots of times in lots of ways). *Each time you read a book of the Bible in its entirety and explore it enough to have and remember a sense of its big-picture view, you put yourself into position to be cured of inkblotitis.* When someone or something (cards, screens, and pastors) quotes a verse or a group of verses from a book of the Bible, you'll know (or you'll be in a good position to find out), if he, she, or it is using it well, as it was intended. Is it being used for God's purposes or has it been re-invented through someone else's subjective, psychological, spiritual looking-glass. The question "What does this mean to you?" becomes "What does this mean?" and this is as it should be. You now carry a part of God's inspired context with you to protect you from Rorschach-like interpretations (theirs and yours); and what you don't carry with you, you know where to find. *Ultimately, only God can cure us because inkblotitis is fundamentally a spiritual disease*; but when you equip yourself with the word of God, you will be illuminating yourself with the views and purposes of God, with pictures and scenes of the kingdom of God—from Spirit to spirit. And what better way to guard against other, ulterior views and purposes. The cure for inkblotitis is the word of God—inspired by the Spirit of God—incorporated into the human spirit.

Does the phrase *Summit Access Bible Reading* have more meaning now? It means we can look at each individual verse or set of verses from the view at the top. Or, in other words, we can see each verse as it fits within its own book-level context, and this makes all the difference in the world. It turns inkblots into snapshots—snapshots of the kingdom. As I said at the beginning, on these two rules—read the whole book and understand the verses as they relate to the book as a whole—hang all the other suggestions, books, and rules of good Bible reading. The "rules" I've been giving are simply suggestions for some of what I think are the best ways to get to the summit. You don't have to do it exactly this way. The method is not what's important. Getting to the top is. There are other ways to the top. These "rules" are my way of summarizing things I believe will help you in your quest to hear God through the Bible. However you chose to do it, the main thing is that you do it—that you discover the written word of God, and therein find God. Or, you can do it the other way around: find God and discover his word. Either way. But let me assure you, the two go together.

Here are all ten rules one more time in condensed form:

1. Read the book (See the picture . . .)
2. Book-level focus the verses (. . . get the point)
3. Discover the shape of the text
4. Highlight key words and ideas
5. Appreciate the genre
6. Tune in to the historical setting
7. Use commentaries with discretion
8. Digest the word
9. Live the word
10. Do it again

And one final thought:

Enjoy the view.

It doesn't get any better than this.

## Chapters 9 and 10: Ten Rules of Good Bible Reading

## Chapter Resources

Aune, David E. *The New Testament in Its Literary Environment*. Philadelphia: Westminster, 1987.

Bjerkelund, Carl J. *Parakalô: Form, Funktion und Sinn der parakalô-Sätze in den paulinischen Briefen*. Oslo: Universitatsforlaget, 1967.

Blume, Frederick E. "The Value of the Papyri for New Testament Study." http://www.wlsessays.net/files/BlumeValue.pdf.

Charlesworth, James H. ed. *The Old Testament Pseudepigrapha*. Vol. 1: *Apocalyptic Literature and Testaments*. New York: Doubleday & Company, 1983.

   *1 (Ethiopic Apocalypse of) Enoch*. Translated by E. Isaac.

   *2 (Syriac Apocalypse of) Baruch*. Translated by A. F. J. Klijn.

Cicero. *De Inventione*. Translated by H. M. Hubbell. LCL. Cambridge: Harvard University, 1949; reprint ed., 1960. In the volume with *De Optimo Genere Oratorum* and *Topica*.

   *De Oratore*. In Cicero 3 and 4:1-185. 2 vols. LCL. Cambridge: Harvard University, 1942; reprint eds., 1967/1968. Book 3 is in the volume with *De Facto*, *Paradoxa Stoicorum*, and *De Partitione Oratoria*.

   *De Partitione Oratoria*. In Cicero 4:306-421. Translated by H. Rackham. LCL. Cambridge: Harvard University, 1942; reprint ed., 1968. In the volume with *De Oratore*, *De Fato*, and *Paradoxa Stoicorum*.

   *Orator*. In Cicero 5:297-509. Translated by H. M. Hubbell. LCL. Cambridge: Harvard University, 1939; reprint ed., 1971. In the volume with *Brutus*.

Deissmann, Adolf. *New Light on the New Testament: From Records of the Graeco-Roman Period*. Translated by L. R. M. Strachan. Edinburgh: T. & T. Clark, 1907.

Dewey, Joanna. *Markan Public Debate: Literary Technique, Concentric Structure, and Theology in Mark 2:1-3:6.* SBLDS 48. Chico, CA: Scholars, 1980.

Fay, Greg. "Introduction to Incomprehension: The Literary Structure of Mark 4:1-34." *CBQ* 51 (1989) 65-81.

Funk, Robert W. "The Apostolic *Parousia*: Form and Significance." In *Christian History and Interpretation: Studies Presented to John Knox*, pp. 249-68. Edited by W. R. Farmer, C. F. D. Moule, and R. R. Niebuhr. Cambridge: Cambridge University, 1967.

"The Apostolic Presence: Paul." In *Parables and Presence: Forms of the New Testament Tradition*, pp. 81-110. Philadelphia: Fortress, 1982.

Gamble, Harry. *The Textual History of the Letter to the Romans: A Study in Textual and Literary Criticism.* Grand Rapids: Eerdmans, 1977.

Long, Lynne. "Scriptures in the Vernacular Up to 1800." In *A History of Biblical Interpretation: The Medieval through the Reformation Periods*, pp. 450-81. Edited by Alan J. Hauser and Duane F. Watson. Grand Rapids: Eerdmans, 2009.

Lund, N. W. *Chiasmus in the New Testament.* Chapel Hill: University of North Carolina, 1942.

Lyons, George. *Pauline Autobiography: Toward a New Understanding.* SBLDS 73. Atlanta: Scholars, 1985.

Malherbe, Abraham J. *Ancient Epistolary Theorists.* SBLSBS 19. Atlanta: Scholars, 1988.

Mullins, Terence Y. "Ascription as a Literary Form." *NTS* 19 (1972-73) 194-205.

"Benediction as a NT Form." *AUSS* 15 (1977) 59-64.

"Disclosure: A Literary Form in the New Testament." *NovT* 7 (1964) 44-50.

"Formulas in New Testament Epistles." *JBL* 91 (1972) 380-90.

"Greeting as a New Testament Form." *JBL* 87 (1968) 418-26.

"Petition as a Literary Form." *NovT* 5 (1962) 46-54.

"*Topos* as a New Testament Form." *JBL* 99 (1980) 541-47.

"Visit Talk in New Testament Letters." *CBQ* 35 (1973) 350-58.

Olson, Stanley N. "Epistolary Uses of Expressions of Self-Confidence." *JBL* 103 (1984) 585-97.

"Pauline Expressions of Confidence in His Addressees." *CBQ* 47 (1985) 282-95.

Parunak, H. van Dyke. "Oral Typesetting: Some Uses of Biblical Structure." *Bib* 62 (1981) 153-68.

Quintilian, *Institutio Oratoria.* 4 vols. Translated by H. E. Butler. LCL. Cambridge: Harvard University, 1920-22; reprint eds., 1980, 1977, 1966, 1979.

Sanders, Jack T. "The Transition from Opening Epistolary Thanksgiving to Body in the Letters of the Pauline Corpus." *JBL* 81 (1962) 348-62.

Shelley, Bruce L. *Church History in Plain Language.* Updated 2d ed. Nashville: Thomas Nelson, 1995.

Schubert, Paul. *Form and Function of the Pauline Thanksgivings.* Berlin: Töpelmann, 1939.

Stowers, Stanley K. *Letter Writing in Greco-Roman Antiquity.* Philadelphia: Westminster, 1986.

Thompson, Mark D. "Biblical Interpretation in the Works of Martin Luther." In *A History of Biblical Interpretation: The Medieval through the Reformation Periods,* pp. 299-318. Edited by Alan J. Hauser and Duane F. Watson. Grand Rapids: Eerdmans, 2009.

Wengert, Timothy. "Biblical Interpretation in the Works of Philip Melanchthon." In *A History of Biblical Interpretation: The Medieval through the Reformation Periods*, pp. 319-340. Edited by Alan J. Hauser and Duane F. Watson. Grand Rapids: Eerdmans, 2009.

White, John L. "Ancient Greek Letters." In *Greco-Roman Literature and the New Testament: Selected Forms and Genres*, pp. 85-105. Edited by D. E. Aune. SBLSBS 21. Atlanta: Scholars, 1988.

*The Form and Function of the Body of the Greek Letter: A Study of the Letter-Body in the Non-Literary Papyri and in Paul the Apostle.* 2d ed. SBLDS 2. Missoula, MT: Scholars, 1972.

"The Greek Documentary Letter Tradition Third Century B.C.E. to Third Century C.E." *Semeia* 22 (1982) 89-106.

"Introductory Formulae in the Body of the Pauline Letter." *JBL* 90 (1971) 91-97.

*Light from Ancient Letters.* Philadelphia: Fortress, 1986.

"New Testament Epistolary Literature in the Framework of Ancient Epistolography." *ANRW* 2.25.2 (1984) 1730-56.

"Saint Paul and the Apostolic Letter Tradition." *CBQ* 45 (1983) 433-44.

"The Structural Analysis of Philemon: A Point of Departure in the Formal Analysis of the Pauline Letter." *SBLSP* (1971) 1-47.

*Studies in Ancient Letter Writing* (Edited). Semeia 22. Chico, CA: Scholars, 1982.

Wiles, Gordon P. *Paul's Intercessory Prayers: The Significance of the Intercessory Prayer Passages in the Letters of St Paul.* SNTSMS 24. New York: Cambridge University, 1974.

## Notes

1.  1 Enoch 60:1-10 illustrates the extreme nature of apocalyptic language, along with other common features:

    "In the year five hundred, in the seventh month, on the fourteenth day of the month in the life of Enoch; in the same parable (I saw) that the heaven of heavens was quaking and trembling with a mighty tremulous agitation, and the forces of the Most High and the angels, ten thousand times a million and ten million times ten million, were agitated with great agitation. And the Antecedent of Time was sitting on the throne of his glory surrounded by the angels and the righteous ones. (Then) a great trembling and fear seized me and my loins and kidneys lost control. So I fell upon my face. Then Michael sent another angel from among the holy ones and he raised me up. And when he had raised me up, my spirit returned; for (I had fainted) because I could not withstand the sight of these forces and (because) heaven has stirred up and agitated itself. Then Michael said unto me, 'What have you seen that has so disturbed you? This day of mercy has lasted until today; and he has been merciful and long-suffering toward those that dwell upon the earth. And when this day arrives—and the power, the punishment, and the judgment, which the Lord of the Spirits has prepared for those who do not worship the righteous judgment, for those who deny the righteous judgment, and for those who take his name in vain—it will become a day of covenant for the elect and inquisition for the sinners.'

    "On that day, two monsters will be parted—one monster, a female named Leviathan, in order to dwell in the abyss of the ocean over the fountains of water; and (the other), a male called Behemoth . . . . And he said to me, 'You, son of man, according (to the degree) to which it will be permitted, you will know the hidden things.'"

2.  Ezekiel 40-48; Isaiah 24-27, 34-35, 56-66; Zechariah 9-14 are sometimes cited as examples.

3.  1 Enoch describes mountains of iron, of copper, of silver, of gold, of colored metal, and of lead that will melt like a honeycomb before a fire in the presence of the Messiah. "It shall happen in those days that no

one will be saved either by gold or by silver; and no one shall be able to escape" (52:1-9).

4. 1 Enoch (chapters 62-63) shows the apocalyptic tendency for the retribution of God to come upon oppressive rulers:

". . . . On that day, all the kings, the governors, the high officials, and those who rule the earth shall fall down before him on their faces, and worship and raise their hopes in that Son of Man; they shall beg and plead for mercy at his feet. . . . So he will deliver them to the angels for punishments in order that vengeance shall be executed on them—oppressors of his children and his elect ones. . . . The righteous and elect ones shall be saved on that day; and from thenceforth they shall never see the faces of the sinners and the oppressors. The Lord of the Spirits will abide over them; they shall eat and rest and rise with that Son of Man forever and ever. . . ." (62:1-16).

5. The passage continues as follows:

"But you ought to know that our Creator will surely avenge us on all our brothers according to everything which they have done against us and among us; in particular that the end which the Most High prepared is near, and that his grace is coming, and that the fulfillment of his judgment is not far. For now we see the multitude of the happiness of the nations although they have acted wickedly; but they are like a vapor. And we behold the multitude of their power while they act impiously; but they will be made like a drop. And we see the strength of their power while they resist the Mighty One every hour; but they will be reckoned like spittle. . . . as smoke they will pass away . . . . like grass which is withering, they will fade away . . . . they will be broken like a passing wave . . . . as a passing cloud they will vanish" (2 Baruch 82:1-9).

6. See, e.g., 2 Baruch 25:1-4.

7. In 2 Baruch 27, the author divides the tribulation of the last days into twelve, mixed and overlapping parts, and displays the dual intentionality (to reveal and conceal) of the symbolism: (1) the beginning of commotions, (2) the slaughtering of the great, etc. "[H]ence, those who live on earth in those days will not understand it is the end of times. But everyone who will understand will be wise at that time. . . ." (27:14-28:1).

163

8. See, e.g., Mark 4:1-34.
9. Compare some of the language from 1 Enoch:

   "At that place, I saw the One to whom belongs the time before time. And his head was white like wool, and there was with him another individual, whose face was like that of a human being. His countenance was full of grace like that on one among the holy angels. And I asked the one—from among the angels—who was going with me, and who had revealed to me all the secrets regarding the One who was born of human beings, 'Who is this, and from whence is he who is going as the prototype of the Before-Time?' And he answered me and said to me, 'This is the Son of Man, to whom belongs right-eousness, and with whom righteousness dwells. And he will open all the hidden storerooms; for the Lord of the Spirits has chosen him, and he is destined to be victorious before the Lord of the Spirits in eternal uprightness. This Son of Man whom you have seen is the One who would remove the kings and the mighty ones from their comfortable seats and the strong ones from their thrones. . . . He shall depose the kings from their thrones and kingdoms. . . .'" (46:1-6).

10. *institutum Neronianum* (Tertullian, *Ad nat*, 1.7).
11. Shelley, *Church History*, 42.
12. The practice of reading and understanding scripture based on what oth-ers have said about it has been around and criticized for a long time. Martin Luther made strong criticisms of relying on what exegetes and theologians of the past have said about a text. As Thompson ("Biblical Interpretation," 304) put it in summarizing Luther's view, "This 'gloss-ing of the glosses,' rather than direct engagement with the biblical text, robbed Christian people of the enlightening treasure of God's word."

# Chapter 11

# Zoomed Out on Philemon

How do you treat a run-away slave—and not a very good slave, mind you? One who was practically useless and even stole from you, but now has had a change of heart and become a Christian? This is what the Bible book of Philemon is about. But I thought slavery was an abominable evil, a blight upon the human race. How can a book of God even deal with such a question and not come right out and condemn it altogether? The short answer is that God deals with us where we are, and slavery was alive and well in Bible days. And what if an answer could be given that would not only affect the institution of slavery but teach us in bold colors how all forms of prejudice and deep hurt can be overcome? The answer to the question in Paul's letter to Philemon—how do you treat a formerly no-good, run-away slave?—transcends the issue of slavery, while it elucidates the meaning of the new community of Jesus Christ.

As big as the challenge might be, given the prevalence of ink-blotitis, the purpose of this book is to encourage, teach, and demonstrate in-context Bible reading. We've looked at the problem and how to solve it in theory. We now need a little hands-on work in the text. The basic principles we've talked about in the last two chapters ("Ten Rules of Good Bible Reading") apply to any book of the Bible, but for several reasons, I've chosen the New Testament books of (Paul's letter to) *Philemon* and (the Gospel according to) *Mark* to apply the things we've discussed. I won't list all the reasons here, but for starters Paul's letter to Philemon is a great example of many of the characteristics of Paul's letters in short or miniature format. Though it's very short in comparison to other books of the Bible, Philemon is a typical, one page letter as illustrated by the common letter tradition discovered in the Greek non-literary papyri. Being a book of the Bible, however, we believe its contents to be inspired by God and to

165

contain important kingdom-life lessons. In addition, the letter illustrates some of the typical shapes of Paul's letters in a brief context, which serves as a wonderful chew toy (or teething ring, to use a people analogy) on which to cut our teeth in discovering and dissecting the contents of a Bible book.

## A Philemon Inkblot

As a way of getting into the book, let's start with an inkblot—or at least a potential inkblot. Here's the New Revised Standard Version's (NRSV) rendering of Philemon 1:6:

I pray          that
the sharing of your faith
may become effective
when you perceive all
the good that we may
do for Christ.

The New International Version (NIV) puts it this way:

I pray that you may be
active in sharing your faith,
so that you will have a full
understanding of every good
thing we have in Christ.

What's that mean? Suppose we're in a small group Bible study and we go around the room, what sort of answers might we get? I've heard this verse used to teach and support the idea that we Christians should be active in "sharing our faith," that is, in evangelism. The NRSV could be used to suggest that we will be effective in our outreach efforts when we serve people and do good ("service" or "friendship evangelism"), and use all the resources available to us. The NIV might suggest that we won't have a full understanding of "every good thing we have in Christ" (how great would that be?) until we are active in sharing our faith. Though these ideas may be true, do you see how I've jumped to applying the verse to our lives and completely out of the context while trying to understand what it's really all about? By taking it out of its book-level context, I've potentially turned this word of God into an inkblot. Even if we don't use it for some harmful or heretical teaching, think of the potential damage we've done to ourselves and to others by letting the Spirit's air out of the full-blown text. We could be losing the word of God, and that's the danger of inkblotitis.

So what does it mean? What does it mean "to be active in sharing your faith" and what is "every good thing we have in Christ"? Answer: How does this verse fit and function in the book of Philemon? This is the literary context. To whom was the book written and for what purpose? That's the historical context. This is the only way to know for sure what the verse means—by reading it within its book-level (literary and historical) context. Answer these questions, and you will be tuning in to one of God's first conversations with his people, aligning your mind and heart with inspiration, and opening yourself to the life-changing power of God's Spirit in his word.

So let's do it. Let's look at Paul's letter to Philemon. As we look at the book together, I'll apply and reference the "Ten Rules for . . . Reading."

(The following analysis of Philemon gets a little technical at times, as we zoom in on the details of the text. So hang in there. We'll pull things together as we go and even more towards the end of the chapter. If you find the presentation overly technical and dry, please skip to the *Changing Our Lives with the Precepts of Philemon* section and see if that will motivate you to want to know more about how we got there.)

# Zoomed-Out Overview: The Picture on the Box

The first thing you should do when reading and studying a book of the Bible is, of course, read the book, the whole book, preferably several times. This is Rule #1 of good Bible reading, and it's easy to do with Philemon 'cause it's so short. I won't reproduce the text here (it's included in the sections below), so pick the version you will use for reading whole books of the Bible—your big picture, enjoyable-for-you-to-read, version—and read the book. Remember, your goal is to get an initial sense of the overall content and purposes of the book, so that you can understand the main points and interpret the verses as part of the book-level context (Rule #2). If you don't understand a word, a verse, or an issue that's brought up as you read, don't worry about it now. You can come back to specifics later. Like looking at the picture on the box of a jigsaw puzzle, the goal here is to familiarize yourself with the landscape.

After you've read through the book a couple of times, it's easy to see that we are, in fact, reading a letter (Rule #5). It's a letter from Paul (the apostle) and Timothy (Paul's companion and apprentice) to someone named Philemon—thus the title—who we learn is Paul's dear friend and co-worker in Christ. We also notice that the letter is addressed to Apphia, Archippus, and the church in "your" house. Though you can't tell in English, "your" is singular in Greek and likely refers to Philemon's house. Even if you didn't know that the earliest churches were "house churches" and met in the homes of prominent members (with houses large enough to meet in), you can glean that historical fact from the text. Thus, we begin to get a picture of some of the historical ingredients lying behind the genesis of this letter.

A first reading of Philemon quickly reveals other details about the historical situation. Paul, who describes himself as "an old man" (which gives some indication as to the time frame in which the book was written), is in prison when he writes the letter. He indicates this several times in the course of the letter, describing himself as "a prisoner of/in Christ Jesus" and "for the gospel" (1, 9, 10, 13, 23). The sheer number of times he mentions this in such a short span provides not only a piece of the historical setting, but alerts us to an immediate (literary) emphasis on this situation. Paul has several people with him, including Timothy, Epaphras, Mark, Aristarchus, Demas, and Luke—Paul's entourage. Knowing that Paul was a missionary who planted churches in Asia Minor and southern Europe explains why he has a team of companions that travels and works with him. Luke, a physician, was Paul's intimate companion and wrote the Bible books of Luke and Acts. So Paul, "an old man and now also . . . a prisoner of Christ Jesus," writes a letter to Philemon, his dear friend and co-worker, and the church meeting in his house.

The letter concerns a man named Onesimus. Paul writes the letter in behalf of Onesimus, who is apparently a run-away slave who belonged to Philemon. It was not uncommon for runaways to steal from their owners in the process (verse 18), since the act of running away was extreme, punishable by death (even crucifixion) or other drastic measures (so you might as well take some things with you—"In for a penny . . ."). Apparently, Onesimus ended up in the city where Paul was imprisoned, heard the message of Christ from Paul, and became a Christian (verse 10). He then began to help Paul while he was in prison. Upon learning of his history (Onesimus comes clean),[1] however, Paul sent him back to his master to face the music of what he had done (living up to his new identity in Christ means resolving some things from his past). Paul sends him back, but not without the knowledge of his radical change of heart and lifestyle (verses 10-12: he was formerly "useless," Paul says, but now is *useful*, both to Paul and Philemon). What's more, he sends with him this letter, a powerful appeal by the apostle Paul to Philemon to accept Onesimus back no longer as just a slave, but as a brother in Christ.

Although there is more we could notice (and will as we delve into the sections), this is the basic story of the letter. Perhaps you noticed that very little of what I just described goes beyond what you can learn from a simple reading of the letter itself. You don't need commentaries or other summaries (Rule #7) to help you understand much of the historical context. A brief introduction to the letter will provide you with the extra details I included and more. (If you like, reading a brief introduction to the book of Philemon would be a reasonable thing to do at this point. Just don't let it keep you away from the text.) Of course, there are other significant questions about the historical setting that we can and should explore more fully at some point; for example, where was Paul when he wrote the letter? Paul was imprisoned several times in the course of his ministry. Was this Rome? Or Ephesus? Or perhaps somewhere else? And where was Philemon and Onesimus's home? When Paul sent Onesimus back, to what city was he going? Most believe it was Colossae, but some think it was Laodicea (Laodicea, Hierapolis, and Colossae were neighbor towns in the Lycus River Valley).[2] Research on the history and nature of slavery in biblical times also provides general insights into the historical background. These are indeed interesting and legitimate questions and issues, but actually have little to do with the major implications and teachings of the letter. Everything you need to get God's point is contained in the context of the letter itself.

# Discovering the Shape of the Text

## Step 1: Find the Introduction and Conclusion

After reading a Bible book all the way through, one of the first things you can do to get a sense of the main points and purposes of the book is to look for the simple three-piece structure: Introduction-Middle-Conclusion. The Introduction to Philemon consists of verses 1-7:

Paul, a prisoner of Christ Jesus, and Timothy our brother,

To Philemon our dear friend and co-worker, to Apphia our sister, to Archippus our fellow soldier, and to the church in your house.

Grace to you and peace from God our Father and the Lord Jesus Christ (1-3).

When I remember you in my prayers, I always thank my God because I hear of your love for all the saints and your faith toward the Lord Jesus. I pray that the sharing of your faith may become effective when you perceive all the good that we may do for Christ. I have indeed received much joy and encouragement from your love, because the hearts of the saints have been refreshed through you, my brother (4-7).

First of all, how do I know this is the Introduction? Several things make this deduction relatively easy. The obvious and most elementary is that it comes at the beginning of the letter—introductions usually occur at the beginning to prepare the audience for a favorable hearing of what's to come. Paul's letters begin with two parts: a Prescript (Address and Greeting), followed by a Thanksgiving section, reporting his gratitude and prayers for certain aspects of the recipients' faith. The Address and Greeting of Philemon get things going by identifying stage-setting relationships, within a setting of Christian faith and community. A little familiarity with Paul's letters demonstrates clearly the introductory nature of his opening Thanksgiving passages. Even if we didn't have any other letters of Paul, however, a close look at the text of Philemon confirms the preparatory function of this Thanksgiving passage (and we'll see this shortly). Finally, like a flashing red light or a beeping alarm, the transition of verses 8-10 ("For this reason . . ." or "Therefore . . .") to a common, highly-significant and stereotyped form/shape within ancient Greek letters (the Petition: "I appeal to you . . .") unmistakably indicates that we are leaving the Introduction and entering the Middle or core of the letter.

That's the Introduction. And how does the letter end? What is the Conclusion? With skilled writers, it's sometimes difficult to tell exactly where a Conclusion begins because the transition is natural and fluid. Sometimes transitions appear to go with the previous section or paragraph and sometimes with the following; therefore, one person might see a particular verse as the end of the Body or Middle, while another sees it as the beginning of the Conclusion. It doesn't really matter. The transitional and concluding function of the final group of verses is clear either way. Specifically, some might see verse 21 as the final verse in the middle section of Philemon, while others include it as part of the Conclusion. Because of its pointed reference to the goal of the letter itself—a final appeal to accomplish its purposes—and the repetition in verse 20 of a key word ("refresh") introduced to us at the end of the Introduction (which I found when I colored the text: Rule #4), I'll include it in our Conclusion:

> Confident of your obedience, I am writing to you, knowing that you will do even more than I say. One thing more—prepare a guest room for me, for I am hoping through your prayers to be restored to you. Epaphras, my fellow prisoner in Christ Jesus, sends greeting to you, and so do Mark, Aristarchus, Demas, and Luke, my fellow workers. The grace of the Lord Jesus Christ be with your spirit (21-25).

This gives us our three-piece shape:

| Introduction (1-7) | Middle (8-10) | Conclusion (21-25) |
| --- | --- | --- |

## Step 2: Divide the Middle into Its Major Sections

Dividing the Middle is a way of coming up with an outline of the book as a whole, since we've already isolated the Introduction and Conclusion. Because the letter to Philemon is short, the Middle is also easy to divide or outline, though there are some interesting rhetorical movements or maneuvers—sort of like curves and protrusions on puzzle pieces. The two biggest "protrusions"—the parts that connect the middle section to the beginning and end of the letter—are fairly easy to spot once we step back and take a look (verses 8-9 and verse 20). We "zoom in" on these transitions in more detail in a minute. For now, we're noticing their place in the shape of the Middle.

Perhaps the quickest way to show some of the contours of verses 8-20 is visually. Like a picture in a puzzle made up of multiple pieces, this is a nice example of a single block of material that's constructed out of several verses. Notice how the Middle is built:

8-9: **Transition/Introduction to the Request, with several mood-altering emphases**
For this reason, though I am bold enough in Christ to command you to do your duty, yet I would rather appeal to you on the basis of love—and I, Paul, do this as an old man, and now also as a prisoner of Christ Jesus.

10: **Start of the official Request with introduction to the background information**
I am appealing to you for my child, Onesimus, whose father I have become during my imprisonment.

11-14: **Background information**
Formerly, he was useless to you, but now he is indeed useful both to you and to me. I am sending him, that is, my own heart, back to you. I wanted to keep him with me, so that he might be of service to me in your place during my imprisonment for the gospel; but I preferred to do nothing without

your consent, in order that your good deed might be voluntary and not something forced.

### 15-16: Implication of the background information

Perhaps this is the reason he was separated from you for a while, so that you might have him back forever, no longer as a slave but more than a slave, a beloved brother—especially to me but how much more to you, both in the flesh and in the Lord.

### 17: Completion of the Request

So if you consider me your partner, welcome him as you would welcome me.

### 18-19: Paul's personal voucher

If he has wronged you in any way, or owes you anything, charge that to my account. I, Paul, am writing this with my own hand: I will repay it. I say nothing about your owing me even your own self.

### 20: Summarizing Conclusion

Yes, brother, let me have this benefit from you in the Lord! Refresh my heart in Christ.

Powerfully motivating expressions pack this passage with such rhetorical skill as to impress even the best practitioners of the art of persuasion. How could Philemon say "No"? And there's more to come in the Conclusion. We'll look at the strategy and content when we explore the purposes of the sections.

For now, we want to notice the shape of this central section. Because of its brevity, it would certainly be legitimate to lump these verses together for outlining as one major section, with no sub-divisions. We could just keep our basic three-part shape:

Introduction (1-7): Philemon as a man of faith and refreshing love
Middle (8-20): Request for Philemon to extend that love to Onesimus
Conclusion (21-25): Continuation of community and cause/purpose in Christ

Adding a couple of sub-divisions displays a little more of the design and logic:

## Introduction (1-7)
    Prescript (Address and Greeting) (1-2): Community and cause in Christ
    Grace Greeting (3): Theological foundations
    Thanksgiving (4-7): Philemon as a man of faith and refreshing love

## Middle (8-20)
    Transition (8-9): Request is based on love (not authority)
    Request Started (10)
        Background Information (10-16)
    Request Completed (17)
    Paul's Personal Voucher (18-19)
    Conclusion: Request in a nutshell (20)

## Conclusion (21-25)
    Confidence: Paul is confident of even more (21)
    Visit Talk (22)
    Final Greetings (23-25): Continuation of community and cause/purpose in Christ

Having a book-level vantage point in terms of shape puts us in a much better position to understand the individual pieces and interpret the verses with book-level focus (Rule #2).

# Step 3: Zoom in on the Transitions

Going through each of these steps may seem redundant and a little pedantic at this point, and with reference to Philemon, it probably is. But let me assure you, it won't be excessive when you tackle bigger books.

Because the book of Philemon is short, it's easy to zoom in on the transitions, especially those between the major sections of our three-piece shape:

| Introduction (1-7) | 8-9 | Middle/Body (8-20) | 21 | Conclusion (21-25) |
|---|---|---|---|---|

The phrase "For this reason . . ." in the NRSV or the word "Therefore" in the NIV helps to show that a transition is taking place (1:8). A special paragraph marker (a Thanksgiving in 1:4 and a Petition in 1:9) highlights each side of the transition, moreover, which confirms that the Middle or Body of the letter does indeed begin with verse 8. The direct address "brother" at the end of verse 7 closes the Thanksgiving paragraph (and the Middle in verse 20). Verses 8-10 thus clearly transition from the opening Thanksgiving to the initial and primary Request of the letter.

Before Paul actually makes his request of Philemon, he chooses his words carefully and delays the content of the request so that he can build upon the spiritual and emotional foundations laid in the Thanksgiving. Though he could be bold or blunt and command Philemon to do what is right on the basis of pure authority, Paul uses several mood-setting conditions to found and cushion his request. "I would rather appeal to you," he says, "on the basis of *love*" (9). If you're highlighting key words, the word "love" stands out in the Introduction as a core characteristic of Philemon (verses 5 and 7). Philemon is known as a man who loves all the saints (verse 5); Paul has experienced his love (verse 7). The word "love" is thus a segue- or link-word: it smooths the movement, links the sections, and provides Paul with the basis for his request.

As he appeals to Philemon on the basis of love, Paul characterizes himself as "an old" or "elderly man" who is now also "a prisoner of Christ" (verse 9)—images that amplify the application of love and present Paul as someone who should be respected, listened to, and perhaps ministered to or helped. Repetition of the petition verb in verses 9-10 (9: "I . . . appeal"; 10: "I am appealing . . .") completes the transition to the formal request of the letter.

The transition between the Middle and the Conclusion is rather fluid and stretches across verses 20-22. Referring to Philemon directly with the word "brother" in verse 20 echoes the same word at the end of the opening Thanksgiving in verse 7 (the repetition helps to identify a circular structure to the letter as a whole; more on this below) and thus concludes the Body of the letter. Referring to the act of and reason for writing the letter in verse 21 provides another sense of moving toward a close, as do other phrases like "One more thing" in verse 22.

The transitions of verses 8-9 and 20-21 thus help to identify the overall shape of the letter as a relatively simple three-piece structure. Verses 8-9 transition from the Introduction to the primary request of the letter—the meat of the matter, you might say—pointing back to the fundamental trait of love and amplifying Paul's intrinsic authority and needful circumstances. Verses 20-21 bring the Middle to a close with a succinct restatement of Paul's purpose, along with other wrap-up phrases and summarizing expressions. These transitional verses thus help to identify the function of verses 4-7 as introductory and of verses 8-20 as the primary request of the letter.

**Hydration Alert:**
You may want to get a glass of water before beginning the next section. Some may find it a little dry and technical—though others will especially enjoy the exercise and benefits of careful analysis of the text.

## Step 4: Determine the Purpose of the Sections

Let's delve a little deeper now into the contents of the Introduction, Middle, and Conclusion as they relate to the purposes of Philemon. This is where we go exploring, where we venture as deeply into the forest as we are inclined or motivated to go. But don't be afraid, the forest is a fertile place of growth and nourishment.

# Introduction

### Prescript: Address and Greeting (1-3)

As we've already noted, the Address tells us whom the letter was from and to whom it was written (Paul . . . and Timothy to Philemon . . .). Though it's directed primarily to Philemon, Paul's including other leaders and the house-church as a whole adds a community dimension to the teaching and admonitions of the letter (how Philemon reacts won't be done in secret). Paul begins almost all of his letters with the phrase "Grace to you and peace from God our Father and the Lord Jesus Christ" as his initial greeting. Though it appears somewhat perfunctory in his letters, the belief that Christians share God's grace and peace in Christ Jesus anchors Paul's theology and serves as the basis of fellowship in the church.

From a literary perspective, the most significant feature of the Prescript (Address and Greeting) is how Paul modifies the basic elements. In other words, he doesn't just say "Paul to you, Greetings." The adjectives and expansions of the basic form reflect the situation and purposes of the letter. This is, in fact, where we get our first glimpse into the setting and purposes of the letter (though we won't be able to see exactly how until we've read the rest of it). So we notice right off the bat that Paul describes himself as "a prisoner of Christ Jesus." He then goes on to mention that he is a prisoner of or for Christ no less than five times in this brief letter. Our question is why. How does Paul's imprisonment relate to or affect the content and purpose of the letter? (". . . . I wanted to keep him with me, so that . . . [verses 11-13]). The opening line prominently introduces this idea.

Philemon is described as "our dear friend and co-worker"; Apphia is "our sister"; Archippus, "our fellow soldier." Then follows reference to the church that meets at Philemon's house. A clear, repetitive emphasis on *community* and partnership in the *cause* of Christ thus fills the Address. Having read the rest of the letter, can you see any reason why Philemon's relationship to Paul as a dear friend (the Greek work is "beloved one") and fellow worker might be relevant to what he will ask of him? It forms a solid piece of the value system and logic on which Paul appeals to Philemon, doesn't it? Looking ahead, Paul uses the same word to refer to Onesimus in verse 16: Philemon is to welcome Onesimus back "no longer as a slave, but as a *beloved* brother." If Philemon is "beloved" and Onesimus is "beloved," then they share the same status and must in some sense be equal. This is exactly what Paul wants Philemon to see and accept.

Further, is the purpose of the letter based in some way on a sense of community and cause in Christ? It depends on it. Close scrutiny of the language of Philemon as a whole reveals the concept of Christian relationship or community to be the pivotal idea on which the theology of the letter depends. Paul clearly and forcefully identifies Onesimus as having a new, spiritual son-like, useful, emotional, vital, beloved, serving relationship with himself—in other words, Onesimus is now a devoted Christian. Paul shares a similar relationship with Philemon. The Christian (Greek) term for this is *koinonia* (= fellowship or community). It's easy to see, then, how the very first words and phrases in the letter help to prepare for what's important to come.

## Thanksgiving (4-7)

The Thanksgiving (4-7) continues the introductory function of the opening with more developed, but still generalized, expression of the key themes and values of the letter.

When I remember you in my prayers, I always thank my God because I hear of your love for all the saints and your faith toward the Lord Jesus. I pray that the sharing of your faith may become effective when you perceive all the good that we may do for Christ. I have indeed received much joy and encouragement from your love, because the hearts of the saints have been refreshed through you, my brother.

Remembering Philemon in prayer suggests a deeply spiritual relationship between Paul and Philemon. The specific items of Paul's appreciation of and prayer for Philemon emerge, moreover, as key concepts in the unfolding logic of the letter. *This is where learning to see the introductory nature of Paul's opening Thanksgivings takes us miles in focusing on the most important points and purposes of his letters—and thus toward getting God's points.*

### ". . . love and faith . . ."

Paul is thankful to God because he hears of Philemon's faith in the Lord Jesus and his love for all the saints. Most modern translations render this sentence as a small circular pattern or shape (a chiasm). A literal translation shows that the Greek sentence reads like this (and I'll structure it in a circle so you can see the balance):

> . . . hearing of
> > your love and
> > > the faith
> > > > which you have
> > > toward the Lord Jesus
> > and for all the saints.

The translators thus associate "faith" with "the Lord Jesus" and "love" with "all the saints," which is the way we naturally think of it. It would be a little odd perhaps to think of having faith in other Christians, but not completely out of the question, especially given the need for Philemon to accept and trust Onesimus again. (So could the circular shape intentionally blur the lines?) Either way, the implication is telling.

Paul thanks God because Philemon is a man of *faith* (in the Lord) and *love* (for all the saints)—characteristics that will prove to be vital if the letter is successful. Philemon's faith is mandatory for the request Paul will make of him. Without it, Onesimus is just a good-for-nothing, run-away slave. Because of faith in the Lord Jesus, however, everything has changed. Faith in Jesus envisions a world where starting over (= new birth) and true change are really possible.

Philemon is also known for his *love for all the saints* (think *Christians*, which is what the word "saints" means); so he's known for his love for all Christians. Interesting. No, more than interesting. What Paul has done with this phrase is set up the premise for a simple form of compelling logic. If Philemon is by nature a lover of *all* the saints, what does that mean about how he would feel and act toward a new saint, a new Christian? How will he thus feel toward and treat Onesimus? As Paul will explain, Onesimus has been reborn and has become a child of Paul and, more importantly, a child of Christ—he is now a "saint." If Philemon loves *all the saints*, he will now also love Onesimus, necessarily. The argument turns on Onesimus's change of identity (". . . my child Onesimus, whose father I became . . . Formerly, he was useless to you, but now . . ."). There is a *then* and a *now*, and they are not the same. The implication is unassailable and unyielding. But notice that Paul doesn't draw the implication here; he simply builds the literary and theological context for the purposes of his letter. (See how important Introductions can be for helping us overhear God's first conversations with his people?)

## ". . . fellowship of your faith . . ."

And that's not all. This is where we come to the potentially vague, somewhat mysterious—inkblot-like—verse that we highlighted (can anyone say "tore out"?) at the beginning of this chapter. (You know, this might be a really good way to conceive of the dangerous potential of inkblotitis: when we take a verse or two out of context, it's as if we tear out a piece of God's word. And isn't it ironic that our efforts to highlight a particular verse or passage can, over time and space, drain it of its intended purpose?)

Let's read it from a literal version now. Here's the English Standard Version (ESV) rendering: ". . . and I pray that the sharing of your faith may become effective for the full knowledge of every good thing that is in us for the sake of Christ." The New American Standard Bible (NASB) has ". . . and I pray that the fellowship of your faith may become effective through the knowledge of every good thing which is in you for Christ's sake." You may have noticed that one version has every good thing "in us," while the other has every good thing "in you." This is one of the relatively rare occasions where our best copies of ancient Greek manuscripts differ. It doesn't make much difference in the overall meaning, though, which is probably part of the reason the variation came into existence in the first place. Nonetheless, we want to think about the place of these ideas in the unfolding logic and function of this introductory passage.

Paul prays that the fellowship or sharing or community (the word is *koinonia*) of Philemon's faith might become active or effectual. Now, given the bit of context-building we've done by reading the whole letter and then looking at how some of these introductory items relate to the picture of the letter ("see the picture, get the point"), these lines immediately begin to come into clearer focus—than when we punched them out of the letter. Does the *sharing* or *community* of Philemon's faith have anything to do with Paul's request for Philemon to accept a run-away slave back as a beloved brother in Christ (from betrayer to beloved—that's a long way)? It has everything to do with it, doesn't it? It's what must happen, if he's to be able to do what Paul asks: "So if you consider me a partner, welcome him as you would welcome me" (verse 17). The word "partner" (*koinonon*) is the same root as "community" or "sharing" of his faith. The *koinonia*—the circle or sphere of his community of faith—must become active—in this case, out-reaching or broad enough to extend to Onesimus, even as it does to Paul. And this is where the force of Paul's references to and descriptions of his relationship to Onesimus come home loud and clear. Paul and Onesimus are one.

But again, notice that Paul doesn't spill the beans in the Introduction. He is preparing the ground, both contextually and spiritually. He doesn't mention Onesimus at this point (that just might spoil the mood), but he does ask God for something—something that must, therefore, be very important. Paul prays that the community of Philemon's faith might become active before he lets Philemon know why—these verses are introductory, which helps to explain why they are somewhat general or abstract and also why they can be easily extracted from the context (inkblotized) to suggest all sorts of possible meanings. Paul did not have all sorts of possible meanings in mind when he wrote to Philemon, although he was intentionally careful about how he prepared the soil of Philemon's heart.

### ". . . every good thing . . ."

Paul prays that the fellowship of Philemon's faith might become active—the relevance of this is now easy to see—but what about the rest of it? ". . . through" or "in the knowledge of every good thing that is in you/us for Christ." Is there knowledge of some new, good thing ("every," implying that there might be something still lacking in Philemon's knowledge) in Christ that might help or motivate Philemon's fellowship of faith to become active? You bet! And Paul is about to share that knowledge with Philemon. It's the knowledge of a new child of God—one who formerly was useless, but not anymore. It's good for the community of Christ. It's good for Philemon. It has been very good for Paul. Just as Paul describes Onesimus as "beloved" a little later in a way that connects Onesimus with Philemon and with Paul, he also refers to the possibility that Onesimus might serve as Philemon's substitute, as a fellow servant to Paul in his ministry and imprisonment for the gospel, in a way that looks back to the Thanksgiving. He calls it "your good thing" in verses 13-14 ("in order that *your good deed* . . ."). Philemon has a new good thing, with amazing new possibilities in and for Christ. The knowledge of this should stir his heart and ignite the sharing (= extending) of his faith.

**". . . hearts . . . refreshed . . ."**

We're still not done with the Introduction. Paul prays these things with a sense of confidence because he knows some things about Philemon. Paul himself has received *great joy and encouragement* from Philemon's *love* because "the hearts of the saints have been refreshed by you, brother" (verse 7)—referring, of course, to Philemon. In Greek the word "heart" refers literally to one's "bowels," which figuratively meant one's deep, innermost feelings (like "heart" does for us). Paul prays that the community of Philemon's faith might become active through the knowledge of the good that he has in Christ because Philemon is known as someone who *refreshes* the *hearts of the saints*.

Again, the letter presents (and evokes) the characteristics of love, compassion, and encouragement to Christians as fundamental, well-known values of Philemon—it's who he is as a follower of Christ. They are also fundamental in the design of the letter. The implication is that such character should impact and control the way Philemon will respond to Paul's request. Again, the logic is unyielding: Paul is one of the saints who has experienced the benefits of Philemon's character in Christ, but, now, so also is Onesimus.

Highlighting recurring words (Rule #4) shows the verbal connections (we look at more of these later) and explicitly reveals some of the logic of the Introduction through a dynamic and powerful turn of phrase. Paul repeats several of these words as a summarizing command at the end of his formal request for Philemon to accept Onesimus back, now as a Christian: ". . . *Refresh* my *heart* in Christ" (verse 20). Receiving Onesimus back this way would indeed refresh Paul's heart, but there's more. In describing the action of sending Onesimus back to Philemon, look at how Paul describes Onesimus: "I am sending him, that is, *my own heart*, back to you" (12). See the word-play: Philemon is a man known for refreshing the hearts of the saints? Paul himself has experienced it and would like to again. But now Onesimus *is* Paul's heart. Refreshing Paul's heart thus has a powerful double meaning that strengthens the request and enhances the logic implied in the Introduction.

## Introductory Thanksgiving

Do you see how this Thanksgiving functions as a skillful introduction? It prepares the ground thematically, emotionally, and spiritually. Because it's introductory—that is, preparatory—it's also generalized, as most introductions are. For such a difficult and potentially complicated request—for Philemon, the slave owner, to welcome the runaway, formerly useless, perhaps thieving slave back, no longer as a slave, but as an equal brother in Christ—the Introduction is truly inspired. Because it's generalized as an introduction, however, what happens if we take a verse or two out of it and make it the center of our understanding and application of the passage, without the context? Put it up on our refrigerators? You know the answer: ink-blotitis. On the other hand, viewing the verses in book-level focus pulls back the shades and lets in the powerful light of the original author—and his Inspirer.

# Middle

Though quite short and relatively simple compared to other books of the Bible, the Middle of the letter to Philemon is a bit more complex than the Introduction and Conclusion. We'll look at it according to the sections that we outlined, which reflect the typical elements of a common letter shape in New Testament times—a Petition. As we saw in the last chapter, the generic Request or Petition form had three basic and two optional elements:

1. Petition verb (request, exhortation): "I beseech/ask/appeal/urge"
2. Addressee (optional): "you"
3. Background
   a. The background may be expressed by one sentence or, more often, by a larger block of material, such as is introduced by a disclosure.
   b. Inferential words like "therefore" and "wherefore" often point to the background.

4. Divine authority phrase (optional): "by the mercies of God"
5. Desired action: "to present your bodies as a living sacrifice"

Each of these is included in one form or another in Paul's request of Philemon:

1. Petition verb: "appeal" (9, 10)
2. Addressee: "you" (8, 10)
3. Background (10-16)
4. Divine authority phrase: "bold enough in Christ to command you" (8); "as an old man and now a prisoner of Christ" (9)
5. Desired action: "for Onesimus . . . welcome him as you would welcome me" (10, 17)

Though it's easy to see the significance of this request in the book of Philemon, it's helpful to keep in mind that the *first* such request in Paul's letters often reflects the main reason for and purpose of the letter.


**Basis of the Request (8-9)**

Since we've already talked considerably about the transitional function of verses 8-9 as a set up or basis of Paul's request, let's look at the developing thought. Paul begins by reminding Philemon of the authority he carries in Christ because of who he is as an apostle (implied) and perhaps because of his relationship to Philemon, of which he reminds him at the end of the section (verse 19: "I say nothing about your owing me even your own self"). Paul thus begins and ends the request from an authoritative perspective (these appeals to authority actually balance each other in the circular structure of the letter; see below), but in each case says, in effect, "I'm not going to play the authority card in this situation." The effect is to give the request a polite but command-like sense, as the use of the imperative verb form in verse 17 implies (". . . receive him . . ."). Paul knows Philemon to be a man of faith and love ("for all the saints"), and

188

would rather base his request on that. Amplifying the potential application of love, Paul describes himself as "an old man and now also . . . a prisoner of Christ Jesus." This again functions to strengthen Paul's esteem, but in a way that connects with the core characteristics of Philemon, reminding him of Paul's dedicated service to the cause of Christ—a cause which Philemon shares.

So here's the question: Why describe himself this way? Of all the things Paul could say about himself, why describe himself this way here in Philemon (he describes himself differently in other letters)? It's because he has a unique purpose in this letter, which calls for a strong emphasis on the community (love) and cause (service) that Philemon and Paul (and now Onesimus) share in Christ. But why emphasize these negative sounding or needful circumstances (Paul is old, in prison)? Perhaps there's more to the intentions of the letter than meets the eye at this point.

## The Request (10)

One of the more fascinating things about the shape and strategy of the request of Philemon is, in my opinion, its skillful use of delay. Verse 10 begins the formal Request, repeating the petition verb from verse 8: "I appeal to you . . ." or "I ask you . . ." But the request is technically not completed until verse 17, so that the sense is "I appeal to you for my child . . . . (for you to) welcome him as you would welcome me." That puts six verses between the start and the end of the request, which might seem strange, if we didn't know how big the request is going to be. The delay is natural and fitting, considering the circumstances. It's like telling someone something good to grease the path or soften the blow before sharing hard or bad news. Welcoming Onesimus back as an equal brother in Christ will take a feat of great faith and graciousness (refreshing love) beyond the norm. It makes perfect sense, then, for Paul to give Philemon the details or background information before making the request. This gives him time to prepare Philemon's heart and soften his reaction.

Several features employ this sense of delay. We're a third of the way into the letter, for example, and Onesimus has not been mentioned. The Introduction and transition to the request have focused on Philemon, Paul, and the community of faith they share. As we've noticed, the request itself doesn't come until verse 17, or about two-thirds of the way through the letter, and the delay is seen even in the wording of the request in verse 10. For English style, most modern versions don't reproduce the delay in the wording of verse 10, as the Holman Christian Standard Version (2004) does:

> I, Paul, as an elderly man and now also as a prisoner of Christ Jesus, appeal to you for my child, whom I fathered while in chains—Onesimus.

He saves "Onesimus" until the end. It's as if Paul waits to the last possible minute—and not until he's expressed the critically important point that Onesimus has become his spiritual child—to reveal the name. He then, without delay, even before finishing the request, fills in the crucial details.

## Background Information (10-16)

In ancient Greek and New Testament letters, formal Petitions always contained some sort of background information that explained the reason for the request. In longer letters, that information is often expressed with (informational) Disclosures ("I want you to know . . .") preceding the Petition. Although we don't have a formal Disclosure paragraph in Philemon, the information of verses 10-16 clearly forms the background to the Request, as Paul builds his case as to why Onesimus should be received as a brother. The foundation is Onesimus's change of identity. The idea that Onesimus has become Paul's *child* who should be accepted as a beloved brother implies conversion and the new birth of the Christian faith; and, according to Paul's reasoning in the letter, this changes everything. Onesimus is not the same man. He has a new identity in Christ and a radical change of character, which may be part of the reason Paul uses the meaning of his name ("Onesimus" means useful) to make his point: "Formerly he was useless to you, but now he is indeed useful both to you and to me" (verse 11). Onesimus's usefulness confirms his change of identity.

Paul amplifies Onesimus's usefulness to him in the verses that follow. In fact, he's much more than useful; he's very dear to Paul. He's become so close to Paul that it's as if he is sending his own heart back to Philemon. Onesimus's change of identity and lifestyle has resulted in a deeply spiritual and emotional relationship with Paul. Identifying Onesimus as his "heart" injects the simple, but compelling piece of logic we noted in the Thanksgiving based on Paul's description of Philemon as someone who refreshes the hearts of the saints. So close and so useful Onesimus has become to Paul, that he would rather just keep him. The statement is emphatic in Greek, more than English translations typically show. I might translate it something like "I really wanted to keep him for myself." That way he could take Philemon's place in ministering to Paul during his imprisonment. But—in contrast to Paul's desire—Philemon's desire or consent was necessary so that his "good thing" might be a free and voluntary act.

The sense of community and cause displayed repeatedly in the opening and closing epithets of the letter ("fellow worker," "fellow soldier," "fellow prisoner") manifests itself in this picture of deeply united purpose in Christ (and need on the part of Paul). To "take Philemon's place" implies a duty on the part of Christians to be engaged in the work or ministry of Christ, though it might relate more to Philemon's history with Paul. Philemon's indebtedness to Paul, at least in a spiritual sense, comes out again in verse 19: "I say nothing about you owing me even your own self." Despite his authority in Christ and Philemon's personal friendship with and indebtedness to Paul, Paul will not presume authority over Philemon regarding Onesimus. He will not tell him precisely what he is to do— even though he really wanted to keep Onesimus—except for one thing: how Philemon must receive Onesimus (verse 17).

Verses 15-16 provide a nice transition back to the heart of the issue as they wrap up the background section. Maintaining the sense of personal freedom in Philemon's final decisions, Paul posits a hypothetical regarding why Philemon and Onesimus were separated for a while: so that Philemon might have him back forever (more on this below)—perhaps. But either way, not like he was. And here we come back to the nature and meaning of what has happened. Philemon is to have him back, "no longer as a slave but more than a slave, a beloved brother . . ." With the use of the phrase "beloved brother," Paul brings the meaning of Onesimus's conversion home with great force, since, as we've seen, Paul has referred to Philemon with both of these terms in the preceding material (1, 7). Philemon is a "beloved brother"; Onesimus is a "beloved brother." In a sense, everything prior in the letter has been building to this point ("more than a slave—a beloved brother"); and, given the circumstances, this is an enormous request.

To anticipate our application of the text, think of the tremendous implications this example of sharing the Christian faith has for how we are to relate to and treat each other. You can't get much lower than a slave in the eyes of society. So no matter what your title or your place in life, when it comes to the community we share in Christ, it's "no longer as a . . . [you fill in the blank], but a beloved brother" or "sister." Living out the implications of Paul's letter to Philemon turns the world upside down—or, perhaps more accurately—erases the stratifying boundaries that thwart true community.

## The Request Completed (17)

Having carefully crafted the preceding parts of the letter, using precisely chosen words and values of the Christian faith, and of Philemon as a Christian; then having delicately detailed the background information regarding Onesimus and his change of life and character; Paul begins his explicit request with a powerful introductory phrase: "If, therefore, you have me [as a] partner . . ." If you "have" me, "hold" me, "consider" me *a what*? It's difficult for an

English word to capture and make clear the significance of the word here. It's from the root word for "community" or "fellowship" in Christ. It's *koinonon*. Remember what Paul prayed in the opening Thanksgiving? . . . that the *koinonia* of Philemon's faith might become active? Relationships in Christ cascade from forgiveness and community in Christ. Paul bases his request of Philemon on the meaning and potential of that new reality, as he now overtly expresses what his earlier (more subtle) choice of words like "beloved brother," "refreshing" of "hearts," "love" for "all the "saints" implied. "If you have community" or "Christian fellowship with me," Paul says. If what Philemon shares with Paul in Christ has meaning toward one person, toward Paul, then it must have meaning for "all the saints." "Receive him as (you would) me." The logic of Paul's rhetoric is more than compelling; his teaching about what it means to be a new person in Christ, more than invigorating—it's life-giving. Like father, like son. Like Paul, like Onesimus. Like Philemon . . .

For Philemon to take Onesimus back, to receive and welcome him as he would Paul himself (no longer as a slave, but as a beloved brother in Christ) is the obvious and explicit request of this letter. It begins in verses 8-10, but is not completed until verse 17, with the important, background information put between the beginning and the completing of the request. Given the uniqueness and difficulty of the request, the sense of delay created by the shape of this passage makes perfect sense. Also, remember that a background-request structure was a common literary (plug and play) shape of the time, what I've called a special paragraph marker. Even without the emphasis given to this material by the Request form, we'd be able to identify the purpose of this section within the overall book-level context as expressing the most important point and purpose of the letter.

## Paul's Personal Voucher (18-19)

He's not quite done, though. Before formally closing the letter, Paul completes the explicit request by continuing the personal identification with Onesimus that underscores the logic in general, but, as if to ratchet up the import of that motif, he takes it to another level by putting himself personally on the line. It would not have been uncommon at the time for a run-away slave to have stolen something from his master in the act of running away (why not, if running away itself could get you killed?). Onesimus might have stolen from Philemon. Or perhaps he's simply been a rather "useless" slave, which, combined with the time that he's been gone, amounts to a sort of debt to Philemon. Either way, Paul says, "If he has wronged you in any way or owes you anything, charge that to me." As if signing a blank check, Paul writes this with his own hand (instead of having his writer or secretary do it), "I will repay it." (Paul doesn't just preach community; he lives it; notice the identification with Onesimus.) But then he reminds Philemon that he owes Paul his very self. The impact of these words gives credence to Paul's story about Onesimus and persuasive force to his request. Paul's personal involvement could not go deeper. He even signs it to say so.

## Summarizing Conclusion (20)

In typical concluding style, verse 20 summarizes the purpose of the letter in a brief, emotionally charged final appeal. Notice that Paul refers to Philemon explicitly as "brother," as he did at the conclusion of the opening Thanksgiving passage (verse 7). He combines this repetition with the key words "refresh" and "heart," also put forward in the introduction with the statement that Paul had much joy and encouragement from Philemon ("because the hearts of the saints have been refreshed through you, my brother"). Noticing the repetition of these key words (Rule #4) quickly displays the literary design of the opening and middle sections, and highlights the conclusive force of verse 20: "Yes, brother, let me have this benefit from you in the Lord! Refresh my heart in Christ." And what is Paul's heart? It's the heart of a man who has experienced and rejoices in Philemon's faith and love for all the saints. It's the heart of an old man and now a prisoner because of his work for Christ. It's the heart of a spiritual father to whom Philemon owes everything. It's the heart of a father to a new child in Christ, one who had come to love and depend on his service while in prison. *Onesimus is Paul's heart* (verse 20). So the question is, *how will Philemon treat Paul's heart?* Will he refresh it? If he acts in character and consistent with the values of their shared faith, he will. And this will provide great benefit and blessing to Paul, in more than one way.

I am intrigued by Paul's choice of words in this succinct appeal. The word for receiving "benefit" or "joy" is in a form or mood of requesting (even praying). The form Paul chooses is spelled *onaiman* (with a long *a* in the last syllable). Compare this to the Greek spelling of Onesimus (*onasimon*). I'm intrigued when you put the words of this sentence side by side. It literally reads:

Yes, brother, I you *onaiman* in the Lord.

Perhaps just a coincidence, but I find the literal appearance of the words fascinatingly similar to the point of the letter. Things really are Paul, Philemon, *onaiman*/Onesimus in the Lord ("through the knowledge of every good thing").

## Conclusion

The Conclusion wraps things up in a final effort to accomplish the goals of the letter. As a conclusion to the middle section, verse 20 restates the request of the letter in an encapsulating brief expression ("Yes, brother, let me have this benefit from you in the Lord! Refresh my heart in Christ") and thus serves as a transition to the closing. When Paul says in verse 21 that he's confident of Philemon's obedience, he's not only complimenting and encouraging Philemon, but he's also using a common expression of the day—a special paragraph marker (see Chapter 9 and Appendix 2)—that carried a persuasive function by creating a sense of obligation through praise and thereby served to support the general purpose of the letter. In addition to the natural encouragement found in such complimentary expressions, using a common manner of emphasizing an important aspect of the correspondence may indicate there's a little more than meets the eye with this statement, especially since the letter contains other potentially suggestive items. Paul is confident that Philemon will do *even more* than he has said. We'll come back to this a little later, but I'm wondering if the book-level context gives us any clues as to *what more* Philemon might do than Paul has explicitly asked.

"One more thing . . ." When Paul asks Philemon to prepare a guest room for him, he's also using a common theme of friendly letters of the day (visit talk), which, nonetheless, carries several persuasive overtones. First, it underscores and seeks to maintain Paul's close relationship with Philemon—a relationship that would certainly be strained if Philemon chooses to disregard Paul's request in the letter. Second, it implies a means whereby Paul's future presence with Philemon will exert a source of accountability (Robert Funk called this "apostolic presence"). And finally, if Paul is released from prison and thus "restored" to Philemon through his prayers, the community remains intact, which holds subtle but powerful implications regarding Onesimus as well (since he's Paul's heart and a beloved brother).

Reference to prayer brings full circle the community of prayer initiated by Paul's praying for Philemon in the opening Thanksgiving. The letter ends, then, as it began with emphasis on the community and cause of Christ, listing fellow prisoners and fellow workers of Paul (verses 23-24). The final grace-benediction (verse 25) reflects the similar "Grace and Peace . . ." in verse 3 and reminds Philemon and his community of the foundation of all that we share in Christ. That Paul desires the grace of the Lord Jesus to be *with their spirit* suggests the deeply spiritual and attitudinal nature of his purposes in writing the letter.

# Highlighting Recurring Words and Ideas

Highlighting key words and ideas throughout a Bible book is a great way to get a feel for important themes and how they relate to one another in the flow of the text. Again, don't let the brevity of my presentation on this fool you into thinking it's not all that helpful or important. It's extremely helpful. In fact, some of the insights in my previous discussion came from this sort of exercise.

Color coding is a little difficult in a word processor (compared to paper and markers) because of the limitation of distinct choices of colors and markings, but you can see the idea. I ended up using these highlights:

> prisoner = pink/rose
> brother = green
> beloved = light blue
> <u>fellow worker</u> = underlined
> **love** = purple
> **faith/fellowship of your faith** = dark blue
> saints/the hearts of the saints = light green
> **knowledge of every good thing** = red
> refreshed = orange

When you highlight key words, it's best to use a literal translation; otherwise, the efforts of the translators to create good English style often hide the repetition of words (like the use of the word "sharing" for *koinonia* in verse 6). The following is the New American Standard Bible's text of Philemon.

Paul, a prisoner of Christ Jesus, and Timothy our brother, To Philemon our beloved brother and <u>fellow worker</u>, and to Apphia our sister, and to Archippus our <u>fellow soldier</u>, and to the <u>church in your house</u>: Grace to you and peace from God our Father and the Lord Jesus Christ.

I thank my God always, making mention of you in my prayers, because I hear of your love and of the faith which you have toward the Lord Jesus and toward all the saints; and I pray that the fellowship of your faith may become effective through the knowledge of every good thing which is in you for Christ's sake. For I have come to have much joy and comfort in your love, because the hearts of the saints have been refreshed through you, brother.

Therefore, though I have enough confidence in Christ to order you to do what is proper, yet for love's sake I rather appeal to you—since I am such a person as Paul, the aged, and now also a prisoner of Christ Jesus—I appeal to you for my child Onesimus, whom I have begotten in my imprisonment, who formerly was useless to you, but now is useful both to you and to me. I have sent him back to you in person, that is, sending my very heart, whom I wished to keep with me, so that on your behalf he might minister to me in my imprisonment for the gospel; but without your consent I did not want to do anything, so that your goodness would not be, in effect, by compulsion but of your own free will. For perhaps he was for this reason separated from you for a while, that you would have him back forever, no longer as a slave, but more than a slave, a beloved brother, especially to me, but how much more to you, both in the flesh and in the Lord.

If then you regard me a partner, accept him as you would me. But if he has wronged you in any way or owes you anything, charge that to my account; I, Paul, am writing this with my own hand, I will repay it (not to mention to you that you owe to me even your own self as well).

Yes, brother, let me benefit from you in the Lord; refresh my heart in Christ. Having confidence in your obedience, I write to you, since I know that you will do even more than what I say. At the same time also prepare me a lodging, for I hope that through your prayers I will be given to you.

Epaphras, my <u>fellow</u> prisoner in Christ Jesus, greets you, as do Mark, Aristarchus, Demas, Luke, my <u>fellow workers</u>. The grace of the Lord Jesus Christ be with your spirit.

Just a few observations. Obviously, this is easier to do with Philemon than with most other books of the Bible. The results are just as effective in longer books, however, if not more so. In this example, highlighting (coloring) key words and phrases clearly shows the importance of the Introduction for finding and following important themes, and thus for preparing the audience both emotionally and thematically (see how all the key words are introduced in the opening Greeting and Thanksgiving paragraphs?). And there are other words or ideas that one might choose to highlight, like Paul's repeated use of something being *to* or *for him* and *to/for Philemon,* for example.

Let me see if I can summarize the letter using these words. The underlined words reflect the fundamental concept of shared new life in Christ, especially that of community and cause or ministry. This is the environment (the community of faith) into which Philemon must now embrace Onesimus. "Faith" and "the fellowship of . . . faith" identify this realm—the "church" ("that meets at your house"). Because Philemon has "love" "for all the saints," it's only natural and mandatory that he take on a new perspective toward Onesimus. Paul uses this love as the basis for his request. Since Philemon is known for "refreshing" the "hearts of the saints," moreover, Paul is confident regarding Philemon's actions toward Onesimus, especially since Onesimus has himself become Paul's very "heart." Bottom line: If Philemon has fellowship with Paul (has Paul as a "partner"), he will welcome Onesimus as he would Paul. (Paul uses his own relationship with Philemon to make concrete the "sharing of the faith" that he expects regarding Onesimus.)

By coming to perceive "every good thing" that he has available or at his disposal for Christ, Philemon should not only be willing to accept Onesimus as he would Paul, but perhaps should consider how he and Onesimus may now participate in the "fellow ministry" of Christ. There may be implications for Paul, since he is old and in prison for the cause, and really wanted to keep Onesimus to help in Philemon's place. Paul would not presume to make such a telling and personal decision for Philemon, however. He wanted to be sure that such a "good thing" would be what Philemon wanted as well.

# Philemon's Circular Structure

Paul, a prisoner of Christ Jesus and Timothy the brother, To Philemon the beloved and our fellow worker, and Apphia the sister, and Archippus our fellow soldier, and to the church at your house. Grace to you and peace from God our Father and the Lord Jesus Christ. **A**

I thank [euxaristo] my God always **B**
    making mention of you in my prayers, hearing
        of the love
           and the faith
                which you have
        toward the Lord Jesus
        and for all the saints,
    [praying] that the fellowship of your faith might become active through the knowledge of every good [thing] which is in you for Christ.
For I had much joy and comfort in your love, because the hearts of the saints are refreshed by you, brother.

    Therefore, having much boldness in Christ to order you to do what is proper, **C**
        on account of love,
        I rather appeal to you,
    being as I am, Paul, an old man, and now also a prisoner of Christ Jesus.

    I appeal to you for my child **D**
        who was born to me while I was in chains, Onesimus—
           the one formerly useless to you
           but now useful to you and to me—
        whom I am sending to you,
    this one, he is my heart,

        whom I would like to have kept [to have] for myself, **E**
        so that he might minister to me for you in the chains of the gospel.

        But without your consent, I did not want to do anything, **E'**
        so that not according to constraint your good thing might be but according to free-will.

    For perhaps for this reason he was separated from you for an hour, so that you might have **D'**
    him back forever,
        no longer as a slave, but above a slave,
           a beloved brother,
        especially to me, but how much more to you,
    both in the flesh and in the Lord.

    If, therefore, you consider [have] me as a partner, receive him as [if he were] me. **C'**
        And if he's done you any wrong or owes you anything, charge it to me.
        I, Paul, am writing with my own hand, "I will pay it back"—
    lest I remind you that you owe me your very self

Yes, brother, I want some benefit from you in the Lord. **B'**
Refresh my heart in Christ.
    Confident of your obedience, I have written to you, knowing that you will do even more than what I say.
And, at the same time, also prepare for me the guest room.
For I hope that through your prayers, I will be freely given [xaristhasomai] to you.

Epaphras, my fellow prisoner in Christ Jesus greets you. [And so do] Mark, Aristarchus, Demas, and **A'**
Luke, my fellow workers. The grace of the Lord Jesus Christ be with your spirit.

A common (structuring) shape in biblical literature is a circle—inverted parallelism. If we look closely at the content and words of Paul's letter to Philemon, I think we can discern a circular structure to the book as a whole. Without going into great depth, let's look at each of the sections above as they relate to and balance each other.

The Yellow sections (A and A') contain the names of people involved in the letter's circle of community. The concepts of community, cause, and refreshing that community/cause in Christ punctuate these verses. Repetition of the words "prisoner," "fellow" ("prisoner," "worker," "soldier") and the grace-greetings make the balance between the sections easy to see.

The Green sections (B and B') connect through the concept of prayer and several ideas and expressions. Paul prays for Philemon in the top section (B) and refers to Philemon's prayers for him in the bottom section (B'). The top section (B) ends with "For I had much joy and comfort in your love because the hearts of the saints are refreshed by you, brother," while the bottom section (B') begins with "Yes, brother, I want some benefit [or "joy"] from you in the Lord. Refresh my heart in Christ." Not only is the repetition of words striking, but the fact that one comes at the end of the top paragraph and the other at the beginning of the bottom clearly shows the technique of inversion. That Paul asks Philemon to "refresh his heart in Christ" and is confident that he will do even more than he asks also reflect the character of Philemon set forth in the Thanksgiving prayer as a man of faith and love for all the saints. Paul's explicit reference to his purpose in writing to Philemon—knowing that he will do even more than he asks—also neatly balances his prayer for Philemon in the Thanksgiving as a summarizing introduction to the material to follow. Other parallels can be seen when looking at the Greek words (like the beginning "I thank" [*euxaristo*] and the ending "I will be freely given" [*xaristhasomai*]), but the balance is rather obvious, even in English.

The parallels in the Blue section (C and C') are also fairly easy to see. Each section begins with clear transitions (inferential particles

202

["therefore" and "if, therefore"]), though the words are different in Greek. Both sections contain strong, descriptive references to Paul and his identity ("old man," "prisoner of Christ Jesus," "partner'), with the explicit repetition of his name. In addition, each of the sections contains an appeal to potential but unused authority ("having much boldness in Christ to order you to do what is proper, on account of love, I rather appeal to you" and "lest I remind you that you owe me your very self").

The Orange sections (D and D') focus on Onesimus's new identity. They also reveal balancing elements; though, as is often the case with circular structures, the relation between the sections is not just repetitive, but contains a degree of contrast as well (Paul versus Philemon). The top section (D) concerns Onesimus's relationship to Paul: that he was born to Paul in prison, how useful he has become, and that Paul is sending his very heart back to Philemon. The bottom (D') focuses on Onesimus's new relationship with Philemon: that he was separated for a while so that he might have him back forever, no longer as a slave, but as a beloved brother (the result of what happened in D). A formerly/now contrast thus characterizes each section (a common motif in Paul's writings), and—as if to clarify that these two units do indeed balance one another—each contains explicit comments regarding Onesimus's relationship to Paul and Philemon in reverse order ("formerly useless *to you*, but now useful *to you* and *to me*," "especially *to me*, but how much more *to you*").

The Red section (E and E') brings us to the center of the pattern, and the center forms a key point of emphasis. The center focuses on Paul's desire for Onesimus and Philemon's free choice. Paul really wanted to keep Onesimus. This would, in effect, allow him to function in Philemon's place in ministering to Paul (a concrete way for Philemon to be a "fellow worker" to Paul in the cause of Christ—a sort of parallel or reversal of Paul's identification with Onesimus). And if Onesimus is serving Christ by ministering to Paul, Onesimus has, in effect, a new master and a new freedom. But—respecting Philemon's relationship with Onesimus—this was not something for Paul to decide. Onesimus must face his past (a choice in keeping with his new identity), and Philemon's offering must also be based on his freedom in Christ. The emphasis here, in a sense, is on freedom and, ironically, on who will *have* Onesimus. The use of the phrase "your good thing" to describe Philemon's action connects back and helps to explain Paul's introductory prayer that the fellowship of Philemon's faith might become active through the knowledge of every *good thing* in him for Christ (verse 6). Onesimus's new identity and usefulness in Christ is certainly a good thing. It will be for Philemon, but it was also for Paul.

Concentric or circular structures in Bible books are sometimes rather fluid, overlapping, and hard to identify precisely—sort of like ripples from a splash in a pond—and, though the general circular structure of Philemon is fairly easy to see, I vacillate on whether the center section could be more precisely defined. I sometimes wonder if the phrase "For perhaps for this reason he was separated from you for an hour, so that you might have him back forever" (15) balances "Whom I would like to have kept for myself, so that he might minister to me for you in the chains of the gospel" (13). With a series of three "so that" clauses, the center of Philemon would then look like this:

> whom I would like to have kept [to have] for myself,
> **so that** he might minister to me for you in the chains of the gospel.

|   | But without your consent, I did not want to do anything, |
|---|---|
| **x** | **so that** not according to constraint your good thing might be but according to free-will. |

> For perhaps for this reason he was separated from you for an hour,
> **so that** you might have him back forever,

This would make a very clear contrast between who will "have" Onesimus, with both sentences actually using a form of the word "have" (*katexein* and *apexais*), and create an emphasis on Onesimus's freedom in Christ to serve Paul and Philemon's freedom to choose. The pivotal focus then lands on Philemon's "good thing," free-will decision.[3]

# "More Than I Say": An Implicit Request

Our goal in reading the book of Philemon is to see what God communicated in this first conversation with his people so that its truths might become a part of us, as the Holy Spirit works in us to teach us to live for God on a daily basis. We're also using Philemon as an example of how to read a book of the Bible in its book-level (literary and historical) context. To that end, I've been illustrating several of the rules for good Bible reading. Our objective is to ascertain the primary themes, message, and purpose of the text. I've taken a detailed approach, moreover, to show you how much you can learn about a book when you take some time to examine it closely.

It is not difficult to see the obvious or *explicit* purpose of Philemon. Paul uses subtlety, emotional ties, fundamental Christian values, direct request, and persuasive rhetoric to counsel Philemon in how he should respond to the return of Onesimus. Couched in a familiar, stereotyped form of the day—the Request form—Paul petitions Philemon to receive Onesimus as he would receive Paul himself (not a small request). He uses the meaning of community in Christ, Philemon's character as a Christian, and his relationship with Paul to bolster the request that this formerly useless, runaway-slave be welcomed back no longer as a slave, but as a beloved brother in Christ. The explicit request and purpose of the letter is crystal clear, and it has strong implications for us as we seek to understand and live by the values of God. We'll explore the application of this amazing picture of extreme community in a few minutes.

In the course of my discussion of Philemon, I've mentioned that I think Paul has something more in mind in this short, but extremely powerful letter than the stated request. Hmm. You may be wondering: "Doesn't looking for secondary, possibly implicit or hidden meanings in a Bible book cut against the grain of what you've been saying about how to read the Bible?" If you're thinking that, then good—you are right. Our goal is to see the first and primary meanings—to protect ourselves against personal, inkblot-like interpretations. On the other hand, biblical writings reflect the characteristics of real life, having been forged in the crucibles of sun-up, sun-

205

down, planet-earth realities. They are, therefore, no less complex than other types of literature. Let me suggest, then, that if the text itself manifests enough evidence for an intended dual or second level meaning, then by all means, we should be open to it. *The key is the text.* Does the writer really lead us to contemplate, explore, or discover a deeper or additional point of view? The question is, does Paul, in the text, lead Philemon (and therefore us) to an addition layer of meaning—something more, a little less direct, perhaps? Was he suggesting something to Philemon without coming right out and saying it? Without being dogmatic, I'd like to suggest that he was. I think the combined effect of several explicit statements, with some suggestive words and phrases would have been an inspired, albeit indirect, help to Philemon in how to handle a complicated and sticky situation.

The explicit statements are the starting point (if all we had were some possibly suggestive or double-meaning phrases, then we'd be on shaky ground). Paul says very emphatically, "I really wanted to keep him for myself so he could take your place in ministering to me in the chains of the gospel" (13). As we saw, he expresses this at the center, emphatic point of the book as a whole. He concludes the letter with a common expression (a Confidence form) that gives strategic emphasis to its content: "Confident of your obedience, I wrote to you, knowing that you will do even more than what I say" (21). "Obedience" suggests a clear and mandatory path—just as we have noticed in the explicit request (treating Onesimus as a brother in Christ is not optional); knowing that Philemon would do even more gives concrete expression to the idea that other courses of action could be considered. "Perhaps he was separated from you for a while so that you might have him back forever" (15), Paul says. But why "perhaps"? Is it a mild reference to God's providential hand in Onesimus's departure and his becoming a Christian? Or, is it a subtle way of suggesting that Philemon might *not* have Onesimus forever? Or both? "*Perhaps* he was separated from you for a little while, so that you could have him back *forever* [my emphasis]"—or perhaps not.

While looking at the letter-opening, I asked why Paul refers to his present, needful circumstances as a prisoner for Christ (he mentions it early and often). It's actually one of the most frequently repeated ideas in the letter. Why? Most of the prominent words and phrases of the letter make perfect sense in the context of Paul's explicit request for Philemon to receive Onesimus as a brother in Christ, but the repeated references to Paul's own imprisonment and the usefulness of Onesimus to him doesn't seem to support that request as readily as the other items. You could argue that it just goes to show Philemon how much Onesimus has really changed and become a part of Paul and his community of Christ (which would make it a form of amplification). On the other hand, Paul's connection of this refrain with his desire to have kept Onesimus seems to imply more. Put simply, why does Paul describe himself as "an old man and now a prisoner of Christ Jesus" and keep repeating how useful and helpful Onesimus is to him ("both to you and to me")? The implication is fairly obvious, isn't it? From Philemon's perspective: "Since Onesimus is so helpful to you, Paul . . . ; since I'm a partner with you not only in community, but in the cause of Christ . . .; since I owe you my very self . . . ." "Furthermore," Philemon might wonder, "what will the other slaves think if I begin to treat Onesimus as an equal . . ." The implied suggestion is that "perhaps" (15) Philemon should send Onesimus back to Paul, to give him to Paul as a sort of gift or contribution to his ministry. This, I believe, is the implicit request of the letter; and if you take these two ideas—welcoming Onesimus as a Christian and giving or releasing him back to Paul ("Confident of your obedience . . . even more . . .")—like the last few pieces of a puzzle, many of the apparent subtleties and ambiguities of the letter fall quickly into place, at times taking on apparently strategic, dual or double-meanings.

For example, the pregnant generality or vagueness of the introductory prayer can certainly be explained by the normal, generic functioning of an introduction, but I suspect there's more to it in this case, something which helps to explain why verse 6 quickly lends itself to an inkblot-like reading. Look at it again: Paul prays that the "fellowship" or "sharing" of Philemon's "faith might become active through the knowledge of every good thing in him/us for Christ." The explicit request of the letter provides a context that sharpens the focus and easily clarifies the meaning, now that we've become familiar with it (a "summit access" view). Paul's prayer is clearly that Philemon's faith would become active (extending far enough) to welcome Onesimus back as a brother, like he would Paul himself. And this can only come about through the knowledge of what Paul tells him in the course of the letter about what's happened to Onesimus—through the knowledge of every good thing that he has in Christ. (Does that phrase make more sense now?) But why "*every* good thing?" Because the last thing on his list of "good things" would be Onesimus. True. But consider the question in light of the explicit description of Philemon's voluntary giving of Onesimus to Paul as a "good thing," and we now have knowledge of a "good thing" that combines the wonder of Onesimus's new birth with his potential freedom for ministry.

And now don't miss this. The word used for "sharing" or "fellowship" in verse 6—*koinonia* in Greek—was sometimes used the same way we use the word "contribution," "offering," or "gift." So now, read the verse that way: "I pray that the contribution/gift of your faith might become active . . ." The New Living Translation leans that way: "And I am praying that you will put into action the generosity that comes from your faith as you understand and experience all the good things we have in Christ." In addition to refreshing fellowship for Onesimus, perhaps Paul is asking for a contribution—a partnering in his ministry—that is more active or comprehensive on Philemon's part than his acceptance of Onesimus. It just might solve several problems. Paul's choice of words at least allows for that possibility.

I'm also struck by how Paul constructs the primary request of the letter. Did you notice that he starts the request in verses 8-10 with the official, stereotyped request form ("I appeal to you . . ."), but never gets around to saying what he's asking until verse 17? Of course, this gives him time to fill in the background information that will help Philemon hear the request more graciously, and thus the delay is strategic (a tactic most of us have used when we need to ask or tell someone something difficult). But why interrupt the request? Why not just give the background first, then the request? Paul often does that in his letters. In addition to the good news about what has happened to Onesimus, the delay also allows him to include how much he would like to have kept Onesimus as part of the background information. But now consider what the request of verse 10 sounds like if you take it by itself: "I ask you *for* my child . . . Onesimus." Hmm. *Maybe he did finish his request*—the preposition here can actually mean either "for," or "concerning" or "on behalf of" and thus appears to function like other words with dual meaning in the letter. Even if we take it to mean that he's appealing "on behalf of" Onesimus, the brief, interrupted statement fits nicely with the idea of an implicit request *for* Onesimus.

Verse 20 contains another strong statement that Paul wants something from Philemon that could be taken either way. I already mentioned how interesting the phrasing is: "Yes, brother, I (of) you, *onaiman* . . ." The statement is again emphatic with regard to Paul ("I myself . . ." or "I really want some benefit from you . . .") Of course, it's perfectly fitting to read this in relation to the very difficult request for Philemon to accept Onesimus as a dear brother, but the continued emphasis on Paul, and his love and need for Onesimus begin to amount to more than just a wink or a nod. The potential, contextually valid, meanings of the phrase "refresh my heart in Christ" add to the multi-dimensional emphasis: of course, Paul wants Onesimus (his heart) to be refreshed; and it will certainly refresh Paul's heart to hear of Philemon's good response (his "obedience") to the letter, but how much more if he sends Onesimus—Paul's very heart—back to him?

Instructing Philemon to prepare a guest room for him, he explains, "For I am hoping that through your prayers to be restored to you" (NRSV). The word "restored" in Greek (*xarizomai*) often means "to offer willingly" or "to freely give" something—like a gift. Given the dual potential of many of the words and phrases in the letter, how interesting and fitting for Paul to end by saying, "For I hope that through your prayers I will be freely given to you." Is Paul implicitly requesting that Onesimus would be "freely given" to him? He almost says as much in verses 13-14, and here in verse 22, he applies the sentiment to himself and Philemon.

There are other things we could notice that suggest Paul gives hints in the course of the letter that beyond treating Onesimus like a brother in Christ, Philemon might considering sending him back to Paul as a "gift" or "contribution" to his ministry—a concrete re-expression of Philemon's identity as a "co-worker" in the cause of Christ. Such an act would not only be a gift to Paul, but may have served as inspired guidance to Philemon about how to handle his challenging situation. Assuming that Philemon has other slaves, how could he treat Onesimus the way Paul requests without causing serious disruption or at least confusing consequences in Philemon's relationship with his other slaves? After all, Onesimus ran away and possibly stole from Philemon as he ran. They didn't. How can Philemon welcome him home and treat him better than he did before he left? How strange and potentially disruptive! Certainly, the situation raises important questions about the practice of slavery itself and the social implications of Christianity, and in a very practical way for Philemon. Short of releasing all his slaves to "faith in Christ," how was Philemon to continue to function as their owner in light of how he must treat Onesimus? The situation is tense and complicated. Paul has put Philemon in the proverbial pickle. Runaway slaves were tortured and even killed as punishment, and as an example to others. What kind of example will Onesimus be? What is Philemon to do?

How wise (and *inspired*) of Paul to give him a possible solution at the same time he creates the problem—an option that goes beyond the explicit request of the letter. If Philemon were to send Onesimus back to Paul, to give him to Paul in effect (as a sharing/contribution of his faith), the disruptive impact on Philemon's household could certainly be minimized, and Philemon still has to deal with the implications of Christianity in his reception of and relationship to Onesimus. If he "were freely given" to Paul, moreover, Paul could set him free—free to serve as a fellow servant in the ministry and work of Christ. Sounds like a win-win: *refreshing and releasing community in Christ.* In the course of the letter, Paul speaks of his own physical freedom (1:22) and of Philemon's freedom in Christ (1:14). Since Onesimus is now an equal follower of Christ, to be accepted in Philemon's community as Paul himself, "slavery" changes necessarily.[4] So, a final question: Does the idea of freedom lurk quietly and emancipatingly behind the explicit words and implicit wishes of Paul's letter?

Here's a list of some potential clues to a secondary or implicit request in Philemon. Some of these are more obvious than others, but the combined effect provides fairly strong, textual evidence as to just what "more than I say" Philemon could do. In the end, Paul leaves it up to Philemon, so that his "good thing" would be a free/voluntary act of community in Christ (such is freedom in Christ):

1.  Paul's emphatic statement that he really wanted to keep Onesimus
2.  Emphasis on Paul's needful situation, in combination with how helpful Onesimus is to him in that situation (thus, a literary function of the prison references)
3.  Repetition of "to you—to me" (which goes with the above)
4.  Emphasis on fellow ministry, in combination with the reference to Onesimus "taking Philemon's place" in "ministering" to Paul (and that Philemon owes Paul his very self)
5.  Philemon's indebtedness to Paul
6.  Repeated use of the word "have" in a context of freedom
7.  Dual potential of the introductory prayer for what Philemon is to do
8.  Meaning of "fellowship" as "contribution" or "gift"
9.  Philemon's knowledge of "every good thing" and Paul's clarification that Onesimus serving him in prison is a "good thing"
10. Interrupted structuring of the request: "I ask you for . . . Onesimus . . ."
11. Phrasing of the initial part of the request: "I ask you for . . . Onesimus."
12. Potential meanings of the phrase "refresh my heart in Christ"
13. "*Perhaps* he was separated from you for a while so that you can have him back forever?"

14. Verse 20: "I want some benefit from you in the Lord; refresh my heart in Christ"
15. "... knowing that you will do even more than I say"
16. "... will be freely given to you"

Is there an implicit request in Paul's letter to Philemon? Even if you disagree with some of the individual clues I've listed, Paul's emphatic statements indicate that Onesimus being and serving with Paul would certainly be a good option. Perceiving an implicit request for Philemon to contribute Onesimus to Paul's ministry clarifies some of the words and phrases of the letter, moreover. The important thing, however, is that we see the impact of the life-changing message of Christ upon the lives of these people and its potential for us if we truly accept the implications of the radical community revealed in Paul's letter to Philemon.

# Digesting the Word

Rule #8 of good Bible reading is to "digest" or "document your experiences in the word" by constructing a summary of some of the key ideas of a Bible book. I'll follow the outline I provided as a way of "digesting" the book of Philemon. The answers I give are my own gleanings and emphases, not meant as an exhaustive or authoritative set of responses.

**Title:** *Extreme Community*
   or *Renewing, Refreshing, and Releasing Community*

If I had to boil it down to a very brief phrase, I think I would call it *Refreshing Love*.

## Purpose

### What is the primary purpose of the book?

To motivate Philemon to accept Onesimus back, no longer as a slave, but as a dear/equal brother in Christ.

### What result or action did it seek from the original readers?

To activate and share the community of Christ. To extend the boundaries of their love and faith in Christ to include Onesimus, and thus to "refresh" him. This would include forgiveness and acceptance into their community of faith.

### What other actions did the book seek from the audience?

To share in the cause of Christ. To continue to participate in the work of Christ as ministry partners with Paul by welcoming Onesimus into that partnership and possibly by "releasing" him (back to Paul) for ministry.

# Message

**What is the major message of the book?**
That renewing faith in Christ transcends all mistakes and all boundaries, creating a community of extreme love and purpose in Christ. That we must forgive others as Christ has forgiven us to share in that refreshing and releasing community.

**What idea(s) or teaching does it convey?**
There is a fundamental equality at the foot and focus of the cross. That new community in Christ comes from the mutual sharing of authentic and devoted faith, and active ("refreshing") love for people.

**What are other key points or messages?**
Anyone (even a good-for-nothing, run-away slave) can be made radically new in Christ, to the point of becoming deeply loved and needed in the community and cause of Christ. How marvelous to think about and apply this principle to myself, that I might be valuable to God and important to fellow followers of Jesus (someone's "very heart") in a fully-devoted community of Christians.

# Themes

**What are the key words and themes of the book?**
Community/Fellowship in Christ
Shared cause/ministry in Christ
Faith
Love (for all Christians)
Forgiveness
Renewal/Rebirth
Encouragement (refreshing hearts)
Equality or non-prejudice
Repentance/Change

Willingness to "go to bat" for another Christian (Paul for Onesimus)
Heartfelt and loyal friendship
Freedom

**Is there a verse or set of verses that seems to capture the core of the book?**
1:6, 15-17

# Shape

**How is the content shaped?**
It has a basic, three-part shape with some additional levels in the structure of the Middle/Request section.

It also appears to have a chiastic/circular shape. (See earlier in the chapter.)

**What are the major sections?**
Introduction (1-7)
Prescript (1-2), Grace Greeting (3), Thanksgiving (4-7)
Middle (8-20)
Transition (8-9), Background Information (10-16), Request and Support (17-20)
Conclusion (21-25)
Confidence (21), Visit Talk (22), Final Greetings (23-25)

**How do they fit together and function in relation to each other?**
1:1-7 function as introduction: key words and concepts are first introduced in the Address and Greeting, while the Thanksgiving highlights key theological foundations, themes, and purposes of the letter

1:8-9 transition to the request

1:8-16 introduce the formal request and provide background information to Paul's request of Philemon

1:16-22 express and support the primary request of the letter

1:20 succinctly concludes the Middle of the letter

1:23-24 function as a conclusion by encouragingly and authoritatively finalizing the request

1:23-25 close with succinct verbal reminders of fundamental values

# Summary

**Summarize the main ideas and primary purposes of the book.**

Paul's letter to Philemon uses the fundamental Christian values of faith, love, fellowship/community and partnership in Christ, forgiveness, equality, renewal, and service/release to support its challenging request. On the basis of faith and love, Paul petitions Philemon to accept Onesimus as an equal brother in Christ. Onesimus—a run-away slave who was formerly useless to Philemon—had run into Paul in prison and become a Christian. Onesimus's life and character were radically altered, as he became a follower of Christ and a very dear helper to Paul. Paul is sending Onesimus back to his former master with a supporting explanation of what has happened and his request that Philemon accept him back no longer as a slave, but as a dear brother in Christ. Paul wanted to keep Onesimus to help him in his ministry, but did not want to presume Philemon's "contribution" to the cause of Christ for him, so that his work and gifts would be given freely. Paul underscores his requests of Philemon with his implied authority and present needs as an "old man" and imprisoned servant of Christ, and by the fact that Philemon is indebted to Paul for his own spiritual well-being.

# Theology

**What does the book teach us about God (the Father, the Son, and the Holy Spirit)?**

> The letter assumes the fatherhood of God and the lordship of Christ.
>
> The book teaches that God is a gracious and forgiving God.
>
> That Jesus, the Christ, provides the spiritual basis for new birth, new life, and new community.
>
> That being a part of Christ radically alters who and what we are in relationship to each other.
>
> That Christ is Lord and expects us to live by what it means to be a part of his person and community.
>
> That being a part of God's community means loving and caring for that community.
>
> That being a part of Christ defines us and is more important than typical goals and patterns of planet earth.

# Kingdom

**What does the book teach us about living for God in the kingdom of God?**

> I think the most direct teaching about the kingdom of God in Paul's letter to Philemon is about the nature of the church as a place of forgiveness, change, renewal, and the amazing new relationships that result. The book is—in a sense—a very concrete expression of the fundamental Christian concept of being "born again." Where else can you find such drastic change in an individual and his relationships to others? From foe to friend? From hurt to healing? From worthlessness to purpose and friendship? The book of Philemon teaches us that as a doorway into the kingdom of God, the church is a place where we can all start over and find life. The character of the kingdom then becomes the foundation for how we live and act toward others. Onesimus

217

displays the initial change of conversion. Paul models kingdom character (in his work with and for Onesimus), as he seeks it in Philemon.

The kingdom of God on earth includes partnership in grace and ministry.
The kingdom of God on earth includes refreshing renewal and release.

# Life

**List the ways that you believe the book should impact and change your life.**

Most directly: I will look upon "all the saints"—all Christians—as equal brothers and sisters in Christ. When given a chance to forgive and accept someone back into the fellowship of my faith, I will seek to do so with the Spirit of Christ, knowing that I owe to him and to others my very self.

I will seek to renew and build community with people who have wronged or hurt me.

I want to live up to Paul's vision of unprejudiced, refreshing, and releasing community.

I want to teach Paul's vision of extreme community to others.

I should remember my roots (figuratively speaking): what it means to have gone from being a "run-away, good-for-nothing" slave outside of Christ to being God's very heart! Now, above all else, I want to be "useful" in service to my master (I want to be free to serve).

I want to be like Paul. I want to help other "run-away slaves" find forgiveness and renewal in Christ.

# Changing Our Lives with the Precepts of Philemon

On the heels of our digest and as one of the last rules of good Bible reading, it's vital to think about how the values and teachings of Paul's letter to Philemon impact our lives today. Some things in the Bible apply directly to today (basic values and actions based on those values). Others—usually specific actions or ways of applying a value or principle—reflect values that need to be ascertained and then applied to situations in today's world. This is the idea behind the triangle of application. Some things slide across the centuries and give us straightforward examples of how scripture should impact our lives (the bottom of the triangle); others reveal values from God that we will apply differently than a particular instance or example in the text (the top part of the triangle). We zoom in on the value or principle and apply it to our lives today.

Several basic principles of Christianity traversing Paul's letter to Philemon apply just as well to us as they did to them. Inspired by their faith in Christ, each of the principal characters display traits of God that should shape our characters and impact our lives today.

The first: **shared faith in Christ**. Perhaps the importance of faith goes without saying, but everything the letter stands for is based on faith in Christ. Without it, the letter would not exist, and Onesimus's history would have been radically different. Given the difficulty of the situation and the extreme implications of shared faith in Christ, Paul doesn't just assume the place of faith, but calls attention to it in various ways, as well as to Philemon's reputation for being a man of faith. He has faith and love toward the Lord Jesus and for all the saints. This is fundamental and critical. All Christian community springs from joint participation in Christ, which is based on faith in Christ; thus, when Paul prays for Philemon, it is for *the fellowship ("partnership") of his faith*. Onesimus's new birth represents a pivotal acceptance of that faith in Christ, and Paul's request to Philemon applies the implications of that shared faith to the circumstances reflected in the letter. So, if we are thinking about how the fundamental teachings of the letter enrich our lives today, we should probably start here, with faith in Christ. After all, there are still

Onesimuses aplenty, who need to come to enjoy the extreme community of Jesus Christ and who face dire circumstances; and there are situations that call for tremendous acts of forgiveness and renewal in our world that would try anyone's faith. Part of the forcefulness of Paul's request of Philemon is the implication that his faith is under test, which implies that our belief in Christ must determine the way we live and act.

The **shared grace of God in Christ** is also fundamental to the content of Philemon. In fact, God's grace is really first—shared faith is based on it. We believe in the saving Christ who loves, died for, and forgives us. New community results. This also lies behind everything in the letter. Paul and Philemon, and now Onesimus, share what they share because of God's grace. We should live with the knowledge of this grace—how much we all owe—and extend similar graciousness to one another. Paul is a model of such gracious living and had apparently so touched the life of Philemon, as he reminds him: "not to mention that you owe me your very self." Philemon's decision to treat Onesimus as Paul requested will be a continuation of the grace of Christ in the lives of believers.

The Bible teaches that God is love and his followers experience and share that love. Thus, our third principle of application: **shared love in Christ**. In bright distinction from the emphasis on feelings in modern culture, love in the Bible typically focuses on a stance or attitude one takes toward someone and on the resulting kind and beneficial actions coming from a fundamental belief in his or her worth. Feelings are certainly involved, but they are not the starting place. In Philemon, "love for all the saints" intensifies the community dimension, and it is on Philemon's nature as a lover of all Christians that Paul appeals to him. Christ creates the new community. By the Spirit's power, our faith in Jesus ushers us into that community. Love—a characteristic of that community—changes the way we treat each other. This doesn't mean that we have to instantly feel wonderful toward every other Christian. That would be great, but it's not realistic in our broken world. It wasn't realistic for Philemon either. But—like I said—that's not the starting point. The starting point is how we act, how we esteem and treat each other. The specific request for Philemon to treat Onesimus no longer as a good-for-nothing, run-away slave, but as an equal brother in Christ applies specifically for Philemon the broader value of love—renewing, refreshing, and releasing (one of the basic meanings of the word "forgive") love—for all saints in Christ. So, broadly speaking, applying the teachings of Philemon to our lives today calls for implementing the value of love for all Christians. I call this "unprejudiced community." It means we do not discriminate in the way we esteem and treat people based on color, social-economic status, education, etc., "for we are all one in Christ Jesus."

But how do *we* apply it more specifically? Obviously, we can't duplicate the specific application of the letter. None of us can accept Onesimus back as an equal brother. There are certainly situations where other forms of mistreatment and "run-away" hurt take place, however. This is where we can apply the values behind Paul's request of Philemon to specific situations where we've been wronged or where various forms of social position/status create barriers between those who can and should share in the new community of Christ. The principle is not unlike the saying, "'Vengeance is mine,' says the Lord . . .," and yet it goes further. It says that in Christ there are fundamentally no artificial, relational barriers erected by planet-earth ways of thinking/living that cannot be scaled in the sphere of Christ's new community through active sharing of (= mutual participation in) our faith. As when Peter asked Jesus how many times should he forgive his brother when he sins against him: expecting maybe seven as an extremely gracious limit, Jesus says, "Seventy times seven," or, in other words, there's no limit.

The issue in Philemon is not so much how many times should we forgive, however, but **how deeply or far can we forgive**. How deeply can we be hurt, how far can we be separated and still be brought together again? To talk like Peter, "How many boundaries, layers, or miles of separation should I cross over, if my brother or sister hurts me and runs away from me?" Personal injury? Cultural norms? Social and economic distinctions? Racial boundaries? Business and financial repercussions? Authority and respect? How deeply must you hurt me before I can never allow you to resurface? Maybe seven layers? Maybe seven miles? In writing to Philemon, Paul says, "Seventy times seven." This, I believe, is a profound application of Paul's letter to Philemon: *extreme community begins with bottomless forgiveness.* Or, perhaps "no-holds-barred" forgiveness—complete release of all debts.

From the book of Philemon, we learn that community in Christ is so extreme and so marvelous that no degree of wrong or distance of separation can nullify the Spirit's ability to create renewing, refreshing, and releasing community, if we respond as Paul petitions Philemon: with **the energizing of the fellowship of our faith**. This is so unlike anything on planet earth that I can't express it adequately. To go from running away, with a past full of uselessness and slavery, to becoming a new child of God, deeply loved, valued, and set free into the community and cause of Christ, is the amazing potential of God's love in Christ. It is definitely extreme—extreme pardon, extreme power, extreme purpose. Sign me up!

I'd like to complete our discussion of the application of Philemon by defining this concept—extreme community—with three examples discernible in Paul's letter to Philemon (discernible because of the careful, contextual reading with which we've approached the letter). The first is **shared participation in full and unprejudiced community**. There can hardly be a greater example of separation and prejudice than when humans put so much distance between one another that one is labeled "master" and another "slave," . . . where slaves are property to be used or abused as one chooses. That's not to say that's how Philemon treated *his* slaves, just that such barriers and boundaries—and their inevitable influences on how we think and act—characterize our world. The message of Christ penetrates even such situations; the gospel of Christ calls for integrity and devotion in the midst of brokenness—ethics beyond our normal imagination.

So Paul sends Onesimus back to Philemon—that, of itself, is a sign of something new. But he can't go back, at least not as he left. He is not the same person because he is now a "saint," a Christian, a fellow member of the community of Christ, where there is and can be no legitimate prejudice. The community of faith is unprejudiced. All are equal. Prejudice is not an option. I must, therefore—if I want to apply the word of God from Philemon to my world—I must seek to know and exemplify full acceptance based on fundamental equality in Christ and love for all Christians—not on my likes or dislikes, preferences and biases; not on my neighborhood or level of education; not on my bank account or my position in life. If I ever think I am better than someone else, through Philemon the Lord says different. In the community of Christ, I cannot treat any person or group as if they are somehow less because of their status, history, or ancestry. I am to love them—him or her—because they are as much a part of Christ as my finger is a part of my hand and my nose, of my face. Each of us is a precious part of the body of Christ. To welcome someone less than completely into the full functioning of the body of Christ is to harm the body of Christ. See what I mean—that unprejudiced community transcends our normal way of thinking? Bottom line: I want to treat any sincere follower of Christ with the sort of refreshing love that Paul asks of Philemon, even if he or she has hurt me deeply, but now comes home.

The second example of extreme community in Philemon is that of **shared commitment to the cause of Christ**—which is the extending of God's new community to places where it doesn't exist. (The kingdom of God is imperialistic in that we want everyone to have the opportunity to find its renewing and refreshing love.) This is community as "gift" or "giving of one's gifts" in Christ: "the knowledge of every good thing we have in Christ," to use the words of the letter. It's our joint privilege of sharing in the cause (mission) of Christ. It's a fundamental part of life in the kingdom of God on earth. Paul was constantly engaged in it; it directed his every step. All the participants in the letter shared this common purpose. Paul wanted to keep Onesimus (he had become that helpful) to take Philemon's place in ministering to him. See the expectation of partnership in ministry? In addition to the releasing of debt that goes with forgiveness, there is a releasing—a freedom to serve—that comes from being made new in the love of Christ.

Coming to know and use one's gifts to serve God in the cause of Christ is a part of the releasing function of the church. Whether Onesimus was to return to work directly with Paul in prison (sort of ironic, don't you think?) or stay with Philemon as a useful, beloved component of God's work there, *Onesimus was to be released for God*. Paul hoped it meant physically, as part of a "sharing" or "contribution" of Philemon's faith. That way, Philemon could show his love for both Paul and Onesimus at the same time. Either way, extreme community in Christ calls out our inherent usefulness to God and our willingness to release others for similar service. If you pause over that thought for a moment, I'm afraid you might begin to feel strangely warmed as a tiny degree of God's extreme love and purpose for you begins to move in your heart—the application of the word refreshes our hearts, as well as our actions. *"Refresh my heart in Christ!"*

None of this could have happened if Onesimus had not met Christ though Paul. It changed his life. This is the beginning of all things extreme community in Christ: **conversion** (to keep our letter-c words) or perhaps **shared new beginning in Christ**. It all starts with conversion, with new birth—the beginning of transformation into renewing, heart-refreshing, debt-releasing, Spirit-enriching freedom in Christ. It's "shared" in the sense that we all must experience it. Nothing we bring can serve as an adequate starting point for this sort of amazing work of God in our lives. Perhaps a better word, then, would be "cross." It all begins with **the shared cross of Christ**.

Community in Christ is so extreme that it requires a brand new start in the form of a new birth that can only come from the Spirit of the Creator himself through the saving work of Christ and the cross. "Except a person be born again," Jesus said, "he cannot enter the kingdom of God." Because the Spirit is free, the potential is limited only by our willingness to accept his grace and renewing power. That shared grace of God produces and uses our shared faith and our shared love for each other (for "all the saints") to create a new person, a new community, and a new world. *To be renewed, refreshed, and released together—this is extreme community.* It changed the life of a run-away slave a long time ago and of those who shared it with him. Those who welcomed him into their fellowship came to know and love him. In a very basic and real way, therefore, Onesimus became a free man the day he met the Lord Jesus, the Christ, regardless of what Philemon did; and Paul's letter to Philemon is, perhaps intentionally and ironically, a document about freedom.

# True Freedom

These, then, are the ingredients of extreme community according to Philemon: (1) shared renewal (forgiveness and new birth in Christ), (2) shared refreshment (accepting and encouraging, unprejudiced community) and (3) shared release into the mission and purposes of Christ in the world. Were a preacher to preach on the steps of extreme community from Philemon with these three words—"cross"/"conversion," "community," and "cause" or "commitment"—or with the three actions of the *renewing, refreshing,* and *releasing* grace of God in Christ, we'd know that his message came from one of God's first conversations with his people through Paul's letter to Philemon.

In route to his martyrdom in Rome, Ignatius (born about AD 35/50), bishop of Antioch and student of the apostle John, wrote a series of letters (sort of like Paul) to various churches in the region as he passed through. He was ordered by the Roman prefect to be chained and sent (from Antioch) to Rome. In his letter to the Romans, he says, "From Syria even to Rome I fight with wild beasts, by land and sea, by night and by day, being bound amidst ten leopards, even a company of soldiers, who only grow worse when they are kindly treated." His most famous quotation also comes from the same letter:

> I am writing to all the Churches and I enjoin all, that I am dying willingly for God's sake, if only you do not prevent it. I beg you, do not do me an untimely kindness. Allow me to be eaten by the beasts, which are my way of reaching to God. I am God's wheat, and I am to be ground by the teeth of wild beasts, so that I may become the pure bread of Christ.

In Ignatius's first and second letter to the Ephesians, he mentions their pastor/bishop by name. His name . . . is . . . Onesimus. Onesimus, Bishop of Ephesus, met up with Ignatius in Smyrna on his journey to Rome. He brought along a deacon named Burrhus, who was a scribe and who helped Ignatius write his letters to the churches. We do not know if this is the same Onesimus as in Paul's letter to Philemon. Some believe it was. Even if he were not this leader in the church of Ephesus, several strands of church tradition hold that our Onesimus, the one-time run-away, useless slave of Philemon, became just such a leader in the church of his day, dying under the persecution of the emperor Trajan (AD 109) as a martyr for Christ. From useless slavery to ultimate freedom—is there anything more free than to give oneself so completely and thoroughly that you gladly lay down your life for it? Such radical potential, revealed to us in Paul's letter to Philemon, shows just how powerful the renewing, refreshing, and releasing community of Christ's love can be for each of us.

When you renew, refresh, and release someone in Christ, there's no limit to what he or she can do and become. I don't know about you, but I want this sort of extreme community. I want to live in it, which means I want to know, respond to, and share the grace of God in Christ. I want to have faith in the Lord Jesus and be a lover of all saints, regardless of skin-color, social-status, or savings account. I want to treat those who have wronged me with the depth of refreshing faith and love that Paul asks of Philemon—an active sharing of my faith that will help them find real the extreme community of Christ that begins to share in Jesus' own love and community with the Father. I won't always feel like it, and, sometimes, I will fail miserably. But God's word spoken to us through the book of Philemon envisions and calls for no less. I must welcome everyone who comes to Christ within the arms of the community in which I serve, no longer as a slave or an enemy or a distant cousin or an acquaintance or an annoyance or someone whom I'm just can't stand. I am to welcome him or her as an equal brother/sister in Christ, remade in the image of God. I get to welcome them as Christ welcomes me . . . as Philemon would have welcomed Paul . . . as Paul asked Philemon to welcome Onesimus.

# An Inkblot No More

Let's finish were we started, with a potential inkblot: Philemon 1:6 (my own translation this time):

> I pray that the fellowship of your faith might become active through the knowledge of every good thing that you have for Christ.

Having done all that we've now done to hear God's first conversation with his people in Philemon, it's difficult to see this verse without connecting it to the rest of the letter, isn't it? We can see how the fellowship of Philemon's faith needs to become active through the knowledge of every good thing he has in or for Christ. This is our goal. Our goal is to put the verses of the Bible back into the Bible: rediscovering the books of God. This is reading the Bible in context. This is reading the Bible in its own literary and historical contexts, its own book-level context. This is good Bible reading. It's Spirit-led Bible reading. It's **S**ummit **A**ccess **B**ible **R**eading. This is what we've tried to do with Philemon. This is what we want to do with all the books of the Bible.

Though our perspectives will always be limited and somewhat distorted, we can now view Philemon 1:6 as it fits and functions in the letter as a whole—its Spirit-inspired context—from the summit, so to speak. From this perspective, we will likely agree on the basic meaning of the text. We see the picture; we get the point. We're much less disposed to see or use the verse as an inkblot—to have our own, independent and personal understandings, which we might very well defend to the point of mutual excommunication (the opposite of Philemon). Pastors will likely use it as more than a "scriptural" exhortation to evangelism or merely a general exhortation to "share our faith." They will model and teach good Bible reading. That is, if we are looking to hear the word of God from the Spirit of God from the books of the Bible. And, from this perspective, SABR can legitimately be interpreted as *Spirit* Access Bible Reading.

From Philemon—among other things—the word of God is

love beyond boundaries,

forgiveness beyond hurts,

community beyond differences, and

purpose beyond failures.

Now, read Philemon again, and seek to live it as you follow Christ.

---

## Notes

1. Perhaps motivated by the arrival of Epaphras from Colossae (Colossians 1:7-8; 4:12-13).
2. See Colossians 4:7-17 for interesting references. Epaphras was from Colossae (Colossians 1:7, 4:12-13). Paul sent Tychicus to Colossae with the letter to the Colossian church, and Onesimus went with him (4:7-9).
3. It's probably over-interpretive, but I find it interesting that, given the importance of the issue of "having" in Philemon, that the concentric structure within the introductory Thanksgiving that we noticed actually centers on the word "have": "hearing . . ."
   of the love
      and the faith
         that you *have*
      toward the Lord Jesus
   and for all the saints
   Philemon's faith and love—the faith and love that he has—form the crucial foundation for how he will respond to Paul's requests.
4. Though, of course, this does not imply that Christianity demands the release of all slaves, as Paul's regulations in Colossians 3:22-4:1 and Ephesians 6:1-9 demonstrate. Like yeast in homemade bread and the smell that permeates the house as it bakes, however, the implications of equality in Christ are so deep and far-reaching as to have gradually contributed to the universal disapproval and extermination of slavery in most modern cultures.

229

# Chapter 12

# Zoomed Out on Mark

## Introduction

### "Sowing an Inkblot"

This time we start with a larger potential inkblot, made up of a brief section of material—a familiar story. It's Mark 4:1-9:

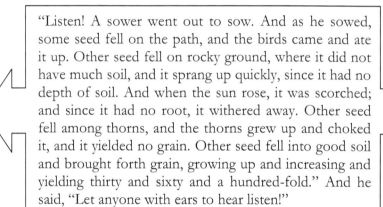

"Listen! A sower went out to sow. And as he sowed, some seed fell on the path, and the birds came and ate it up. Other seed fell on rocky ground, where it did not have much soil, and it sprang up quickly, since it had no depth of soil. And when the sun rose, it was scorched; and since it had no root, it withered away. Other seed fell among thorns, and the thorns grew up and choked it, and it yielded no grain. Other seed fell into good soil and brought forth grain, growing up and increasing and yielding thirty and sixty and a hundred-fold." And he said, "Let anyone with ears to hear listen!"

If you've ever read the books of the Bible known as Gospels (Matthew, Mark, Luke, John) or spent much time in church, you're probably familiar with the parables of Jesus and with this story called "the parable of the Sower." The word "parable" is a Greek word for a short story or saying used to compare something to something else, similar to the English word "analogy" or "illustration." Jesus often used parables—analogies or comparisons—to teach about the nature of the kingdom of God. In Mark 4:20, for example, he said, "With what can we compare the kingdom of God, or what parable will we use for it?" The Hebrew word for parable (*mashal*) could also be used for symbolic actions that served as living parables—the Old Testament prophets sometimes acted out God's messages for the people. In this case, Jesus tells the parable of the Sower while teaching a large crowd of people from a boat on the edge of the Sea of Galilee (he's in the boat; they're on the shore). The disciples apparently don't understand it very well and ask Jesus in private what it means.

So what does the parable of the Sower mean? Jesus gives an explanation, but no application, of the details to the disciples in Mark 4:14-20:

> "The sower sows the word. These are the ones on the path where the word is sown: when they hear, Satan immediately comes and takes away the word that is sown in them. And these are the ones sown on rocky ground: when they hear the word, they immediately receive it with joy. But they have no root, and endure only for a while; then, when trouble or persecution arises on account of the word, immediately they fall away. And others are those sown among the thorns: these are the ones who hear the word, but the cares of the world, and the lure of wealth, and the desire for other things come in and choke the word, and it yields nothing. And these are the ones sown on the good soil: they hear the word and accept it and bear fruit, thirty and sixty and a hundred-fold."

Puzzled and perhaps a little disappointed that the disciples need help understanding the parable (4:13), Jesus clarifies the comparison of a farmer sowing seed with the word sown or planted in the hearts of people: different types of people (soils) yield different sorts of responses or results. The analogy is profound and easy enough to grasp, given Jesus' explanation. And so you have likely heard a sermon or two (or maybe many) about the preaching, spreading, or "sowing" of the word of God. Some hearers are like an asphalt-hard, dirt path. The word bounces off and is taken away by Satan. Some are like rocky soil. These respond quickly, but their faith is shallow and short-lived in the face of hardship. Others are like thorny soil, choked out by more pressing and more valued things. Some, on the other hand, are good soil—the word of God takes root and produces a bountiful harvest. No doubt this makes a great sermon, encouraging us to be good soil, subtly reassuring many of us who are listening—we Christians—that we *are* good soil; otherwise, we probably wouldn't be there.

But is this Mark's point? Is this what he (the author/story) hoped to accomplish by relaying this event in the life of Jesus at this point in the story? Why does Mark tell the story of Jesus' teaching via the parable of the Sower here? How does it relate to what's going on in the context? . . . to what's come before and what comes after? How does it relate to the other parables in the context, like the lamp and the lampstand (4:21-23), the measure (4:24-25), the growing seed (4:26-29), and the mustard seed (4:30-32)? What does it have to do with the fact that at this point Jesus began to teach them *only* by parables, "as they were able to hear" (4:33-34)? And why don't the disciples understand the parable? Doesn't "good soil" hear and understand the word of God?

In other words, we should seek to answer The Question: how does the parable of the Sower fit/function in the book of Mark as a whole? From a negative perspective, is it possible that we have made an inkblot out of one of Jesus' most important parables by taking it out of Mark's story-setting? Is it possible that by reading or preaching on the parable of the Sower without its Holy Spirit-inspired context, we could be missing something of the power and intent of God's word in our lives? And are we at that moment . . . sowing an inkblot?

We'll keep these questions in mind as we begin to explore the Bible book of Mark. But let me warn you, the answer is more challenging than we probably want to hear. Mark certainly intended more than a generic message about how the word is received differently by different people. *Casually or implicitly reassuring followers of Jesus that they are good soil is the opposite of Mark's purpose.* In fact, just as the first followers of Jesus had a great deal of trouble figuring out who Jesus was and the real meaning of his presence and message, the book of Mark seeks to challenge our core—root-deep soil—conceptions of

233

what it means to be a follower of Jesus, the Christ (= the Messiah). So, can you handle it? If so, then journey on.

## The Gospel of Mark

As I've mentioned, when you first read a book from the Bible, a little background information can be helpful to get you started and give you some idea of the historical context—but only enough to propel you to the text (Rule #7). You'll build your perception of that context more as you read, and you can look to study guides, commentaries, and other books later. To that end, here's a little about Mark.

The Bible book of Mark is a story about Jesus. More specifically, it's a book about what it means to be a follower of Jesus: Who was Jesus? What did he stand for? How did people respond to him? How should *we* respond to him? How do we follow him? Mark's story about Jesus is one of the four books of the New Testament (Matthew, Mark, Luke, John) referred to as "Gospels." The word "gospel" comes from the Greek word *euaggelion,* meaning "good news." Mark's first sentence may have provided the impetus for the use of the word to describe similar writings about the ministry of Jesus: "The beginning of the *good news* of Jesus Christ." Although the identity of the author is not revealed in the text, Christians have always held Mark to be written by John Mark (sometimes called Mark the Evangelist), the cousin of Barnabas.[1] Mark was a missionary companion of Paul and probably of Peter. Ancient citations of Irenaeus (2nd century AD)[2] and Papias (120/130 AD) in Eusebius's *Church History*[3] suggest that Mark's Gospel may have been based on the preaching of Peter. Consistent with his missionary experience, Mark is believed to have founded the very influential church at Alexandria.

Obviously, *Mark* is very different from *Philemon*. (From here on, unless otherwise stated, I use the word "Mark" to refer to the content of the book and not the physical author.) Instead of a brief, personal letter to a friend, Mark is an artfully constructed literary composition (though some scholars didn't used to think so). It was written to a group of Christians during the days of the early church, but we do not know exactly which group, when, or where (though many think it was written in Rome, sometime before the destruction of Jerusalem by the Romans in AD 70). The specifics of the historical context have thus been lost, and we must depend on implications within the story itself to envision how it spoke to Christians of the first century. In distinction from Matthew's Gospel, Mark appears to be written for a more non-Jewish or at least non-Judean audience and has sometimes been labeled the "Greek" or "Gentile" Gospel. Compared to some biographies or narrative works, the story is rather brief, but contains a skillfully designed plot, highly developed themes, vivid and profound use of symbolism, with extremely challenging theological implications.

From a literary perspective, Mark's story of Jesus is just that—a *story* or *narrative* of key events, scenes or episodes during the life and ministry of Jesus, containing considerable dialogue and a few, more extended monologues or speeches (teachings) of Jesus. Many of these episodes appear to be based on "oral tradition"; that is, before the author of Mark or his sources wrote down these stories, they were remembered and told often as part of the preaching (Peter, perhaps) and developing history of the early church by those who had experienced them first hand. They were a part of the treasured, living memories of Jesus' time on earth. Some of the scenes thus tend to reflect the conventions of story-telling in the oral culture of the first century. These scenes, like miracle stories, for example, amount to a sort of sub-genre or sub-shape that went into the overall construction of the book. As with New Testament letters (as we saw in Philemon), characteristics of these sub-shapes can sometimes aid us in perceiving the structure and impact of a given section. In addition, Mark uses several literary/oral techniques to arrange the material, interrelate ideas, and highlight important points. For example, Mark is well known for putting one event or story inside of another, sometimes referred to as a "sandwich." Looking closely at the contents of the "sandwich" often reveals additional layers in circular or chiastic patterns (a common technique in oral storytelling and biblical literature in general).

With similarities to and differences from ancient biographies or "lives" of important figures, ancient novels, and other popular literature of the day, Mark intends to present an historically accurate and spiritually compelling portrayal of the nature, actions, teachings, and meaning of Jesus. Mark is, therefore, an historical and theological narrative. Its gene is not so different from modern short stories or books, moreover, that we can't connect with and understand the movement and intent of the text, especially if we're willing to apply the principles of good Bible reading that is our focus. Reading a narrative is different from reading a letter (Rule #5), however, and that's why we're going to spend some time together on a New Testament Gospel.

So what does Mark say of Jesus? Who is he? Can he really be the promised Messiah? Is he more than human? Is he the Son of God? . . . especially in light of his death on a cross? How can God's Anointed die in such a shameful way? And if he is the "Christ of God," what does that mean? What does it mean to be a disciple or follower of Jesus? What constitutes a disciple? Isn't everyone who responds to Jesus in a positive fashion a follower, at least to some extent? What does it mean to be a *faithful* or *good* disciple? How does one learn and grow as a follower of Christ? And of course, what does all this mean for us? How do we follow Jesus today? These are some of the tremendous questions that come from reading Mark's story of Jesus.

Regrettably, the length of Mark prevents me from undertaking a thorough study in the scope of this book. Our purpose, moreover, is to illustrate how to apply some of the principles of good Bible reading to a longer, narrative context. For these reasons, I'm going to adjust how we approach the book, which illustrates the point that you don't have to follow a single regimen when you read, as long as you apply the fundamental principles that we're learning. After finding the Introduction and Conclusion, and looking at the basic shape of the text (Rule #3); highlighting some key words and ideas introduced in the beginning (Rule #4); I'll then combine our rules and steps of good Bible reading into some observations about each section, especially the early part of the book, always keeping a watchful eye on our primary question: how does this material/section fit into the overall content and purpose of the book. Though we can't cover everything in depth, I'm confident that our journey in Mark will provide enough hands-on experience for you to take it further; and, it's my prayer that it will help motivate you to want to rediscover Mark and all the books of the Bible—books that lie hidden under layers of traditional dust, Christian familiarity, and contextual disconnection.

Okay, let's get started. What's the first thing you should do? Of course, it's read the whole book, preferably several times. That's Rule #1. That way you begin to develop a big-picture perspective, within which you can see how the individual chapters and verses fit into Mark's overall context and purposes. That's Rule #2. Our goal is to reduce and eliminate inkblots by seeing how all the individual parts fit together—for you to become an inkblot zapper. Remember, if you don't know how a part fits, you're not sure you're getting God's point; you're not sure that the Holy Spirit-inspired context is shaping the meaning. But when we "see the picture," it's much, much easier to "get the point." If you'll always remember and apply this basic principle—see the picture, get the point—you'll be embracing more and more of the Spirit-given perspective of God when you read the Bible.

Would you like to know who Jesus is? Would you like to know what it means to follow him? Would you like to be the best follower you can? Are you willing to weigh carefully what you hear (4:24)? Then the book of Mark is for you. Open its pages honestly and completely, and I believe you will never be the same.

# Zoomed-Out Overview

Mark's story of Jesus takes place with a broad-based movement, reflecting a circular framework in the text: it moves from the Wilderness or **Desert** (1:1-15) through **Galilee** (1:16-8:26), on **the Way** to Jerusalem (8:27-10:45), in **Jerusalem** (11:1-15:39/41),[4] and finally the **Tomb** (15:42-16:9/20).[5]

| | |
|---|---|
| Desert/Wilderness (Gospel/Desert/Baptism) | 1:1-15 |
| Galilee | 1:16-8:26 |
| On the Way | 8:27-10:52 |
| Jerusalem | 11:1-15:39 |
| Tomb (Tomb/Resurrection/Gospel [16:15]) | 15:40-16:8/20 |

The movement reflects the actions and purposes of Jesus, and the sections overlap and interrelate, as one would expect in any good story.

Encircled by references to the "gospel" or "good news" of Jesus Christ, the Son of God (1:1, 15), the story begins with the preparatory ministry of John the baptizer (1:1-8) (you have to read Matthew or Luke to get the birth stories), and ends with the resurrection of Jesus (16:1-8) and the sending out of the disciples with the gospel (16:15).[6] After the initial calling of the first disciples (Simon, Andrew, James, and John) to follow Jesus (1:16-20), Mark takes us with those disciples on a journey that leads from the initial, exuberant reaction of the crowds to the final rejection and crucifixion of Jesus at the hands of the religious and political leaders. From the outset, we are invited to follow Jesus and the disciples on this journey, referred to by Mark as "the way."

## Mark 1:16-3:12: Called to Follow

After the call to follow Jesus and "become fishers of men," the journey begins with the crowds' extreme excitement about the authority and power of Jesus to heal and cast out demons (1:21-45). They flock to him and spread "the word" (1:45) of their experiences of Jesus. As Simon puts it, "Everyone is looking for you" (1:37). *The crowds want Jesus.* The response was so great that "Jesus could no longer go into a town openly, but stayed outside in lonely [that is, desert] places. Yet the people still came to him from everywhere" (1:45: NIV).

In contrast to the crowds, the religious leaders respond to Jesus with growing suspicion and animosity. His authoritative acts of forgiveness and healing (2:1-12), his intentional pursuit of and association with the "dregs" of society ("tax-collectors and sinners") (2:13-17), his joyful freedom to eat and celebrate with the disciples (2:18-22), his perceptive understanding of the real purpose of religious rules (2:23-28), and his resolute willingness to do good and heal, even on the Sabbath (3:1-6) drive a wedge between Jesus and the entrenched, hardened leaders of the religious community. Their ever-increasing hostility reaches an initial climax in 3:6: "The Pharisees went out and immediately conspired with the Herodians against him, how to destroy him." *The religious leaders want Jesus dead.*

## Mark 3:13-6:6: Chosen for Purpose

Needless to say, Jesus' methods and actions would necessarily be influenced by such a climate where those in power are seeking to destroy him. This is the impact of the religious reaction to Jesus, and, as if to remind us of the contrasting, enthusiastic reaction of the crowds, Mark summarizes their almost crazed pursuit of Jesus (3:7-12) and then returns to a focused emphasis on the disciples. It's within this environment—one of impulsive excitement and intense hostility—that Jesus must continue his work. In this venue, those who follow him must come to know who and what Jesus is, and to be trained as ministers and missionaries for God; and this may not be as easy as it sounds because they all have strong images and expectations of the Messiah. Jesus thus withdraws and chooses twelve to be with him and to be sent out to proclaim God's message with authority. They are to follow him intimately, as we follow them in the story. *Disciples follow.*

These various emphases come together in the next section (3:19-35), as boundaries begin to be drawn and a new community forms around Jesus. The crowd converges on the house where Jesus was, "so that they could not even eat" (3:20). The religious leaders accuse him of being possessed. Members of his own family think he's out of his mind and try to take him home. Looking at those who were sitting around him, those close to him, his intimate circle, literally; Jesus proclaims his new, real family to be those who do the will of God. This new community or family of Jesus (= followers)—and I would add those of us who follow him closely in the story and want to do the will of God—becomes the primary target of the actions and teachings of Jesus in the book of Mark.

As the disciples follow Jesus around in this context—rampant and sometimes superficial enthusiasm from the crowds, hostile opposition from religious leaders, confusion and concern from his family, fearful obedience from demons and evil spirits, along with apparently sincere seeking of individuals for life and health—Jesus teaches them about the kingdom of God, or at least he tries to teach them. In the midst of such a complex and dangerous environment, Jesus begins (in chapter 4) to teach the people more exclusively through parables and his own actions, which function as sort of living parables, in order to meet them where they are spiritually, so to speak: "With many such parables he spoke the word to them, as they were able to hear it; he did not speak to them except in parables . . ." (4:33-34). And though we might expect the good soil (from the parable of the Sower) to understand the parables, the disciples don't (4:13) and so Jesus picks up the slack: ". . . but he explained everything in private to his disciples" (4:34).

In the next major section (4:35-6:6), each of the episodes highlights a fundamental tension created by the coming of the kingdom of God, one of the first challenges of being a follower of Jesus. When Jesus calms a storm threatening violently to engulf him and the disciples in the sea of Galilee, they are filled with fear. But even more so when the winds and the waves obey Jesus: "He said to them, 'Why

240

are you afraid? Have you still no faith?'" (4:34-41). On the other side, when legions of demons flee into a herd of pigs from a man whom Jesus heals, the Gerasene people are so afraid that they ask Jesus to leave their territory (5:1-20). A leader of the synagogue named Jairus begs Jesus to come and heal his daughter. On the way to his house, a woman with a twelve-year illness touches Jesus secretly, is healed, and when found out falls before him trembling with fear. "Your faith has made you well," Jesus says, "Go in peace and be healed of your disease" (5:24-34). In the meantime, Jairus's daughter dies. To the heart-stopping terror of the news of her death, Jesus speaks simple but powerfully challenging words to this religious leader—words that briefly capture the message of this section: "Do not fear, only believe" (5:21-24, 35-43). In stark contrast to this call to child-like faith, the people of Jesus' hometown are astonished and "scandalized" by Jesus to the point that he, in a dramatic reversal of the amazement/faith theme, is "amazed at their unbelief" (6:1-6).

When it comes to the radical call of Jesus, the Messiah, this is, in a sense, the first word of the kingdom, as this section of Mark graphically highlights the ever-present challenge of *fear versus faith*. How will we respond to the words and deeds of Jesus? He is certainly no ordinary teacher. He teaches and acts with great authority and power. His words and actions are often "astonishing"; his requests, radical. Following him means experiencing things that reach into the deepest places of life and death, fear and pain; and push the boundaries, sometimes farther than some are willing to go. The disciples are witness to this, as they follow Jesus.

(Did you notice that in the last paragraph I slipped into application of some of the things we are discovering in Mark's story? Rules #8 and #9 of good Bible reading remind us to *digest* and *live* the word. Though we need to contextualize everything we read in a Bible book in order to prioritize the messages, some applications are easy and suggest themselves almost immediately.)

# Mark 6:7-8:21: Sent Out with Authority

The next section (6:7-8:21) takes the journey further and deeper, as the disciples continue to follow Jesus around the Galilean countryside, witnessing his teaching and power. Mark actually shapes and punctuates the first half of his story with three major episodes or scenes that zoom in on Jesus' relationship with the disciples. **Mark 1:16-20** sets forth the initial call to follow him and become fishers of men (Simon, Andrew, James, and John). **Mark 3:13-19** expands the focus to 12 disciples, whom Jesus chooses carefully for intimate attention and training, designating them "apostles," which means to be sent as a messenger. (I refer to the 12 apostles as "the twelve.") He then sends them out by twos on their first preaching mission in **Mark 6:7-13**. Each of these paragraphs prefaces a major section within the first half of Mark's Gospel, and together they set forth a basic outline of the early stages of discipleship: (1) responding in faith to the call of Jesus, (2) listening and learning (being with Jesus in order to be sent out), and (3) imitating Christ in ministry by going forth in faith with the life-giving word and power of God.

In Mark 6:7-8:21, Jesus feeds the people. As the twelve become more intimately engaged in his work, however, having been sent out on their first ministry tour, the results, reactions, and complications multiply. Crowds explode with enthusiasm for the healing power and potential of Jesus. 5,000 men run around the Sea of Galilee to assemble with the disciples for what Jesus would do next (ready for the kingdom revolution, it appears the disciples have done a good job of "fishing for [= recruiting] men"). Religious leaders grow more agitated and virulent in their opposition, as Jesus challenges the framework of their positions and influence. At times, hungry, good-hearted (= good soil?) individuals step forward with sincere faith and reap great blessings. In the midst of it all, Jesus feeds the people (Jews and non-Jews) both physically and spiritually, "for they were like sheep without a shepherd" (6:34).

Continuing the emphasis on the vital importance of the heart ("soil") for understanding and responding to the word of God, the need to listen and understand (or at least to grow in one's understanding) resounds and echoes throughout these stories. As with the parable of the Sower, however, the disciples display a tendency—a surprisingly dark tendency—not to understand. Their dullness or closed-mindedness reaches a climax at the end of this section when a frustrated Jesus asks them a series of pointed questions: "Do you still not perceive or understand? Are your hearts hardened? Do you have eyes, and fail to see? Do you have ears, and fail to hear?" (8:17-18).

## Mark 8:22-10:52: The Way

Mark 8:22-10:52 is the center or core of Mark's Gospel. It takes place geographically "on the way" to Jerusalem (8:27; 10:32, 52), as Jesus teaches his disciples "on the way" of following him. "Following Jesus on the way" thus crystallizes here as a central, key theme of Mark's Gospel, and we find some of the most clearly articulated characteristics of life in the kingdom of God. Just as Jesus took special time and effort to work intimately with his inner circle of followers—"he explained everything in private to his disciples" (4:34)—so the center of Mark's book takes us as readers into that inner core. As if we were with them privately in a house or on the boat, and now "on the way," Mark invites us to see and hear Jesus unpack the heart of who is as the Messiah and what it means to follow him as a disciple. No longer just in parables, but now he speaks the word "plainly" to them (8:32).

If you have responded to the call of Christ with faith, have followed him around the Judean and Galilean towns and countrysides, have witnessed the impact of his words and power, have pressed in and received the sprouting and ever-growing word of God implanted into the soil of your heart—as you listen carefully to Jesus to learn and grow—perhaps you are ready to hear plainly what it means to follow Jesus. Bottom-line stuff about following Jesus on the way is only palatable (think spiritual food) to those who have eyes to see and ears to hear. Is that you?

Stories of a blind man receiving his sight surround the central section of Mark (8:22-10:52), displaying, not only the power of Jesus

243

over physical illness, but also metaphorically (or "parabolically") illustrating the spiritual healing of the person as a whole—persons in the story who don't see the true nature of the kingdom of God and his Christ. Though both blind men are healed, it takes two touches for the first—a somewhat surprising yet narratively and spiritually appropriate illustration of the blindness of the disciples and their need for further growth and healing. The disciples have been with Jesus for some time now, but things are still rather blurry, to say the least. They need another touch of his presence and power to see clearly; even so, their lack of perception and closed-mindedness continues throughout the section.

In another important disciple paragraph, the followers of Jesus come to a crucial point in their journey when on the way to the villages around Caesarea Philippi, they profess their faith that Jesus is indeed the Messiah (or Christ) of God (8:27-30). Others may think he is Elijah, a prophet, or John the Baptizer, but they believe he is the promised one from God.

Then, as if building on this realization, Jesus teaches them "plainly" or "openly" the destiny of his journey/way and the nature of the Messiah. Three times Jesus graphically predicts what's about to happen to him—he must suffer, die, and rise from the dead—and after each prediction, the disciples display their serious lack of understanding about the nature of the kingdom, Jesus, and his ministry. Jesus predicts his suffering and death—Peter begins to rebuke Jesus (8:31-33). Jesus predicts his suffering and death—the disciples argue about which of them is the greatest (9:33-34). Jesus predicts his suffering and death—James and John come to him with a request for the right- and left-hand seats of power when he comes into his kingdom (9:35-40). Clearly, the disciples don't see clearly. So Jesus must teach them, or "touch" them, again, with important first principles of the kingdom. The way of God is not the way of the world or its religious conceptions: instead of focus on the present and on oneself, a follower must pick up a cross and follow Jesus (8:34-38); instead of special treatment, a follower is to be last, a servant of all (9:35-37); instead of glory and commanding authority, a follower must wait for the voice of God, as he shares in the experiences of Jesus, the Christ

(10:38-46). Humility . . . servanthood . . . child-like, enduring faith . . . suffering and self-sacrifice—these are traits of a child of God.

Since Jesus is speaking plainly, the disciples' lack of under-standing—on top of the numerous displays throughout the course of the story—sounds a reverberating question about their own spiritual condition. In other words, *what kind of soil are the disciples?* Are they good soil, or is their following merely an example of one of the other types that sprouted and grew quickly, but didn't last? Understanding or "insight" is a fundamental trait of a good follower; how will he or she know the way, otherwise? To help the disciples see that he has not come to set up an earthly kingdom of physical priority, position, and power, Jesus foretells the way, his way, while on the way to Jeru-salem where he gives us the supreme model of a devoted follower of God. As in all things, Jesus leads the way through his words and his actions.

## Mark 11:1-13:37: Jesus versus the Establishment

In the latter half of Mark's Gospel, things change dramati-cally. In keeping with the movement of his life and purpose, Jesus' strategy also changes as he enters Jerusalem (11:1). Instead of keeping his identity a secret and working privately with his disciples, as in the last section (9:30-31: "He did not want anyone to know it; for he was teaching his disciples . . ."), Jesus enters Jerusalem with the shouts of the people identifying him as the coming Messiah, son of David (11:1-11).

This openness translates into head-to-head confrontation with the religious leaders in the temple: Jesus "cleanses" the temple, driving out those who have turned God's "house of prayer for all the nations" into a "den of robbers" (11:15-19); the religious leaders question and challenge his authority to do the things he's doing (11:27-33); Jesus directs the parable of the Evil Tenants at them, boldly articulating their corruptness and predicting his death yet sub-sequent victory (12:1-12). The result: The chief priests and the scribes look for a way to kill him (11:18). A series of theological challenges—

laced with poisonous political and legal traps—by the leaders of various religious groups (Pharisees, Herodians, Sadducees, scribes) exhibits the conflict, while Jesus continues to bring light to fundamental teachings about the real character and purposes of the kingdom of God. A poor widow gives her last pennies and in so doing gives more than those from the crowd who put money in the treasury out of their abundance. With humility and devotion, she gave her all. Such is at the heart of a true follower of God.

The intensifying confrontations between Jesus and the religious leaders reflect his rejection of what they stood for and were doing as leaders to the teachings of scripture, the temple, and the spiritual health of the people. Jesus brings new wine that can only be placed in new wineskins (2:18-22); his blood would be poured out for the sins and salvation of the people. As the fig tree withers, never again to provide fruit (11:12-14, 20), and as the owner of the vineyard will destroy the wicked tenants and give it to others (12:1-12), so Jesus foretells the coming of "the Son of Man" in power, and the destruction and dismantling of the temple itself (13:1-37).[7] In addition to reminding all followers to be in a state of readiness, Mark's emphasis on Jesus' repeated appeals to be alert and keep watch may suggest that Mark's audience was itself experiencing these turbulent times.

## Mark 14:1-15:39: The Passion of the Christ

The story of Jesus' death—the passion of the Christ—makes up a comparatively large portion of Mark's book. Fulfilling in graphic detail the three-fold prediction of the central section that Jesus must suffer, die, and rise from the dead (8:31, 9:31, 10:33-34), Mark 14-15 not only provides heart-wrenching details about the suffering and death of Christ, but also illustrates the hard-core truth of the meaning of following Jesus *on the way*. Sharing the Passover meal ("the Last Supper") brings to culmination some of the bread/food themes of Mark, foreshadowing the ongoing presence of Christ with his people in the kingdom: "Truly I tell you, I will never again drink of the fruit of the vine until that day when I drink it new in the kingdom of God" (14:25). When Jesus prays in the Garden of Gethsemane just before he's arrested (14:36), we're privileged to witness the ultimate example of a child of God's relationship with the Father, overhearing the sound of supreme commitment (". . . not what I want, but what you want"), as Jesus drinks the bitter cup of betrayal, heart-breaking rejection by those he loved, tremendous suffering at the hands of those who opposed him, and of brutal and bloody death on a criminal's cross. Ironically, the soldiers' epithet, summarizing the charge against him, read, "The King of the Jews" (15:26).

The latter pages of Mark give further indications of how some of the various groups we've seen throughout the story do in critical moments of faith and following. In other words, we begin to see some of the outcomes of the seed sown into various types of soil. Like seed sown on rock-hard path, the religious leaders repudiate and completely reject Jesus, often acting on the basis of jealousy and the reactions of the crowd (11:18-19, 32; 12:12, 38-40). Like seed sown among thorns, some individuals/groups from the crowds turn out to be servants of the moment, converting from rampant enthusiasm for the immediate enjoyment, potential, and benefits of Jesus' ministry into pawns of the authorities who seek Jesus' destruction (12:41; 14:43; 15:6-15, 29-30). (Is there any potential comparison here with those of us who limit God to the moment in our approach to scripture and elsewhere?) In stark contrast to Jesus' response to the crowd (prayer and steadfast focus on his mission), as Herod sought to please his guests (6:26), Pilate seeks to please the crowd (15:15) by ironically releasing an insurgent rather than releasing Jesus.

And what about the disciples? How do they do? It's almost as if their lack of understanding throughout the story flowers into full bloom during the arrest, passion, and crucifixion of Jesus. Jesus' closest followers and friends can't stay awake and pray during his most passionate prayer in the garden of Gethsemane (14:32-42). Judas betrays Jesus (14:17-21, 43-46). The disciples vow loyalty, but "all of them deserted him and fled" (14:50). Despite his vows to stay loyal, three times Peter denies that he knows Jesus (14:26-31, 66-72), which is ironically true at that point in time (given all the examples of misunderstanding). He really doesn't know Jesus. He follows at a distance (14:54), however, as do some of the women (15:40). So what kind of soil are they? Can seed take this long to spout and grow strong? Must Jesus somehow touch them yet again?

## Mark 15:40-16:8/20: The Resurrection

The same women who followed at a distance, having noticed where the crucified body of Jesus was put, go to the tomb early on the first day of the week to anoint the body (16:1-2). They then witness first-hand evidence of the greatest event in the history of the world. The angel tells them that Jesus has risen, that they were to go and tell the disciples and Peter that he was going ahead of them into Galilee where they would see him, as he had said. Given the history of Jesus' predictions in the story, we have no reason to doubt the outcome. But notice what they do: they flee from the tomb with terror and amazement, "and they said nothing to anyone, because they were afraid" (16:8). Does the story end here? And does this (their fear) sound familiar as a kind of reaction to Jesus that we've seen in the story? Do the disciples never learn of or proclaim the good news of God that Jesus—the one they followed, learned from, and saw die—has in fact been raised from the dead? Do they meet with Jesus in Galilee and, after his ascension, begin to take the gospel into all the earth?

Of course, the story of Jesus didn't end at the tomb, with the fear and silence of the women followers. We know this from the other Gospels; the history of the church; and from the longer ending of Mark, which recounts several resurrection appearances of Jesus, the disciples' unbelief, and their commission to go to all the world. We know differently, and so did Mark's original audience. How ironic that when it's time to proclaim the good news of the messiahship of Christ—in stark contrast to the occasions throughout the story when men and women were told to be silent but would not—that "they said nothing to anyone." And how does trembling and fear square with the lessons of faith (versus fear) in response to the amazing person/power of Jesus that we've learned in our journey? (How does "disbelief" fit with the pattern of the disciples within the story?) In other words, in some of the most defining moments of Mark's story of Jesus, the followers of Jesus don't look or act like good soil. Do they produce a bountiful crop of understanding and behavior consistent with the heart and teachings of the gospel of Jesus Christ, the Son of God? In the end, they do, and we know this. *But faithful following wasn't always certain, and it was never easy.* And this is Mark's point, if you and I want to be followers of Jesus. What are we thinking and how are we acting in response to the life, teaching, death, and resurrection of Jesus?

As transition to a closer look at some of the features of Mark's story, I'll anticipate briefly a bit of application (Rule #9). When Mark's audience heard the Gospel read and identified with the first followers (the historical context: Rule #6), I believe they were being challenged with hardcore questions of what it means to be a follower of Jesus, especially relevant if they were experiencing persecution and suffering for their faith, as Christians were during the time of Nero from 64-68 AD (during which Peter and Paul were likely killed). Here's the point: the Gospel according to Mark is not an elementary retelling of the life and actions of Jesus of Nazareth. It's not children's literature. On the contrary, it's a serious challenge to would-be followers of Jesus to respond to the call, to listen carefully to him, to learn from him, to come to understand what the good news of the kingdom of God is really all about, and to make gut-level, heart-felt, deep-soil decisions as to whether they will indeed follow him on the way: to be with him and go forth with power—to become fishers of men.

If any want to become my followers, let them deny themselves and take up their cross and follow me. For those who want to save their life will lose it, and those who lose their life for my sake, and for the sake of the gospel, will save it (8:34-35).

To use images from our inkblot passage, the Gospel of Mark stands as a deeply probing challenge to those who follow Jesus not be like seed sown on rocky ground or among the thorns. We must follow Jesus on the way, all the way, and the end is worth the journey. To Peter's honest question about the rewards of leaving everything and following him, Jesus said,

> Truly I tell you, there is no one who has left house or brothers or sisters or mother or father or children or fields, for my sake and for the sake of the good news, who will not receive a hundredfold now in this age—houses, brothers and sisters, mothers and children, and fields with persecutions—and in the age to come eternal life (10:28-30).

# Discovering the Shape of the Text

## Introduction

### Mark's Introduction

Finding the Introduction and Conclusion of a text is fun and almost always quite revealing. Most will agree generally on what makes up Mark's Introduction. The Conclusion is another story.

We can designate Mark 1:1-15 fairly confidently as the Introduction. Because verses 14-15 contain a synopsis of the initial movement of the story (from John/Jordon to Jesus/Galilee) and an emphatic summary of the beginning of Jesus' proclamation of the good news, some like to take verses 14-15 as the beginning of the story proper and thus see Mark 1:1-13 as the Introduction. On the other hand, you may likely have noticed the transitional nature of these verses. They clearly connect with the opening scenes (John and Jesus) and point forward. They're also obviously compact in their content, as the overarching summary—a 10,000 foot view—of Jesus' message displays. The pace then changes dramatically in verse 16, as Mark zooms in on the actions of Jesus in calling the disciples to follow him. Mark 1:13-14 are, therefore, clearly transitional and can thus be positioned at the end of the Introduction or at the beginning of the Middle/Body of the story. Because of the repetition of the very important word "gospel" introduced in the first verse and a structure/shape this helps to create (more on this in a minute), I like to put verses 14-15 with the previous and think of Mark 1:1-15 as the Introduction. It doesn't really matter as long as we see how the opening of Mark's Gospel prepares us for the content and style of the story to come.

A brief side note. As I've said before, good writers hide the seams of their outline in the final product (making it "seamless"). This is especially true in narrative material. Throw in the overlapping tendencies of oral, circular structures, and it's not surprising that some sentences and even sections seem to fit or go in both directions. This is part of the reason it's good to "zoom in on the transi-

251

tions" and see how the material functions in the flow of the text (Rules #2 and #3). The minute details of our outline are not all that important. What's important is that we catch the meaning within the flow and internal connections of the text. Okay, back to Mark.

Mark tells us in the first verse that he is in fact starting with an "Introduction," as he boldly pronounces—almost title-like—"The *beginning* of the gospel of Jesus Christ." (Unless, perhaps, somehow the whole book is only the beginning—something worth thinking about. The continuation would then rest with the hearts and lives of the audience—and thus with us.) Beginnings are important. So Mark says that the good news about Jesus, the Messiah, begins with predictions from the Old Testament about one who would precede him and clear or prepare the way. John the baptizer comes in the desert, preaching a baptism of repentance, implying that one (John in the desert) connects with and fulfills the other (the Old Testament prophecy). The description of John's clothing (1:6) further connects him with the Old Testament character of Elijah (2 Kings 1:8). That *all* of Judea and the inhabitants of Jerusalem were coming to John to be baptized in the Jordan River suggests that something major (in God's plan) was happening by means of John's ministry. In addition to the opening Old Testament citation, Mark provides a summary of John's message: a far greater one is coming who will baptize the people, not with water but with the Holy Spirit of God. Again, John is seen as preparing the way (or getting things ready) for the coming Messiah. (This suggests an important question: if this identifies Jesus' purpose or effect, what does "baptism with the Holy Spirit" mean in the course of Mark's Gospel?)

Jesus comes to John in the desert or wilderness and is baptized. Immediately, the heavens split apart, the Spirit lands on Jesus in the form of a dove, and the voice of God pronounces Jesus to be his beloved son, with whom he is pleased. Old Testament prediction, prophetic fulfillment and anticipatory proclamation, voice of God affirmation: the beginning of the good news is extraordinary. Like many good introductions, these ideas not only introduce the foundations and first part of the story, but give us key ideas that will unfold as we turn the pages.

Jesus' ministry will not be easy. Mark 1:12-13 shows from the beginning that testing and temptation are a part of Jesus' path/way as the Messiah. The Spirit of God who descended on Jesus at his baptism now "drives" him into the desert/wilderness to be tested by Satan for 40 days. Mark provides no details of these temptations, which is interesting and perhaps significant in the unfolding development. In spite of the lack of specifics, we do learn, however, that the desert/wilderness setting contains and represents transcendent (= above-the-earth), difficult and defining moments (in this case, involving the Spirit, Satan, testing, wild animals, and angels). In short, the desert is a place of testing, decision, and focus.

Mark 1:14-15 then initiates the preaching ministry of Jesus in summary fashion, similar to Mark's synopsis of the message of John (1:7-8). It begins when John ends (when he was arrested)—thus separating and connecting their roles—and it begins in Galilee where Jesus proclaims the good news of God, saying, "The time is fulfilled, and the kingdom of God has come near; repent, and believe in the good news" (1:15).

It's difficult, if not impossible, to elucidate all the significant features of Mark's Introduction. There are many more things than we can begin to capture. So I'll just point out a few.

In narrative stories, the first words of a character are often significant for defining or setting the stage for that character. Mark presents four actual quotations in the Introduction: (1) the Old Testament, (2) John, (3) the Father from heaven, and (4) Jesus. Each of these citations contains valuable content for Mark's story and is worth examining in detail. Without time to do that now, let's use the practice of highlighting recurring words and ideas (Rule #4) to focus on some of the key themes and motifs of the Introduction. The highly skilled design of the Introduction becomes apparent when we combine our focus on key words with the structure of this opening section (Rule #3).

Like many biblical passages, Mark 1:1-15 has a circular shape—one that makes repeated use of some key words. Here is the basic pattern:

| | |
|---|---|
| 1:1 | Gospel |
| 1:2-4 | Desert/Wilderness |
| 1:5-8 | Baptism (John) |
| 1:9-11 | Baptism (Jesus) |
| 1:12-13 | Desert/Wilderness |
| 1:14-15 | Gospel[8] |

The concave shape of Mark's Introduction begins and ends with "gospel" or "good news." These are the only times this extremely important word occurs in the opening, and the occurrences serve as book-ends (an "inclusio") to mark off the segment. The desert or wilderness location underscores the role of the desert in the opening events and in the book as a whole. John's baptism in water engages all the people, his message points toward the Holy Spirit baptism of Jesus, while the baptism of Jesus itself splits the heavens as the voice from heaven identifies him as the very pleasing son of God. Reading Mark 1:1-15 as introduction—which is certainly legitimate given the content of what follows—all of this must somehow be a part of the "good news" of Jesus, the Christ.

A color-coded version of Mark 1:1-15 helps to show the placement of these and other key words in the Introduction. The diagram of the text uses these highlights:

gospel = green
Christ/Son of God = light blue
messenger/angels = purple
the way/kingdom of God = orange
voice/proclaiming = underlined
what is quoted or proclaimed = italics
wilderness/desert (similar) = red
baptize/baptism (water) = blue
repentance/forgiveness/believe = pink/rose
Judea/Galilee = light green
Holy Spirit/Satan = gray

The beginning of the gospel of Jesus Christ, the Son of God. **A**

As it is written in Isaiah the prophet, **B**
  "Behold, I send my **messenger** before your face,
    who will prepare your way,
      the <u>voice</u> of one <u>crying</u> in the **wilderness**:
    'Prepare *the way* of the Lord,
*make his paths straight.*'"

  John appeared, baptizing in the **wilderness** and <u>proclaiming</u> a baptism of repentance for the forgiveness of sins.

  And all the country of Judea and all Jerusalem were going out to him and were being **baptized** by him in the river Jordan, confessing their sins.

Now John was clothed with camel's hair and wore a leather belt around his waist and ate locusts and wild honey.
  And he <u>preached</u>, <u>saying</u>,
    *"After me comes he who is mightier than I, the strap of whose sandals I am not worthy to stoop down and untie. I have **baptized** you with water, but he will **baptize** you with the **Holy Spirit**"*

In those days Jesus came from Nazareth of Galilee and was **C**
baptized by John in the Jordan.
  And when he came up out of the water, immediately he saw
  the heavens being torn open
    and the **Spirit** descending on him like a dove.
  And a <u>voice</u> came from heaven,
*"You are my beloved Son; with you I am well pleased."*

The **Spirit** immediately drove him out into the **wilderness**. **B'**
  And he was in the **wilderness** forty days,
    being tempted by Satan.
  And he was with the wild animals,
and the **angels** were ministering to [serving] him.

Now after John was arrested, Jesus came into Galilee, <u>proclaiming</u> **A'**
the gospel of God, and <u>saying</u>,
  *"The time is fulfilled, and the kingdom of God is at hand; repent and believe in the gospel."*

## Key Words and Ideas

It would take another whole book, or more, to unpack the rhetorical skill, content, and meaning of this succinct but incredible Introduction.[9] As we would expect, many of the most important themes and motifs of Mark's Gospel are carefully arranged and artfully introduced to prepare the reader/listener for the story to come. Similar to the role of John the baptizer within the story, Mark prepares us for "the good news of Jesus Messiah, Son of God." Journey with me, then, as we look at how some of the key ideas of the opening are fleshed out in the following pages.

## John the Baptizer

Almost everything in this Introduction plays an important part in the pages that follow. Take for example, the character and role of John the baptizer. His work begins in Judea and Jerusalem—the heart of Jewish country—and, more specifically, in the desert, as a prophetic messenger of God, proclaiming the need for the inhabitants of Judea to start over with repentance, baptism, and the forgiveness of sins. And they came—all the Judean countryside and the inhabitants of Jerusalem—and were baptized by John in the Jordan. Something major is happening in the scope of salvation history, and God is using John to get it started. John's message and role is thus preparatory. It's to get Israel ready for something even bigger—for someone much greater who will baptize them, not with water, but with the Holy Spirit. John comes ahead of Jesus.

The coming one comes "after" or "behind" John (1:7). He follows John, and he begins his ministry after John is arrested (1:14). This is why John is often called the "forerunner" of Jesus, but the relationship goes deeper from a literary perspective. Following Jesus becomes a crucial, if not the most important, theme of Mark. The concept of "following" actually begins then with Jesus and John. John is like Jesus and vice versa in several ways. Though John precedes him, we find similarities in their ministries, here in the wilderness/desert opening and in the endings.

Though prominent initially, we only hear of John a couple times more in Mark's story, particularly in Mark 6:14-29 where we have an elongated—flashback—description of his gruesome death, surrounded by the first mission (sending out) of the apostles. John is portrayed as a fully committed, outspoken man of God. Herod respects John, likes to listen to him, is confused or perplexed by him, but values other things more—especially the opinions of powerful and manipulative people around him. (Any recollections of the parable of the Sower in Herod's response to John, especially since this comes as the apostles have been sent out for the first time to sow the seed like Jesus?) In summary, two things stand out in this scene: (1) what happens to proactive, faithful followers of God, as John goes "before" or "ahead" of Jesus; and (2) characteristics of human kingdoms—kings, rulers, methods of leadership and decision-making, etc. And this . . . in the middle of following Jesus in proactive mission and ministry. (Herod and later Pilate provide great examples of human, non-Jesus-like ways of leadership.)

Who is John the baptizer? The power (from Jesus) at work when the twelve are sent out to preach causes Herod and others to believe that John has been raised from the dead. (Note the literary foreshadowing of what actually happens to Jesus. But John is not Jesus; John is not the Christ.) Others think the power on display might represent the coming of Elijah (6:16). The description of John in 1:6 with the clothing of Elijah, the belief that Elijah was to come first, and Jesus' confirmation of this belief and association with John (9:11-13) continue to define the role of John as the coming Elijah, the forerunner of the Messiah. In the middle of his focused teaching about the way of God that includes the prediction of his own intense suffering, Jesus' terse commentary sums up the purpose and outcome of John: "But I tell you that Elijah has come, and they did to him whatever they pleased, as it is written about him" (9:13).

The more general point is that John prepares the way of Jesus as a servant/follower of God and his ministry puts him at odds with ways and standards of the world. Like Jesus, John's ministry leads to death and a tomb. The central section of Mark (8:27-10:45) concentrates on the idea that following Jesus means following him in the way of suffering and a cross. Unfortunately, that's what discipleship often entails. Jesus graphically predicts this for himself (8:31, 9:31, 10:33-34) and for his disciples (10:38-39, 13:9-13). In the central section, Jesus also teaches the disciples intensely about the nature of true leadership: it is faith, humility, and service; not fear, power and manipulation. We see these tensions foreshadowed in John, and one thing we know for sure about the way-setting role of John the baptizer: he displays what can happen to intensely devoted followers of God. But remember, after John was arrested, Jesus came . . . (1:14-15). In what he preached and what he endured—persecution, suffering, death–John prepared *the way*.

**The Way**

Let's look at this idea as introduced in Mark's opening. On first glance the word "way" or "the way" might seem to be an incidental part of the Old Testament citation that Mark uses to introduce the role of John the baptizer. Reading Mark's citation closely, however, suggests that a way or "path" (". . . make straight his paths") is an important part of John's preparatory ministry (for what he is getting the people ready). The famous wilderness journey of Israel ("the wilderness way") from Egyptian slavery to the promised land of Canaan lurks behind the image from an historical perspective, as the potential sources of Mark's citation suggest (Exodus 23:20; Isaiah 40:3-5; Malachi 3:1-2) and also the language of Deuteronomy 8:2: "Remember how the Lord your God led you all the way in the wilderness these forty years, to humble and test you in order to know what was in your heart, whether or not you would keep his commands" (NIV). Following his own "crossing of the Jordan" (his immersion), Jesus being tempted for 40 days in the desert solidifies the connection (1:12-13). A "straight" path in the wilderness/desert implies success in getting through its challenges and dangers, as

Psalm 107:4-7 illustrates (compare Mark 8:3 where the word "way" is also used):

> Some wandered in desert wastes, finding no way to an inhabited town; hungry and thirsty, their soul fainted within them. Then they cried to the Lord in their trouble, and he delivered them from their distress; he led them by a straight way, until they reached an inhabited town.

For Israel, "the way" in/through the desert has a deep history, and for Mark there is a coming new course, a new direction, journey or way. John the baptizer is to help create a "straight" path for that way because the wilderness is obviously a dangerous place of difficulty, temptation, and testing—it's the way of the desert. The coming of John, and all of Judea and Jerusalem out to John highlights the significance of "the way," moreover, as does the emphasis on the "gospel . . ." and the critical and often repeated word/phrase "kingdom of God" (1:15). What's more and decisive, Mark uses the word as a structural and thematic motif in the pages to come.

You can find the word "way" (*hodos* in Greek) in the following locations in Mark: 1:2, 3; 2:23; 4:4, 15; 6:8; 8:3, 27; 9:33, 34; 10:17, 32, 46, 52; 11:8; 12:14. Tracing its use reveals its significance in the message of Mark (though, not surprising, some of the occurrences have different connotations). The highly focused central section (8:22/27-10:52), where Jesus is teaching his disciples "openly" or "plainly" (8:32) about his coming suffering and death, shows clearly its literary and thematic importance:

> Jesus went on with his disciples to the villages of Caesarea Philippi; and **on the way** he asked his disciples, "Who do the people say that I am? . . . ." (8:27).

> Then they came to Capernaum; and when he was in the house he asked them, "What were you arguing about **on the way**?" But they were silent, for on **the way** they had argued with one another who was the greatest. . . . (9:33).

As he was setting out on a **journey** [while going **on his way**], a man ran up and knelt before him, and asked him, "Good Teacher, what must I do to inherit eternal life?" . . . . (10:17).

They were **on the road** [**way**], going up to Jerusalem, and Jesus was walking ahead of them; they were amazed, and those who followed were afraid. . . . (10:32).

They came to Jericho. As he and his disciples and a large crowd were leaving Jericho, Bartimaeus son of Timaeus, a blind beggar, was sitting **by the roadside** [**beside the way**]. . . . Jesus said to him, "Go; your faith has made you well." Immediately he regained his sight and followed him **on the way** (10:46-52).

Many people spread their cloaks **on the road** [**way**] . . . Then those who went ahead and those who followed were shouting, "Hosanna! Blessed is the one who comes in the name of the Lord! Blessed is the coming kingdom of our ancestor David! Hosanna in the highest heaven!" . . . . (11:8-10).

. . . . And they came and said to him, "Teacher, we know that you are sincere, and show deference to no one; for you do not regard people with partiality but teach **the way** of God in accordance with truth . . ." (12:14).

Mark presents Jesus as the one who travels and teaches the "way of God"—the one who baptizes in the Holy Spirit. In the pivotal central section of Mark's story, Jesus and his disciples are literally *on the way* to Jerusalem, which symbolizes the journey/way of Jesus, where they are taught by Jesus what the way of God and following Jesus is really all about. When you read and study the book of Mark as a whole, it is difficult to miss the importance of this metaphor and the force of its application to those of us who are attempting to follow Jesus on the way. (On the other hand, the lack of consistency in the NRSV's translation of the word makes it difficult on occasion to observe the repetition. This is why it's good to use a literal version and a concordance in tracing out repeated words and phrases—Rule #4.) In fact, it's so important that I might title or subtitle the book of Mark, "Following Jesus on the Way" (Rule #8). With some of the first words of the text, then, the Introduction prepares us for this theme: *the desert way of the Christ*. It's rich and exciting, even if a little foreboding, and I challenge you to trace it out and explore it deeply as you read Mark.

## Desert/Wilderness

Let's look at another key word: the desert. This one is closely associated with "the way," but takes the thought further. It occurs in 1:3, 4, 12, 13; 1:35, 45; 6:31, 32, 35. The first thing you might notice from this list is that there are no occurrences of the word beyond chapter six. This may be relevant thematically, or not. Remember that a single word is just that—one word or idea. Words have synonyms and can easy be associated with other words and ideas in a written text. (Mark associates things like mountains, prayer, and possibly the tomb with the desert theme.) A concrete list of the actual occurrences of a word is, however, the right place to start when tracing out recurring words and ideas.

The word "desert" or "wilderness" is obviously a key word in the Introduction. It is the home base, so to speak, of John and his baptizing work. The prophecy of God's prepare-the-way messenger describes him as "the voice of one crying out in the *wilderness*" (1:3). Immediately (as though to help us make the connection), Mark then says that John the baptizer comes proclaiming and baptizing in the *wilderness* (1:4). All the people of Jerusalem and Judea come out to him to be baptized in the Jordan river. The prophecies of Israel, the use of "the way," and now "the wilderness" connect with Israel's past—the wilderness way in their journey from slavery to the promised homeland. That John is a desert-personality, wearing camel's hair and eating locusts and wild honey, further connects John with prophetic figures of Israel's past, especially Elijah. For prophets, as well as Israel as a nation, the desert has a sort of sacred history as a place of testing, trial, and cleansing (thus the coming to John to be baptized).

Perhaps the more striking use of "the wilderness/desert" in Mark's introduction comes after Jesus' baptism. Immediately following his baptism, with the accompanying voice from heaven declaring him to be God's beloved son, the text says that the Spirit of God—that had just landed on Jesus as a dove—"casts" or "drives" Jesus out into the *wilderness/desert* (1:12). "And he was in the *desert* 40 days being tempted by Satan . . ." (1:13). Whatever historical associations might have accompanied the theme word "desert" in the original audience, Mark makes clear that not only is the desert a place for John and for Jesus (taken there no less than by God's own Spirit), but it is a place of struggle and temptation. Tracing out the use of the word in Mark, along with associate places and actions, like mountains and prayer, highlights some defining moments in Mark's story of Jesus. As we'll see, *the way of Jesus is a desert way.* We'll look further at some of these when we examine one of the first sections shortly.


**Baptism**

(Don't forget that we're focusing on how the opening of Mark functions as introduction—how it fits in the puzzle of Mark as seen in the development of key concepts.)

Another prominent word (and action) in the Introduction deserves our attention. It's the word "**baptism**." In a sense, the dominant focus of Mark's Introduction is on baptism. The inhabitants of Jerusalem and Judea are going out to be baptized by John. John describes Jesus as the one who will baptize with the Holy Spirit. Jesus is baptized by John, and it's at that moment that the voice of the Father affirms Jesus' sonship. The concept of a new beginning—starting over, so to speak—is certainly a foundational idea in Mark. As if a new era of history is dawning on the human race, John the baptizer prepares the people for the coming of Jesus. They participate through repentance, confession of sins, and baptism. Jesus announces that "the time is fulfilled, and the kingdom of God has come near" (1:14). In the midst of the initial, growing opposition from the religious leaders that Mark displays in the early pages of his story, Jesus describes his coming as something new, like new wine that must be put into new wine skins (2:18-21). In Mark 4, teaching about the kingdom of God is presented as seed—seed that must be planted into the hearts of people before it can grow and produce fruit (4:1-9, 14-20, 26-32). Other moments and ideas in Mark suggest the need for a follower of Jesus to make a radical break from his or her past and be "immersed" in the life and teachings of the Messiah.

The word "baptism" itself is used sparingly in the following story, however. It's found fittingly and powerfully in 16:16 ("The one who believes and is *baptized* will be saved . . ."), but we're not sure if these verses (16:9-20) were a part of Mark's original document (more on this in our discussion of the Conclusion below). Besides references to John (6:14, 24; 11:30) and the Pharisees "washing" (= baptism) of items from the marketplace (11:30), the word doesn't occur—*with one notable exception*. It's used *six* times in two verses in the pivotal "on-the-way" section (Mark 8:22-10:52) where Jesus is teaching his disciples what the way of the Messiah—and thus the way of the kingdom of God—is really all about. Jesus will not become a powerful king of Israel, ruling over the world on a throne like David, defeating their enemies and ushering in an eternal kingdom of peace—at least not now. On the contrary, three times—which makes it very emphatic and important—Jesus predicts that he will go to Jerusalem, suffer intensely, die, and on the third day rise from the grave (8:31-33; 9:30-32; 10:32-35).[10]

Following the final prediction (10:32-34), seemingly oblivious to the meaning of Jesus as the serving and suffering "Son of Man," James and John want to know if, like chief administrators, they can sit on his right and left hand of power and authority when he comes into his glory. The other apostles hear about it and get angry. Jesus uses the occasion, then, to teach them about the true nature of leadership in the kingdom: self-sacrificial service, just as Jesus came to serve and give his life as a ransom for many (10:45). Before reiterateing these fundamental kingdom values, however, Jesus asks James and John a sobering, soil-tilling question that reflects the overarching theme of this critical section of teaching, using our key word "baptism":

> ". . . . You do not know what you are asking. Are you able to drink the cup that I drink, or be **baptized** with the **baptism** that I am **baptized** with?" They replied, "We are able." Then Jesus said to them, "The cup that I drink you will drink; and with the **baptism** with which I am **baptized**, you will be **baptized** . . ."

Like leader, like follower. Like teacher, like student. *Following Jesus means following him on the way that leads to Jerusalem and a cross*, symbolically speaking. Just as Jesus was fully immersed—that is, *baptized*—in suffering as a result of his resolute commitment to God and the purposes of God, so his disciples will undergo similar persecution and suffering. Following Jesus on the way thus leads through the desert, sometimes involves intense obstacles and opposition, and can even end in death (like John and Jesus). As Jesus began his ministry literally, baptism in the desert thus becomes a sort of spiritual symbol for his way. It doesn't end there, as the transfiguration (6:2-13) and resurrection (16:1-8/20) promise. But in the meantime, as with the seed sown on the rocky ground, the question is what will happen to one's faith "when trouble or persecution arises on account of the word" (Mark 4:17).

## Who Is Jesus?

A decisive question in Mark is—as we would expect—"Who is Jesus?" The question comes up in various ways throughout the story, with a little more explicit emphasis in the first half, as the disciples grapple with the question. An important turning point comes when **on the way** to the villages of Caesarea Philippi, Jesus asks his disciples, "Who do people say that I am?" They respond with various answers that have to do with Jewish expectations regarding God's messianic plan—John the Baptist, Elijah, one of the prophets. "But who do you say that I am?" Jesus then asks. Peter's reply—"You are the Messiah"—acts as a secure stepping stone for the next (unstated but clear) crucial question of the text: "What does that mean?" (8:27-30). Jesus then begins to answer the question by teaching them about his/God's true way.

Though we don't know it's a governing question the first time we read Mark's Introduction, we do know that the identity of Jesus is extremely important. Mark announces it in the first verses. John the baptizer's whole ministry functioned to point towards and identify Jesus as the one powerful enough to baptize in the Holy Spirit. Mark then positions the baptism of Jesus as the center-piece of the Introduction (1:9-11); in that moment, we see the Spirit of God come upon Jesus as a dove and God the Father ("a voice . . . from heaven") affirm Jesus' identity: "You are my Son, the Beloved; with you I am well pleased" (1:11). Mark tells us this at the very start. The people in the story don't know it. They have to come to decisions about Jesus as we go, and we frequently hear them asking identity questions: "What is this? A new teaching—with authority!" (1:27), "Who can forgive sins but God alone?" (2:7), "Who then is this, that even the wind and the sea obey him?" (4:41), etc.

This identity theme receives one of its strongest expressions as part of the pivotal, central section of Mark in what's called the "transfiguration" of Jesus (9:2-13). Jesus takes Peter, James, and John with him on a high mountain by themselves. Jesus' clothes become dazzling white. Moses and Elijah appear talking with him. The disciples are overwhelmed and don't know what to do or say. A cloud comes over them and again the voice of the Father, "This is my Son, the Beloved; listen to him!" The foundation is still the same—the identity of Jesus as the Christ, the Son of God—but in this case, there's another step—the logical and spiritual implication of the answer to the first question: "Listen to him!"

At the end of the story, when Jesus dies, a Roman centurion who stood facing Jesus said, "Truly this man was God's Son!" Then comes the account of Jesus' resurrection—the ultimate indication of who Jesus was and is. And here's my main point: Mark skillfully introduces us to the importance of the question of Jesus' identity in the Introduction. His baptism, transfiguration, and resurrection (prefaced by the centurion's statement, "Truly this man was God's Son") provide a sort of identity—Jesus is the Christ, the Son of God—shape to the whole of Mark's book, as the very first sentence forecasts: "The beginning of the good news of Jesus Christ, the Son of God."

## Other Key Words

Tracing several other words from the Introduction through Mark's story helps to sharpen the prevailing focuses and emphases of the text. Just as Mark highlights places like **Jerusalem, Judea, the Jordan River**, and **Galilee** in the opening, geographical locations and movements are significant throughout the story. The words **"gospel"** and **"kingdom"** of God are two obvious key words. The "gospel" or "good news" of Jesus summarizes the message of the book as a whole, as Mark tells us in the first verse and Jesus in verse 15. You'll find it again in 8:35; 10:29; 13:10; 14:19, and 16:15. The "kingdom of God" is an important topic throughout, frequently used in association with Jesus' teaching in parables (and in contrast to kingdoms of earth [6:17-29, for example]). The last phrase of Jesus' first words to us in Mark sets the tone for some highly significant themes: **"repent and believe** in the **gospel"** (1:15).

In conclusion, though it doesn't explicitly mention every important word or theme in his story, Mark's Introduction clearly sets the stage ("the beginning of the gospel") for much of what is to come. Reading it as an Introduction puts our minds on the right track as we look to hear God's word to us in Mark.

## Mark's Use of Symbolism

From a stylistic and strategic perspective, Mark alerts us in the opening to his intention to make points or associations that he doesn't express directly. For example, the juxtaposition of John with the Old Testament citation shows that he intends the audience to associate John the baptizer with the prophecy. He does the same with Jesus in relation to John's prophecy. "One is coming . . .," John says; then Mark says, "Jesus comes." Though obvious and easy here, the interpretation is left to us. That Mark doesn't make the connection explicitly suggests, from the beginning, that he will sometimes be indirect. The strategy is taken further with the description of John the baptizer as one "clothed with camel's hair, with a leather belt around his waist . . .": the prophet Elijah is identified in 2 Kings 1:8-9 from a similar description ("He had a garment of hair and had a leather belt around his waist": NIV). This sort of indirection progresses into symbolic associations of one thing with another (aided at times by Mark's "sandwiching" or concentric structures) and becomes an intrinsic part of Jesus' teaching through the parables. (Parables are comparisons between one thing and another, where the specific interpretation or associations are left to the listener.)

Though somewhat more subtle and less obvious perhaps than the use of symbolism in John's Gospel, Mark is very fond of indirectness, metaphor, and symbolism. At times, he likes to use brief phrases as word-pictures and summarizing metaphors of key concepts. Several words and ideas set forth in Mark's Introduction thus become symbols/metaphors for important thematic notions as the text unfolds (like "the way" of Jesus and the "desert," for example). As we read Mark's story, then, it becomes a part of the process of good listening to become familiar with Mark's parabolic (= parable-like) style and purposes.

## Conclusion and Shape

Isolating the Conclusion in Mark is more difficult than in other books of the Bible because we're not exactly sure where Mark ended. This might come as a surprise to you, though most versions of the Bible have some explanatory notes regarding Mark 16:9-20 in particular, explaining that some of our oldest and best manuscripts of Mark end with 16:8: the women "fled from the tomb, for terror and amazement had seized them; and they said nothing to anyone, for they were afraid." This seems like such an odd way to end that some scholars have supposed that somehow the last page/section of the original copy of Mark was lost. We actually have several other alternative endings in the manuscript tradition, which shows that some early readers of Mark didn't think the story should end at verse 16 either. Some Bibles thus print "the longer ending" (16:9-20) and perhaps "the shorter ending." We know historically from the other Gospels, and from the existence and growth of the church that the report of Jesus' resurrection did not die on the lips of the women who ran in fear from the tomb. Whatever initial silence accompanied their first reaction to this world-changing event, the good news was and continues to be told.

This may, however, provide a clue as to how Mark's "odd" ending could have functioned with the original audience, if Mark's story did indeed end with 16:8. Several of the words describing the women's reaction to the resurrection are recognizable theme words seen throughout Mark's story. Reacting to Jesus with amazement is constant. The new potential—the new wine presence of the kingdom of God—is so beyond normal, planet-earth experiences that we can't help but be amazed. Nor can it be contained in old wineskins. Fear is also common, and, on the other hand, a problem throughout the story. Fear contrasts faith in all five stories from 4:35-6:6. Believing the good news is at the heart and core of Jesus' message (1:15). The teaching, preaching, and spreading of the word of the good news of Jesus is also a prominent theme, coming to a degree of climax when Jesus exclaims that he will be ashamed of anyone who has been ashamed of him and his words when he comes in the Father's glory with the holy angels (8:38). Given all that they had seen in Jesus—up close and personal—hearing his teachings and the predictions that he would rise from the dead . . . yet now when looking into the face of that amazing moment, the text says *"they said nothing to anyone because they were afraid."*

If Mark were originally written to a group of Christians who were undergoing severe persecution, even death because of their belief and spreading of the good news about Jesus, the Christ, what effect might such an ending have had on a group of followers—followers (readers and listeners) who had identified with the disciples throughout the story? Knowing that the story didn't end there and it was now *their* responsibility to continue to share the good news in spite of the growing torrent of opposition and suffering (think of what Jesus had to experience—probably the most consistent theme in Mark), what a profound impact a truncated ending such as this might have had on a group of devoted followers who want to be good soil and live up to their commitments to follow Jesus "on the way"? *What if they had stopped or were tempted to stop telling the good news because they were afraid?* And who wouldn't be afraid, staring into the vicious eyes of the violent persecutions suffered by the early Christians? Mark's story may not have originally ended with 16:8, but if it did, the ironic and compelling contrast with what should and ultimately did happen would have acted like an electric jolt to remind these early Christians of just how important, how wonderful, and how challenging following Jesus really is—even if it means suffering and death. After all, their Lord led the way. And what was more important to Jesus in the course of his wilderness journey than taking and telling and touching and living the good news of God's kingdom? Nothing! After all, Jesus called the disciples "to become fishers of men." Following Jesus means sharing the good news, regardless of the circumstances and the consequences (Rule #9).

For us, then, Mark's story ends with 16:8 or with 16:20, if we include the longer ending (in light of the big-picture of the book as a whole and our other Gospels, the overall impact and teaching is not changed either way). I would suggest that the Conclusion begins with 15:40 (or perhaps 15:42)—the actual death of Jesus—with the pronouncement of the centurion that Jesus was truly God's Son, drawing the body or Middle of Mark to a close (remember the Father's affirmation of Jesus' identity in 1:11 and 9:7). The summary of 15:40-41 of the women who followed Jesus ("looking on from a distance") functions as a transition, setting up the coming of the women to the tomb to anoint Jesus' body (16:1). We could say, then, that Mark's Conclusion consists of 15:40-16:8/20, making our simple three-part shape look like this:

| Introduction (1:1-15) | Middle (1:16-15:39) | Conclusion 15:40-16:8/20 |
|---|---|---|

The ending of Mark emphatically reminds us that this is not the end of the story. It's the beginning, in a sense, of the ultimate message of Jesus the Christ, the Son of God. The persecution, suffering, and death of the Messiah on the cross did not defeat him and put an end to his work and message, as the religious authorities had hoped. On the contrary, like a seed planted in the ground, it brings it to completion and germination, and Mark's Conclusion sets the stage for the growth and spreading of the good news in the early church and through followers of Jesus throughout the ages. Just as Jesus repeatedly predicted in the central section, he rose from the dead, and the angel forecasts, he will now go ahead of his disciples (we are always to be "followers") into Galilee where they would see him. Similar to the other Gospels, Mark 16:9-20 reports some of these post-resurrection appearances—Mary, two disciples walking in the countryside, the apostles. Each time there is an element of unbelief, stubbornness or hardness of heart, echoing a vital theme, prominent in the course of the story. Then, as when he sent the disciples out as they were learning to follow him (6:7), Jesus now sends them on the "great" or border-less commission: "Go into all the world and proclaim the good news to the whole creation. The one who believes and is baptized will be saved; but the one who does not believe will be condemned . . ." (16:15-16). Key words fill the command. Mark 16:19-20 concludes that they went everywhere proclaiming the good news, working with the power and presence of Jesus.

Prior to this nicely packaged ("longer") ending, Mark takes us with some of the earliest followers of Jesus to the tomb in 15:40-16:8 in a way that powerfully completes some of the themes, promises, and motifs introduced to us in the Introduction and developed in the course of the story. As the story began with God's herald or messenger ("I will send my angel . . .") pointing to the one who would baptize with the Holy Spirit, so Mark ends with an angel ("a young man, dressed in a white robe") announcing Jesus' resurrection, presence, and leadership into Galilee (where Jesus began his ministry [1:14-15]). The death, burial, and resurrection of Jesus, the Christ, the son of God is indeed the good news of the gospel, as well as the basis for germinating, growing, and fruitful new life in the kingdom of God (continuing our connections with the Introduction). Since the act of Christian baptism came to symbolize the death, burial, and resurrection of Jesus, it's not difficult to see a relationship between the empty tomb passage and the key theme of baptism introduced to us in the beginning of Mark.

What began in the desert ends in a tomb—places of hardship and death, but which function as launch pads, so to speak, for the gospel of God: from death to life. Both John the baptizer and Jesus trod the wilderness of desert testing, and both were placed in a tomb. Unlike John, however, who some *thought* had been raised from the dead, Jesus rises from the dead. Like uncontainable wine bursting the strongest skins . . ., like newborn Christians rising up from the watery grave of baptism, Jesus leads the way. Jesus *is* the way. The gospel/desert/baptism triad of the Introduction finds literary resolution in the tomb/resurrection/gospel combination of the Conclusion. Here the good news begins (again), as Jesus goes ahead of his disciples into Galilee and to all the world with the news of forgiveness, resurrection, and the dawning presence of the kingdom of God.

Adding the clear division of the Middle of Mark into Galilee, Jerusalem, and between or "on the way" (to Jerusalem) sections gives us a fuller, though admittedly still broad, shape to Mark. We can thus see a five-part outline:

| | |
|---|---|
| Desert (Gospel/Desert/Baptism) | 1:1-15 |
| Galilee | 1:16-8:21/26 |
| The Way | 8:27-10:52 |
| Jerusalem | 11:1-15:39/41 |
| Tomb (Tomb/Resurrection/Galilee/ Gospel [16:15]) | 15:40/42-16:8 |

Each of these sections can be broken down further into sub-sections and sub-shapes, but I'll leave that for later and for your own reading.

# Mark 1:16-3:12: Scattering the Seed

Rather than trying to cover all of Mark in detail, I'd like to walk briefly through the first few sections after the Introduction in order to provide some framework for our inkblot passage—the parable of the Sower (Mark 4:1-8). In combination with our overview (having read the whole book—Rule #1), this will help provide an initial context for putting together the pieces of Mark chapter 4 and connecting them with what comes before (Rule #2). Having introduced us to some very important figures in the story (John, Jesus, God, Satan), their perspectives and messages, including fundamental themes and concepts like the kingdom and gospel, the desert/ wilderness, baptism, and others; Mark transitions (1:14-15) into his story with a summary of Jesus' activity and message in Galilee: "The time is fulfilled, and the kingdom of God has come near; repent, and believe in the good news."

Each of the first three major sections in Mark begins with a paragraph that focuses on the disciples and their journey with Jesus—in particular, their calling, training, and mission (1:16-20; 3:13-19; 6:7-13). It's as if, from the beginning, Mark wants us to see that Jesus is about calling and training disciples to be good followers. Whatever Mark reveals about Jesus' teaching and actions in the stories to come, it happens under the watchful eye and purpose of disciple-making. This also helps us as readers to identify with the story— that is, if we, too, want to be followers of Jesus.

The first major section, Mark 1:16-3:6, provides the first block of material dealing with the work of Jesus, packaged within the theme of discipleship. Following the opening summary of Jesus' preaching, the pace screeches to a zoomed-in halt on Jesus' initial calling of the disciples, with focused detail. Walking beside the Sea of Galilee, Jesus calls four fishermen—Simon (= Peter), Andrew, James, and John—to follow him, which means to become his disciple (to come or walk behind him) in order to learn from him; and with an end in mind: "Come, follow me, and I will make you become fishers of men" (1:17). And that's exactly what they do. Immediately, they begin following him around the towns and countryside of Galilee.

273

As we begin to read, we're going to see Mark open several different windows or views on how various people react and respond to Jesus. The windows aren't mutually exclusive. They overlap and eventually merge into one comprehensive view of the complex environment in which Jesus had to do his work. That doesn't mean that people quit reacting to Jesus differently. On the contrary, like plants in a field, multiple sorts and sizes grow in the same general location; and, like a scenic view on the side of a mountainous highway, highlighted by a sign and a place to pull off to the side of the road, Mark's "windows to a view" highlight various ways Jesus impacts the hearts and lives of individual and groups.

## Window 1: Disciples—Called to Follow (1:16-20)

The disciples'—and most everyone else's—initial encounters with Jesus are powerful and intriguing. He's preaching about the kingdom—we know that—but the first specific incident Mark narrates (1:21-28) takes us into the synagogue in Capernaum on the Sabbath day (first things—events, words, actions—are often significant by way of trend/theme setting). The people are astonished at Jesus' teaching because, unlike the scribes (copyists and authorities on the Jewish scriptures), he teaches as one who has authority. Introduced here, being "astonished" and "amazed" at the teaching and actions of Jesus is a constant throughout Mark. Jesus is not like the present expressions of Jewish religion; the contrast is strong and evident from the beginning.

Not just his teaching, but also its effects: "Just then," or "immediately," Mark says, Jesus encounters a man with "an unclean spirit" in *their* synagogue (my emphasis)—perhaps the last place authoritative and effective spirituality should encounter a demon. The demons know Jesus, underscoring his authority ("Have you come to destroy us?") and identity ("the Holy One of God"). But Jesus silences them—as he will other premature, confusing, and/or inadequate expressions of his identity—which is an important and interesting theme (the suppression of expression about Jesus), but one we'll save for another day. Highlighting and supplementing the spoken contrast between his teaching and that of the scribes, Jesus heals the demon-possessed man. The impact is immediate and clear: the people are amazed and provide a nice summary of what we just saw: "What is this? A new teaching—and with authority! He commands even the unclean spirits and they obey him" (1:27). The summarizing result: His fame or report spread like wildfire through the surrounding region of Galilee.

## Window 2: The Crowds Want Jesus (1:21-45)

The next incident shows the speed with which the talk about Jesus spread (1:29-34). Jesus goes home with Simon and Andrew, along with James and John (notice they are "following"). Simon's mother-in-law lay sick in bed with fever. They tell Jesus about her (indicating intentionality—they've apparently learned something about Jesus), and he heals her. He lifts her up by the hand, the fever leaves, and "she began to serve them" (1:31). (Could this represent another window in the text? Individuals from among the people/crowds who are touched by Jesus and respond to him in various ways? Perhaps we should be open to a *window on individuals*, where Mark zooms in on a particular person or group of people who respond to Jesus.)

Now watch this. We've seen one healing of a demon-possessed man in a synagogue and one healing of a sick person inside a house, but now, "That evening, at sundown"—which means the Sabbath day has officially ended and folks can travel, which means this is the very first opportunity since the healing in the synagogue on the Sabbath day—"they brought to him all who were sick or possessed with demons. And the whole city was gathered at the door" (1:33). Not surprising. Isn't this the way any people at any time in history would react to a person who could genuinely heal them of their illnesses and diseases? The response is understandable, yet dramatic and potentially subversive—yes, I said "subversive." At least that's what Jesus thinks. Let's read on.

275

In his typical love and compassion for people, Jesus cured many who were sick and cast out many demons the night the whole town flocked to Simon and Andrew's door. But then something interesting and defining happens—a defining moment in Jesus' early ministry. Jesus gets up very early the next morning ("while it was still very dark") and goes off to pray. (Now this is an inkblot passage, if I ever saw one. Perhaps you've heard people speak of Jesus' prayer-life, using this passage to illustrate his regular practice or "habit" of getting up early for his prayer/quiet time?) If you look through all of Mark, you'll find that we're told of Jesus praying on only three occasions, and each occasion represents a critical juncture or potential turning-point in his ministry—Mark 6:46 after feeding the 5,000 (John's Gospel tells us that they wanted to make Jesus king at that point), Mark 14:32 in Gesemane just before he's arrested and killed, and here: after the crowds' initial, rapid, explosive, light-speed, reaction to his power to heal. They all want to be healed. (And who wouldn't?) While Jesus is praying, Simon and those with him, acting much like their own summary of the crowd's response to Jesus, come looking for him and say, "Everyone is searching for you" or "seeking you" (1:37). Jesus' reaction is profound and path-setting (or perhaps we should say *way*-setting).

Before looking at Jesus' response, however, let's back up. We may have missed something. Mark tells us that when Jesus gets up early to pray, he didn't just pray, but he got up very early and went off to "a deserted place, and there he prayed" (1:35). In other words, he got up very early and went to "the desert" to pray. This is one of our key words from the Introduction: the desert/wilderness. And do you remember how Mark used it? Just a few verses back, we learned that after Jesus' baptism, the Spirit of God drove Jesus into the desert to be tempted (1:12-13). The desert was presented as a place of trial, testing, and even temptation—the place where Jesus meets Satan in battle, so to speak. As such, it's certainly an appropriate place of prayer, as this passage indicates.

So what's the point? The rapid response of the crowd to Jesus' teaching with authority and the healing that goes with it (a natural response that the disciples imitate) pushes Jesus into a time and place of prayer—into the desert—which implies that something's not right, challenging, or even unintentionally subversive within their response to Jesus. Couldn't Jesus just heal everybody? Wouldn't everyone want to make him Lord and king, if he did? Couldn't Jesus just be the type of leader and Messiah that the people want? After all, just a couple of reported healings, and everyone's at the door: "Everyone wants Jesus," to paraphrase Simon and his companions. The point is that the crowd's initial reaction to Jesus represents and could help to create, therefore, a particular understanding or viewpoint of Jesus and what he should do as God's Messiah. He could in fact be a great healer of physical weakness and disease, and, I dare say, the people would "love" him. After all, the healing of disease is a part of how they would know the time of the Messiah had arrived (Matthew 11:1-6; Luke 7:18-23). But Jesus goes *to the desert to pray.* He then responds to Simon's summary of the crowds' initial reaction ("Everyone is looking for you"). He says, "Let's go somewhere else—to the nearby villages—so I can preach there also. That is why I have come" (1:38: NIV). A purpose statement for the ministry of Jesus—quite profound, yet out of sync with some elements of the current setting.

So he does. For a moment, Mark zooms out to give us a summary of this activity: "And he went throughout Galilee, proclaiming the message in their synagogues and casting out demons" (1:39). (This is a common technique of Mark: zoom out and give a summary; zoom back in on specific instances and events.) But then he quickly zooms back in to continue the current thematic development: the people's response to Jesus and its impact.

A man with leprosy comes to Jesus, on his knees begging Jesus to heal him. Filled with compassion, Jesus touches him (an act that would make him "unclean" from a contemporary religious perspective) and heals him. But then Jesus acts with a forcefulness we've not seen in the story to this point, even a touch of harshness. He immediately leads ("drives") the man out and gives him a very stern warning: *"See that you say nothing to anyone . . ."* (1:43). Why so hard a warning? Because we've seen what happens when the word of Jesus' healing power gets out. Look what happens. Instead of saying nothing, the man goes out and begins to proclaim it freely and "spread the word," almost as if he were preaching a counter-message to Jesus: another word. He was "preaching the word"—a word that carried subtle but serious misconceptions about who and what Jesus was. . . . a view of Jesus, the Healer.

And here's the punch line: because of "the word" that was being spread about Jesus, he was no longer able to enter into a town openly, "but was outside in desert places—and people came to him from everywhere" (1:45). In other words, the radically enthusiastic response of the crowd to Jesus—remember Simon's summary: "everyone wants you"—actually prevents Jesus from doing what he came to do freely (1:38) and forces him to stay *in the desert*. And the desert is a place of what? A place of testing and temptation (Mark tells us in his Introduction that the Spirit of God "drove" Jesus to the desert to be tempted). What this means is that one sort of reaction to Jesus becomes a perpetual obstacle, struggle, and even temptation in the ministry of Jesus. The people hurt, and they want a Messiah who will heal them and take away their sufferings. Jesus does—it's part of the coming kingdom and he has compassion on the people—but there's something more; and the threat is real—it's a *desert* struggle. Jesus has a purpose and message much bigger than just physical healing or comfort. It includes that, but there's something more important and fundamental, which implies that some things—shallower or near-sighted things—can keep us from deeper, eternal things.

The initial reaction of the people to Jesus thus implies and represents a particular view or definition of "the Messiah": Jesus could be a man of the people—the people's Messiah. Jesus, the Healer! Like bees to honey, they would flock to him, as they are doing. But that's not the essence of who Jesus is or what he came to bring (contrast Herod [6:26] and Pilate who want to please or satisfy the crowd [15:6-15]). The word, desire, and actions of the people thus become a persistent obstacle in the ministry of Jesus, the Messiah, the Son of God. This is Mark's window on the crowd. And Mark highlights this for us, thematically and metaphorically, with the desert theme. (See how important the Introduction has already become in our reading?)

Let's jump to application for a second (Rule #9). When we begin to apply the things we learn from Mark to our lives, we want to open a window on our own motives for responding to the call of Jesus. Do we ever respond to Jesus like the crowds? Sometimes our belief in the goodness and faithfulness of God depends on what he does for us *now*, doesn't it?—a "what-have-you-done-for-me-lately" sort of thing. When things are difficult and don't go the way we hoped and planned, we begin to doubt the goodness and even the existence of God. So the question becomes *is there something I need even more than physical healing, health, and comfort?* And *what does Jesus, the Messiah, have to offer?*

## Window 3: The Religious Leaders Want Jesus Dead (2:1-3:6)

At least, the religious leaders want Jesus dead by the time we get to the end of this section. Mark 2:1-3:6 is a collection of stories, featuring the religious leaders' reactions to Jesus' continued ministry of preaching and healing. The section has a circular or concentric structure that has been carefully set forth by Joanna Dewey in her book, *Markan Public Debate*.[11] The shape of Mark 2:1-3:6 looks like this:

2:1-12: Healing of the Paralytic
   2:13-17: Call of Levi/Eating with Sinners
      2:18-22: Sayings on Fasting/Old and New
   2:23-27: Plucking Grain on the Sabbath
3:1-6: Healing on the Sabbath

These are meaningful events in the ministry of Jesus that highlight various characteristics of his teaching about the kingdom of God and the growing antagonism of the religious authorities toward him. In addition to some highly important tenets and practices relating to the kingdom of God—or true religion, we might say—the fundamental conflict of established religion versus the new wine of

Christ raises its head and grows to a point of impending harvest (plotting to kill Jesus) in this block of material. I'll summarize the stories briefly and then highlight the reactions of the religious leaders.

In the first episode (2:1-12), the frenzied enthusiasm of the people toward Jesus continues as so many people gather outside a house that four men, carrying a paralyzed man on a mat, couldn't even get to the door. That didn't stop them, though. Their faith led them to dig a hole through the flat adobe roof so they could lower their paralyzed friend to Jesus. As if to speak to the heart of the man's (and our) deepest need—not just to heal physical infirmities—seeing their faith, Jesus tells the man that his sins are forgiven. Some of the scribes silently accuse him of blasphemy, supposing that only God can forgive sins. To provide proof that he has authority on earth to forgive sins, Jesus then heals the paralyzed man, who picks up his own mat and carries it out in front of them; "so that they were all amazed and glorified God, saying 'We have never seen anything like this!'" (2:12).

In 2:13-17, Jesus calls Levi, a tax collector—viewed by many as about the lowest you could sink in that culture—and then goes home to eat with him, along with many "tax collectors and sinners" (2:15). And here's a key statement: "for there were many who followed him." When the scribes of the Pharisees challenge these actions, Jesus retorts that those who are well don't need a doctor, but those who are sick. (Notice that the meaning of healing has shifted to the healing of the person as a whole—the soul.) This is a basic part of who and what Jesus is, as he expresses it: "I have come to call not the righteous but sinners" (2:17).

In the next encounter (2:18-22), Jesus faces questions about why his disciples don't fast like the disciples of John and of the Pharisees. They will, Jesus says, but not now, not while the bridegroom (that is, Jesus) is with them. (Note Jesus' and Mark's use of metaphor.) As the first indication in the story that he will be killed because of his work, Jesus says that the bridegroom will be taken away from them and they will fast on that day. Continuing his answer to the question about why his disciples aren't performing some of the same religious activities as others (fasting in this case), Jesus gives two similar, compelling analogies about his ministry: (1) you don't sew a piece of unshrunk cloth on an old cloak and (2) you don't put new wine in old wineskins. The unshrunk cloth will tear away from the old and the new wine will expand and burst the old skins—both the wine and the skins will be lost. In other words, what Jesus brings in his person and presence can't fit into traditional religious viewpoints or constraints. He is new wine and can only be received as such.

The disciples pluck and eat heads of grain as they make their way through the grain fields one Sabbath day (2:23-28). The Pharisees openly accuse them of doing "what is not lawful on the Sabbath"; to which Jesus responds with an example from the Old Testament showing that even King David did something that was "not lawful" when a sort of higher law—a basic human need—was at stake, explaining that "the Sabbath was made for man, not man for the Sabbath. So the Son of Man is Lord even of the Sabbath" (2:27-28: NIV). In other words—and this is the point—one shouldn't forget the meaning and purpose of the Sabbath while observing it, which is often the problem when religious ritual begins to take the place of the heart and purposes of God. And beyond all that, the presence of the source of true religion trumps legalistic applications of religious rules. In other words, rules serve the ruler, not the other way around.

Finally, applying the previous principle in a slightly different way, Jesus heals a man with a withered hand in the synagogue on the Sabbath day (3:1-6). By this time, the religious leaders were intentionally looking for a way to accuse Jesus. Aware of their duplicity and utter lack of concern for the well-being of the man with the withered hand, Jesus calls the man up, center stage, and confronts them with a fiery question about whether being "lawful" has anything to do with doing good (versus doing harm). They were silent. Jesus looks around at them, angry and deeply disturbed by their callous hearts; then heals the man. The contrast is striking; the clash, overt. In response the opposition of the religious leaders opens its dark and sinister bloom: "The Pharisees went out and immediately conspired with the Herodians against him, how to destroy him" (3:6), ironically, plotting to do "harm" on the Sabbath. They've had enough of Jesus, and now they want him dead.

Several key ideas about the nature of Jesus as the new wine of God versus the old, traditions of legalistic religion present themselves in this block of material. Healing involves not just healing the flesh, but the soul (as in forgiveness of sins), and Jesus has such divine authority. Healing is for everyone, tax collectors and sinners included, not just important looking and sounding religious characters. The "rules" of religion are not just ritualistic repetition, but have purpose for the health and well-being of people. And people matter, such that the most authentic form of religion comes from the heart, seen in doing good and not harm or evil, especially perhaps on the Sabbath day. Just as Jesus stood for something deeper and more eternal than the frenzied clamoring of the crowds for physical healing would have imposed upon him (which he rejected or transcended by maintaining his primary focus), so here Jesus rejects outright the implications of the religious leaders' view of a good Messiah. Were they to superimpose their expectations onto Jesus, he would have followed all their traditions and become an orthodox rabbi or religious figure of the day. Such was not possible or desirable—you don't put new wine in old wineskins. Jesus, the Christ, stood for something radically different from relentless and heartless religion. He was and is the bridegroom, whose coming brings the presence of the kingdom of God.

The contemporary religious traditions couldn't contain the new wine of Jesus, the Christ. He was bursting those skins in each of the stories in 2:1-3:6. He still bursts them—something for us to think about and apply as we seek to follow Christ in the kingdom of God today.

## Window 2: The Crowds Grow (3:7-12)

As if to remind us of the previous window/reaction to Jesus, Mark 3:7-12 returns to the ever-present and growing enthusiasm of the crowds, forming a type of thematic bracket around the hostility of the religious leaders (1:21-45; 2:1-3:6; 3:7-12). In summary form (a 5,000-foot view), Mark tells us that the crowds were hearing what Jesus was doing and began coming from places even beyond Galilee in great numbers, "from Judea, Jerusalem, Idumea, beyond the Jordan, and the regions around Tyre and Sidon" (3:8)—that's south and north. So many came and tried to touch Jesus that he asked the disciples to have a boat ready for him so the people wouldn't crush him. The demons recognize and proclaim him "the Son of God," but Jesus continues to silence them.

## Window 1: The Twelve (3:13-19)

Resolving his typical circular patterns, Mark moves his focus back to the disciples in the next section, giving our "windows" (= literary focus) the following flow/shape:

Disciples (1:16-20)
    Crowds (1:21-45)
        Religious Leaders (vs. Bridegroom/New Wine) (2:1-3:6)
    Crowds (3:7-12)
Disciples (3:13-19)

Also in typical overlapping fashion, the next paragraph presents a new stage in the journey of the disciples, as we begin a new major section in Mark.

# Mark 3:7-6:6 Sowing the Gospel

## Window 1: Calling the Twelve (3:13-19)

Mark's focus on the disciples continues in the next major section, which, like the previous one, begins with a key disciple paragraph. In Mark 3:13-19, Jesus goes up on a mountain ("mountain" appears at times to be associated with the desert solitude/prayer theme: see 3:13; 6:46; 9:2, 6) and calls to himself 12 disciples "whom he wanted, and they came to him" (3:13). This again suggests the calling-following theme, introduced in the initial calling of Simon, Andrew, James, and John (1:16-20). But now Jesus calls *the twelve* and appoints them to be "apostles." An apostle is one who is sent out on a mission; the twelve are thus called for specific purposes: "to be with him, and to be sent out to proclaim the message, and to have authority to cast out demons" (3:14-15). This is the purpose and plan for these first disciples. They are (1) to be with Jesus—this continues our "following" theme, adding a note of intimacy—and (2) to be sent out to preach and to have authority to cast out demons. In other words, they are to be *with* Jesus so they can be *like* Jesus. A few of the apostles (the inner three: Peter, James, and John) are given new names ("nicknames")—a significant event in the history of Israel—that capture something of their character and personality. Simon was named "Peter" (which in Greek means rock); James and John were called "Sons of Thunder." Judas is identified as the one who betrayed him, giving us our second and more nuanced foreshadowing of Jesus' fate. A second Simon is distinguished from Simon-Peter as "the Canaanite" or "Zealot" (a Jewish nationalistic sect).

## The Gang's All Here: New Community around Jesus (3:20-35)

Mark 3:20-35 brings our window views on the early reactions to Jesus to a degree of climax, coalescing and amplifying various attitudes toward Jesus in one compact setting, within which something new emerges. Jesus again enters a house (or "went home," as the NRSV has it), and, as we would expect by now, the crowd converges—this time with such numbers and enthusiasm that "they couldn't even eat" (3:20). Word about him had spread so far and so fast that when his family heard about it (this is the first we've heard of "his family"), they came to "restrain" or "take charge" of him (we would likely say "they came to *get* him"), for they/some were saying, "He is out of his mind" (3:21). Even worse, the scribes from Jerusalem were saying he was possessed by Beelzebul and casts out demons by the ruler of demons. We assume disciples/followers are here as well, since they've been called to be with Jesus and have been following him around the countryside. We learn a little later that a "crowd" is sitting around Jesus, and he speaks favorably of those "sitting around him" at the end of the section (3:34). In other words, the gang's all here. With all the ingredients of a highly combustible recipe thrown in, the place is filled with people of all types, views of all sorts, desires of all kinds—centered "around" Jesus.

So Jesus calls the people and begins speaking to them "in parables" (a crucial feature of Mark's story). This is the first mention of Jesus speaking to the people in parables, and the makeup of the audience (of all types, with some who are very hostile) is significant for this development. We'll learn more about Jesus' use of parables in the next chapter, but for now, the emphasis is on Jesus' responses to the groups and their views toward Jesus. He offers a powerful analogy to those who believe he's acting by the forces of evil: a kingdom or house divided against itself cannot stand. He can't possibly be casting out Satan by Satan, or Satan is divided and so is he—he would be "out of his mind," as some thought, if that were the case. Jesus' (often) troubling statement about an "eternal sin" then pronounces an ultimate judgment: to those who think that the very work of God's kingdom though God's Son is from Satan himself, to those so blind that they see white as if it were black, to those who believe and thus pronounce Jesus to be the very embodiment of darkness, to those who see that which is holy (from the Holy Spirit) as evil (from Satan), they cannot be forgiven. They don't want to be—they don't recognize the need. In other words, they have made their choice in response to Jesus. (Mark goes on to portray this sort of response to Jesus as having "hard hearts": eyes that don't see and ears that don't hear.) The statement actually has a wonderful counter side as well. To everyone else—and this would include many levels of understanding and types of responses to Jesus in the audience that day—Jesus says that all sins and blasphemies of people can and will be forgiven (3:28).

After Jesus responds to the charge of those who reject him as evil, Mark returns to Jesus' family. They were "standing outside," as compared to those "sitting around him" (Mark loves to use brief symbolism and metaphors), and they called him. (This almost looks like a reversal of Jesus' call—the call he's issued to the disciples to follow him—a counter call, so to speak; a sort of cease and desist order.) His family is calling him because they want to get him and take him home, to save him from all the talk and the potential ramifications of his explosive teaching and actions (3:6: the authorities are plotting to kill him). To their call, Jesus makes an extraordinary pronouncement, which, in very succinct form, gives his feelings about those who have come to him and have pressed in close enough to be sitting around him. For all who respond to Jesus with enthusiasm and hunger, there is the potential for forgiveness and welcome into a new family or community with Jesus himself. "Who are my mother and my brothers?" Jesus says, "Here are my mother and my brothers! Whoever does the will of God is my brother and sister and mother" (3:35).

Responding to the call of Christ and following him as we experience his life-changing character and power—this is phase one of being a disciple. The next phase of our journey with Jesus, so says the next section of Mark, is listening carefully and learning about the kingdom of God, as Jesus teaches with verbal and action parables—with pregnant (Spirit-filled) words and deeds.

# Sowing the Word in Parables (4:1-34)

## Jesus Teaches in Parables

"Again he began to teach beside the sea" (4:1). The crowd was so large that the boat—the one Jesus asked the disciples to get ready to keep the crowd from crushing him (3:9)—become useful now as a stage or platform for teaching. Jesus is in the boat, the crowd is on the shore, and Jesus begins to teach them "many things" in parables (I think the Greek word *polla* should perhaps be translated here with something like "intensely" or "fervently": Jesus teaches them "intensely" or even "passionately in parables," rather than "many things"). "Parable" is a Greek word for a brief story or example that serves to express or illustrate a point. It's a way of saying something by way of comparison or analogy—an indirect way of communicating, especially if you don't say clearly to what the point or concept is being compared. And this brings us to our inkblot sample: Jesus then tells them the parable of the Sower.

Mark chapter 4 (4:1-34 to be more precise) is often referred to as "the parable chapter," since it introduces us to the use and purpose of parables. Why does Jesus begin teaching publicly in parables? Why here? Why now? We know that he's been preaching and teaching throughout the towns of Galilee and in more open places where the crowds came to him. We saw the first use of parables in the last section in a mixed setting in response to those who accused Jesus of being possessed by Satan. We've already learned that powerful people are plotting to kill him (3:6). Toward the end of the book, we learn that they attempt to use Jesus' own words against him in order to have him executed (14:55-64). We also know that there are various types of responses to Jesus and his message: in the last section, we saw crowds, opponents, family, those around Jesus, and those who do the will of God—his new family. Throughout this first part of Mark's story, we've looked briefly through windows on disciples, crowds, religious leaders, and individuals who respond to the work and call of Jesus. And now, in an open setting with one of the largest

287

crowds to date, Jesus teaches by parables. In fact, the conclusion of this section (4:33-34) says that at this point, he *only* used parables: "With many such parables he spoke the word to them, as they were able to hear it; he did not speak to them except in parables . . ." (4:33-34). Again, I ask about the parables.

Guess what? The disciples asked the same thing: "When he was alone, those who were around him along with the twelve asked him *about the parables*" (4:10). And in response, Jesus explains the parable of the Sower. Hmm. That means that the parable of the Sower answers their question about parables, and what's more, it discloses something fundamental about teaching about the kingdom of God given in parables. "Don't you understand this parable?" Jesus asks. "How then will you understand any parable" (4:10)? The parable of the Sower is fundamental, and it's about parables. And the disciples don't understand it. Again, hmm. This is a surprising and potentially telling development.

## The Parable of the Soils

This is the context in which Jesus tells and explains the parable of the Sower—a parable that might better be named, "the parable of the Soils." It comes in the developing context of Mark that we've seen to this point. It comes as crowds respond to Jesus with an enthusiasm so intense that it threatens his purpose and message. It comes as powerful, religious authorities have become so offended at the teaching and actions of Jesus that they are actively trying to figure out the best way to get rid of him. It comes as individuals with good hearts press in for healing, more than just of the body—to hear and learn about the kingdom of God. It comes as Jesus works intimately to train his disciples for the continuing mission of the kingdom, of calling and preaching and healing. In this complex, multi-faceted environment, Jesus still has much to do. Thus, he begins teaching in parables. Like the parable of the Sower itself, the summary at the end of the chapter (verse 33) helps to give the answer to the question and explain the meaning. He spoke to them in parables "as they were able to hear." What does that mean? How can you speak to people—varied, diverse, multi-motived people—as they are able to hear? Answer: In parables. Mark chapter 4 is, in fact, a new stage in the ministry of Jesus and at the same time an explanation of that beginning.

(Have you ever read the parable of the Sower within this context? You can see how easily it can become a dislodged analogy—an inkblot.)

Mark 4:1-34, to resume our train of thought, is about listening to the word of Jesus spoken in parables.[12] Does it make sense then that before he starts the parable, Jesus says, "Listen!" or "Hear! . . ." (4:3)? And then when he's done, he says, "Let anyone with ears to hear listen!" (4:9)? Now comes the parable of the Sower itself and its explanation privately to the disciples (even though they don't seem to get it; Jesus is working with them intimately and graciously).

> "Listen! A sower went out to sow. And as he sowed, some seed fell on the path, and the birds came and ate it up. Other seed fell on rocky ground, where it did not have much soil, and it sprang up quickly, since it had no depth of soil. And when the sun rose, it was scorched; and since it had no root, it withered away. Other seed fell among thorns, and the thorns grew up and choked it, and it yielded no grain. Other seed fell into good soil and brought forth grain, growing up and increasing and yielding thirty and sixty and a hundredfold." And he said, "Let anyone with ears to hear listen!"

Given what we've seen in Mark thus far, does this fundamental parable about the kingdom of God, one that helps to answer the question that the disciples (and we) ask about parables, about understanding the word of God, spoken at this time only by parables—does it say something about the ministry of Jesus? Does it say something about how Jesus works and can be effective in an intensely complex environment? (And what will happen when the disciples begin sowing the word?) Does it say something about the various types of reaction to Jesus that we've seen in the text to this point? And about what will happen as we go forward? For, in fact, the parable tells us that there are different types of soil and different responses to the seed (the word of God) scattered upon the different types of soil. Could our "windows" be related to "soils"? (Think about that for a minute.) *Within the literary context of Mark, the parable of the Sower lives as an insightful summary of what has been and an illuminating forecast of what will be in response to the teaching and preaching ministry of Jesus.*[13] Not just generally, whenever and wherever the gospel is preached. This may be true. But before we reach that conclusion, we must listen to the word of God spoken to us in the context of Mark's Gospel. To do so is to be guided by the Spirit of God.

## What about the Parables?

When they were alone, "the ones around him with the twelve" asked Jesus "about the parables" (4:10). This is the inner group—disciples, followers, learners—those who have responded to his call and have pressed in close enough to hear all that Jesus would teach them. To their question, Jesus gives a direct answer in verses 11-12 and several parabolic or analogical clarifications in verses 13-32.

The direct answer: Parables reveal and they conceal. (Isn't that the nature of a parable or analogy? The point is expressed, that is, "hidden" or "concealed" in another, metaphorical, way of saying it.) "To you has been given the secret of the kingdom of God . . .," Jesus says (4:10)—by parables (and also by Jesus' intimate teaching and private explanations). "But to those on the outside . . ."—this reflects the lines that we saw drawn in the last chapter by decisions various groups and persons have made about Jesus (remember, there were literally those sitting inside/around Jesus, those calling for Jesus *from the outside*, and those accusing him of being possessed). To those on the outside, parables conceal the messages of God's kingdom so that they can look and look but not see, listen and listen but not understand (4:12). (Sounds harsh, but the point has to do with decisions already made, soils already defined.) To those on the inside, parables reveal the mystery of the kingdom of God, or at least they should, which helps to explain Jesus' puzzlement or surprise that the twelve and those on the inside were asking him about the parables ("Don't you understand this parable and how you will understand all the parables?"). In other words, parables function to confirm and deepen who and what they already were: inside or out.

See, the parable of the Sower actually answers the question. That's why Jesus explains the parable in response to their question about parables. Understanding parables is a method for going deeper and coming to understand more of the real nature of Jesus and the kingdom of God, in a very mixed and even dangerous environment. See why the parables are so appropriate? They allow Jesus to keep teaching "many things" or passionately (*polla*) and effectively ("as they were able to hear") in this explosive setting, based on the interests and hearts of the listeners. This is why the conclusion of the chapter says that he didn't speak to them without using parables and at the same time was teaching them "as they were able to hear." Everything in this chapter is about effective listening, and it's based on the heart and ears of the listener and the inherent power of the word of God. Now, do you see how the parable of the Sower answers the question about the parables, and how they are to understand all or any of the parables? *It depends on the soil.*

If we look at the parable more closely, we learn that there are different types of soil into which the seed (the word of God, now being sown through parables) implants itself . . . or not. Concrete-hard, path-soil—birds eat the seed. Rocky soil—comes up quickly but dies under the heat of the hot sun. Thorny soil—the thorns/weeds choke out the gain. And finally, good soil—it sprouts, grows, and produces abundant harvests. Two clear kinds: bad (path-soil) and good (good soil). Two not-so-clear kinds (rocky and thorny): sprouts and looks good to start with, but doesn't endure and produce a harvest. Jesus elaborates with his explanation to them:

> The sower sows the word. These are the ones on the path where the word is sown: when they hear, Satan immediately comes and takes away the word that is sown in them. And these are the ones sown on rocky ground: when they hear the

word, they immediately receive it with joy. But they have no root, and endure only for a while; then, when trouble or persecution arises on account of the word, immediately they fall away. And others are those sown among the thorns: these are the ones who hear the word, but the cares of the world, and the lure of wealth, and the desire for other things come in and choke the word, and yields nothing. And these are the ones sown on the good soil: they hear the word and accept it and bear fruit, thirty and sixty and a hundred-fold (4:14-20).

Does this sound anything like what we've been experiencing in response to Jesus in the narrative thus far? And, since you've read the rest of the book already, what happens as the story unfolds? We've seen various types of responses to Jesus and his teaching. We've seen some who seem to be so hard-hearted that they've already rejected Jesus and begun to plot his demise (the religious authorities). We've seen others who have responded favorably, with enthusiasm and apparent commitment (the disciples, the crowds, people from the crowds). But at this point in the story, we don't yet know how it all turns out. We don't know for sure who bears fruit and who doesn't. We can't say for sure what type of soil each person or group is.

*The point I want you to see is how Mark uses the parable of the Sower with a literary, contextual, Bible-book, story-connected purpose.* In addition to the fundamental nature of the parable as an explanation as to what happens to the word sown in the hearts of people, it's a picturesque summary of where we are in Jesus' ministry at this point in Mark. It connects to everything that's happened *and* to what comes, and, in this context, raises the very probing question of what kind of soil the people are (and what kind of soil are the listeners—including us). What kind of soil are the disciples who respond immediately and devotedly to the call of Jesus to follow him? (Of course, at this point in the story, we assume they are good soil.) What kind of soil are the crowds, as they respond to the healing power of Jesus with tremendous enthusiasm and desire? What kind of soil are the religious leaders as they . . . That one's easy. Or is it? (Later, we see a scribe interact with Jesus in a way that causes Jesus to say, "You are not far from the kingdom of God" [12:34]; and a synagogue ruler, Jairus, comes in faith to Jesus for the healing of his daughter [5:21-24, 35-43].) And what about individuals who step forward and display striking examples of faith or understanding? We've yet to see how all this turns out, and remember, Jesus is now teaching only in parables, which means that understanding parables becomes vital as a means of nourishment and growth of the word in the hearts of the listeners.

## More Parables about Soil, Listening, and Growing

Let's look briefly at the other parables in this context. They all relate to this theme of the word sown or implanted in the heart. As if to respond to the question about the apparent (moral) harshness of using parables to hide truth from some, Jesus tells the parable of the Lamp and the Lampstand (4:21-25). He didn't come or teach in parables in order to hide or conceal the light he brings. The real purpose, the reason things are hidden (or put into parables, in this case), is so that they might be disclosed. That's the real purpose, but it depends on the listener: "Let anyone with ears to hear listen!" (4:23). Because—and this is tremendously important—you're going to get out of it what you put into it, to what you listen and how you hear it—with what measure you use. "For to those who have, more will be given; and from those who have little to nothing, even what they have will be taken away" (4:24-25). Isn't that saying something very similar to the answer Jesus gave to their question about parables (for some they conceal; for others they reveal) and the parable of the Sower (the harvest depends on the soil)? But it takes it a little further. Parables are a tool for piercing, discerning, employing—farming— the heart/soil of the listener.

And he's not done. Jesus gives two more parables on this same topic. The parable of the Growing Seed (4:26-29) highlights the inherent, progressive, and mysterious power of the good-seed/good-soil combination. It doesn't happen all at once, or overnight. But over the course of time—naturally, yet supernaturally—the seed sprouts, grows, ripens, and bears fruit. And the results can be magnificent, the parable of the Mustard Seed says (30-32). Though it starts out very small (as a tiny seed), it grows, and when it's full grown, it has large branches, "so that the birds of the air can make nests in its shade."

Such is the kingdom of God sown in the hearts of men and women through parables. The repeated emphasis on "listening" throughout this section (4:3, 9, 12, 23, 33) underscores the synergistic relationship between the seed and the soil. Like the sower, Jesus has been sowing the seed of the kingdom—now, with parables. The result of the word sown in the soils of individuals depends on the type of soil. Just as we've seen different reactions to Jesus in the early part of Mark's story, so the seed will continue to grow and produce fruit in the good soil. It may take a little time and occur in steps or stages, but over time good soil produces a good harvest. In fact, an amazingly plentiful harvest: from the tiniest seed grows a full-grown, bird-nesting bush. God's power resides in his word, and, therefore, in the parables of Jesus. Planted in a good heart, the word of God bears fruit *"automatically"* (4:28). Because it's presented in an indirect or concealed way, it doesn't work for everyone. In fact, it heightens what you are, multiplies what you bring to the table, turns up the volume on where your heart is tuned, calls forth your deepest motives. The intent is to shine the light of Christ, but hearers must listen closely and carefully.

Thus, the question becomes, *do we really want to hear and see what Jesus has to offer*. Or will we allow our own views of what the Messiah should be to filter and block what we're able to hear? Do we want to create God in our own images, in other words? Like sharp, suffocating thorns, will "the cares of the world, and the lure of wealth, and the desire for other things" (4:19) choke out the lifeblood of the word? Or, like seed sown on rocky soil, will the onset of "trouble or persecution . . . on account of the word" (4:17) cause us to wither, sapping our ability to thrive and bear fruit? As you read the book of Mark, see if you notice a rather undiscovered theme about what a person *really wants*, culminating, on the positive side, in Jesus' famous statement in the Garden of Gethsemane: *". . . not what I want, but what you want"* (14:36).

Not everyone is a good listener; not everyone is good soil. And here's the challenging point: *the first stages look very similar in rocky soil, thorny soil, and good soil.* So what sort of soil are the disciples? What sort are the crowds? Things must play themselves out over time before we know for sure, but at this point in Mark's story, a subtle and potentially dark characteristic begins to break through the sod and raise its ugly head in the story of the disciples. They don't understand the most basic parable. . . . a parable about understanding parables. Jesus, though a little surprised, takes up the slack. He explains it to them, and he keeps doing that, as verse 34 says (". . . but he explained everything in private to the disciples"), since his goal is to train them to be fishers and healers of men and women. Jesus' surprised response to the incomprehension of the disciples initiates what will become an increasingly (ironically, like a growing seed) prominent theme in the pages to come—*the disciples don't get it.* But good soil understands, doesn't it? The text thus raises a subtle (at this point) but probing question for the audience—a question Mark wants us all to face squarely and honestly: What sort of soil are the disciples? And, by way of application, what sort are we?

All of this thematic development is marvelously interrelated by Mark's arrangement. Like most sections, Mark 4:1-34 has a concentric shape. Summarizing paragraphs surround parables, which surround questions and statements about the purpose of parables, with the interpretation of the parable of the Sower coming at the center:

4:1-2: Introduction: Jesus Teaches in Parables
    4:3-9: Parable of the Sower
        4:10-13: About Teaching in Parables
            4:14-20: Interpretation of the Parable of the Sower
        4:21-25: About Teaching in Parables
    4:26-32: Parables of the Growing Seed
4:33-34: Conclusion: Jesus Speaking in Parables

The concentric development supplements the linear movement of the text, and without trying to be overly precise, this shape actually puts the very center focus on the two types of mixed—start-out-one-way, end-up-another—soil. Bad and good soils flank the two that start out well, but fall victim to temptation and struggle in the end.

I believe this is a major purpose of Mark's Gospel. Mark wants Christians—those who have responded to the call of Jesus in faith—to follow him closely and to the end. . . . to listen and learn what Jesus is really all about, so that when times of trouble, persecution, testing, planet-earth allurements, and temptations come their way—as they will; it is a desert journey—they will be empowered not to be like seed sown upon the rocks or among the thorns. Over time, the seeds of understanding will sprout, grow, and produce a fruitful harvest of new wine, kingdom presence. After all, it's not always or only how we start that matters most, but how we end.

# Section Highlights

## Mark 4:35-6:6: Sowing the Word in Living Parables

Since studying Mark is not our primary goal, I won't journey with you through the rest of the story now—perhaps another time. Our main goal is for you to learn to do it on your own, for you to become an inkblot-zapper. So I'll paint with broad strokes the rest of the way through Mark's narrative.

The next section of Mark takes the journey further and deeper—deep into frightening, even dark places. It begins by crossing "to the other side." Here, Jesus doesn't teach as much in parables, but he presents himself a living parable of the kingdom. As you read the stories in Mark 4:35-6:6, pay careful attention to how each scene makes use of the concepts of *fear* versus *faith*. Encountering Jesus, the living word of God, always brings amazement to the people, but, on many occasions, it also creates fear—sometimes intense, defining-moment fear. In this section, Jesus crosses boundaries in an effort to begin teaching the disciples that the kingdom is bigger than they had imagined. Fear naturally arises, but, of course, it's not the ultimate goal. Jesus summarizes that goal when to Jairus, one of the leaders of the synagogue, at the news that his young daughter had died, Jesus said: "Don't be afraid; just believe" (5:36: NIV). As Mark announced to us in his initial summary of Jesus' preaching message (1:14-15), change of heart/life and faith in the good news is essential to following Jesus on the way.

## Mark 6:7-8:21: Bread for the World

Like the previous two, the next major section of Mark begins with a discipleship paragraph. It's time to put what they've learned to practice; hands-on doing is, after all, a vital part of learning. Remember, he called Simon, Andrew, James, and John to become fishers of men; and he chose the twelve to be with him and to be sent out to preach with authority. The disciples have been following Jesus, listening to his messages, witnessing his healings, hearing his discussions and encounters. So now, it's their turn. Applying the principle of faith that was underscored boldly in the last section, Jesus sends them out with instructions to take nothing for their journey ("for the way"): "the way" is based on faith. How do they do? What do they preach? How do the people respond? In your own reading, take note

- . . . of the results,
- . . . of the super-excitement of the crowd (5,000 men run around the lake and arrive before Jesus and the twelve),
- . . . of the significance of Jesus feeding the 5,000 . . . and in a desert (6:32, 35),
- . . . of Jesus sending the disciples away in the boat, as he dismissed the crowd,
- . . . of Jesus going onto a mountain to pray,
- . . . of the reaction of the disciples to Jesus when he comes to them on the water.

And be sure to notice what Mark says about the disciples at this point. After pointing out that they had not recognized Jesus walking on the sea, that they were terrified and utterly astounded, he explains: ". . . for they did not understand about the loaves, but their hearts were hardened" (6:52). Such language has been used for outsiders, those furthest away from God who even seek Jesus' death.

As you read chapter 7, notice the strong confrontation between Jesus and the religious authorities over "cleanliness"—what makes someone right and valuable: "Then he called the crowd again and said to them, 'Listen to me, all of you, and understand . . .'" (7:14). Then watch how the focus of Jesus' ministry shifts toward non-Jewish places and people—toward Gentiles—whom many Jews at that time would have considered unclean and unworthy of concern, much less targets of the word and grace of God (from the Messiah). What does it mean that Jesus extends his teaching and healing ministry to non-Jews? Is it "fair to take the children's food and throw it to the dogs" (7:27)? What's it mean when Jesus feeds another great crowd of 4,000, but this time in Gentile country? Jesus appears to have plans "for the other side" that go beyond what many people of the day were able to hear, and like a good shepherd, he provides bread (think spiritual nourishment, as well) for Jews and non-Jews alike. (If we used the seed analogy from earlier, we might say "he waters . . .") He is, in fact, healing and spiritual nourishment *for the world*. Then see how the disciples respond.

In a very important paragraph at the end of this section (8:14-21), Mark gives us a deeper view of the disciples than we've seen thus far in our journey with them. They get in the boat to go to the other side, and the disciples forget to take bread, except one loaf (that sounds sort of odd, doesn't it?). Jesus tells them to beware of the leaven or yeast of the Pharisees and of Herod (look back in the previous paragraphs to see what that "yeast" is like). The disciples think it's because they didn't bring any bread. Now, remember, at the beginning of this section, Jesus sent the disciples out and told them *not* to take any bread, and then we saw him feed crowds of 5,000 and 4,000 with a very small amount of food. We might say, "What are you thinking?" Similarly, Jesus responds with deep concern and frustration:

> "Why are you talking about having no bread? Do you still not perceive or understand? Are your hearts hardened? Do you have eyes, and fail to see? Do you have ears, and fail to hear? And do you not remember? When I broke the five loaves for the five thousand, how many baskets full of broken pieces did you collect?" They said to him, "Twelve." "And the seven for the four thousand, how many baskets full of broken pieces did you collect?" And they said to him, "Seven." Then he said to them, "Do you not yet understand?" (8:17-21).

Since we were introduced to the theme in Mark 4, *understanding* the messages (= word) of God taught by Jesus through his parables and actions has been a key theme in Mark. Without it, one's path and beliefs will be determined by distortions of all types; Mark's story shows that even those who seek God can be led astray by their own desires and conceptions (compare our concept of inkblots). (Considering how much emphasis the Gospel of Mark places on listening and understanding, and on how the disciples and others couldn't see or hear Jesus because of their preconceptions and expectations, how much more should be our concern about turning God's written word to us into brief reinforcements of what we already think!) The word preached and demonstrated by Christ is like seed sown into the hearts of men and women. In good soil, it takes root, grows, and over time produces a bountiful harvest. Using another metaphor, it's like bread, spiritual nourishment from heaven. Jesus takes small amounts and multiplies them, even in difficult times and places (in the desert), where people hold conflicting views of what good, spiritual nourishment consists; yet people come away full and satisfied. (Jesus is in fact—as John puts it in his Gospel—"the bread of life.") Those following Jesus, the disciples, those learning from him so that they can become fishers and healers of men must also learn to provide similar nourishment for the people.

After the disciples went out preaching and the crowds came together like mad into a desert place, Jesus said to them, "You give them something to eat" (6:37). But they're not there yet. Not by a long shot. In fact, when Jesus extends his spiritual planting and feeding to those "on the other side" of the sea, they have trouble making the trip. Planting, feeding, growing—these are basic activities of the kingdom of God on earth. They are part of the way of Jesus, the Christ. But, along the way, the disciples respond with fear (6:47-52: "for they didn't understand about the loaves, but their hearts were hardened") and now a serious lack of understanding that makes them sound like those on the outside who can't see or hear (8:14-21; 4:10-12). And so my question—and I think it's Mark's question, as well—is what kind of soil are the disciples?

## Mark 8:22-10:52: The Way

I would be remiss if I didn't underscore Mark's central section where Jesus speaks "openly" or "plainly" to his disciples about "the way"—in contrast to his public ministry in parables. Peter's confession (8:27-30) of the disciples' belief that Jesus is indeed the Christ represents a sort of threshold or turning point; such faith is really the basis for everything else, especially for coming to understand the true and sometimes difficult journey of a follower of Jesus. Several features highlight the importance of this material as pivotal for Mark: (1) it's central placement between the two locations of Jesus' activity (Galilee and Jerusalem); (2) Mark's surrounding of this core unit with stories of the healing of a blind man—highlighting its importance for true spiritual insight; (3) the thematic repetition of "the way" motif, as the true way of the Messiah and the kingdom of God; (4) articulation of the fundamental belief—a critical step in the disciples' development—that Jesus is indeed the Christ; (5) clear teaching about the heart and soul of being a follower of Jesus and a leader among God's people; and (6) the threefold repetition of Jesus' prediction that he must suffer, die, and be raised from the dead—the foundation and pattern of "the way."

Differences between kingdoms of the earth (Herod, Pilot, even the disciples' expectations of the messianic kingdom) and the kingdom of God come through loud and clear in this section of Mark. As you read, be sure to notice the pattern Mark establishes with Jesus' predictions of his impending suffering and death, the disciples inability to comprehend such a thing, followed by further teaching from Jesus on what sort of Messiah he is. In sharp contrast to the judgments of the religious leaders (Window 3), the desires of the crowds (Window 2), and even the hopes and expectations of the disciples (Window 1), with resolute focus, Jesus repeatedly underscores his characteristics as the suffering, servant, Messiah of God and applies those traits to those who would be like him (compare his initial focus when the crowds forced him into desert prayer [1:35-39] and religious authorities tried to squeeze him into old wineskins [2:21-22]). For example, after Jesus predicted his suffering and death the first time, Peter began to rebuke him to the point that Jesus calls Peter "Satan." Peter's view cannot at this point represent the way of God. Instead,

> He called the crowd with his disciples, and said to them, "If any want to become my followers, let them deny themselves and take up their cross and follow me. For those who want to save their life will lose it, and those who lose their life for my sake and for the sake of the gospel, will save it. For what will it profit them to gain the whole world and forfeit their life? Indeed, what can they give in return for their life? . . ." (8:34-37).

I urge you to trace out the teachings of Jesus carefully in this section of Mark, hear them in the context of Mark's developing story, digest them (or "feed" on them, as Mark might put it), and apply them to your life. This part of scripture is at the heart of what it means to be a Christian; that is, if you, like the formerly blind Bartimaeus, want to gain your sight and follow Jesus on the way (10:52). I suspect that Mark 8:22-10:52—in conjunction with Mark's Gospel as a whole—has a lot to do with what John the baptizer predicted when he said that the one coming after him would baptize in the Holy Spirit. As Jesus said to Nicodemus in John's Gospel: "I tell you the truth, no one can see the kingdom of God unless he is born of water and the Spirit" (3:5: NIV).

## Mark 11:1-13:37: New Tenants

In the next section, pay careful attention to the tension between Jesus and the religious leadership of the day. Conflicts that we saw in 2:1-3:6 re-emerge, intensify, and reveal more of the differences between God's way and that of the Jerusalem-led religion. Some questions to ask:

How does "the triumphal entry" (11:1-11) function in Mark's developing story, as a beginning of the latter half?

What about the cleansing of the temple (11:12-19) and the graphic predictions by Jesus of its future (13:1-37)?

What does the parable of the Tenants say about the future leadership of God's people (12:1-12)? And who is Jesus in relation to God's vineyard?

What is Jesus' view of the Old Testament law of Moses in this section and why is it emphasized as it is? (Similar to the Sermon on the Mount in Matthew, be sure to notice how Jesus affirms the Old Testament and the teachings of the law in this section, while reminding us of what true devotion to God looks like.)

Finally, why does Jesus curse the fig tree (11:12-14) and encourage the disciples with the power of faith and prayer (11:20-26)?

These are the kinds of questions that will keep you on track for hearing and getting God's points, as they come from the text itself.

## Mark 14:1-15:39: The Seed Is Sown

The last sections of Mark contain world-changing stories and events. Just as the Passover lamb was prepared and slain in Israel as an annual reminder of God's gift of deliverance, so Jesus was anointed for burial (14:3-9) and instituted the Lord's Supper (14:22-25) as an ongoing reminder of the depth of his sacrifice for our salvation and of his continuing presence with his followers, promising that he would not drink of the fruit of the vine again until he drank it new in the kingdom of God. As you read, notice the intimacy of his last hours with the disciples in the Passover meal and in the Garden of

Gethsemane. How do these settings and stories fit with the pattern of the disciples being with and learning from Jesus? The detailed descriptions of the rejection, suffering, and death of Jesus are excruciatingly extraordinary, moreover—the passion of the Christ. As readers, we should ask how Mark's rendition of Jesus' suffering and death functions in the context of his overall story. What does it mean for Mark's purposes? For our salvation? For learning to be a follower of Jesus? As the central section tells us, remember that what was happening to him was a pattern or paradigm of what following him on "the way" means—not in each minute detail, but in how the world treats servants of God.

Finally, be sure to watch how the authorities, the crowds, and the disciples act and respond during this time. In fact, it may well be quite insightful to see if the fundamental question raised by the parable of the Sower receives some clarifying answers during these last scenes. What kind of soil are the religious authorities? What sort are the crowds? What kind are the disciples? And—even more importantly, as we experience and apply the message to our lives—what sort are we? "What kind of a follower of Jesus am I?"

What does it mean to follow Jesus on the way, all the way to the end? Does Mark imply something, figuratively, when he says that Peter (14:54) and some of the women (15:40-41) were following "from a distance?" There is much Spirit-filled understanding, insight, and stimulation to be gained by carefully reading and re-reading these last sections in Mark—by letting Jesus touch us again and again—as they bring to conclusion vital teachings and themes of Mark's Gospel.

## Mark 15:40-16:8/20: The Good News of the Gospel

One last thought about Mark's Conclusion (in addition to what we discussed earlier) and a reminder. I recommend that you think about the ending of Mark from both perspectives, as if it ended with 16:8 and with 16:20. These are our best preserved options, and it's certainly worth asking The Question from both perspectives. And remember, conclusions are highly important for driving home the most important point(s) of the text. So consider deeply how the story of the resurrection brings to climax and resolves the message and meaning of Mark. What about the angel/messenger's reminder that Jesus would go ahead of his disciples into Galilee? What about the women's reaction to the news? How does it fit with how folks have reacted to the amazing deeds of Jesus throughout the story? And doesn't this transcend them all? What about the disciples' slowness to believe as part of the longer ending? How does that fit with what we've seen in the story? And finally, what about the sending forth of the disciples into all the world with the good news ("gospel") and the promise that those who believe and are baptized will be saved? How does Mark's ending complete his story of the good news of Jesus, the Christ, the Son of God? And, of course, what does the message of Mark mean for you?

Mark announced to us from the lips of John the baptizer that Jesus would baptize with the Holy Spirit. This is why I want to read Mark carefully and often. I want to be baptized in the Holy Spirit, touched by Jesus as many times as it takes, to see more clearly and follow more closely. How about you? Careful, contextual reading is in fact careful listening, as Jesus and God the Father exhort us in the pages of Mark's Gospel: "This is my Son, whom I love. Listen to him!" (9:7).

## Chapter 12: Zoomed Out on Mark

### Chapter Resources

Boucher, Madeleine. *The Mysterious Parable: A Literary Study.* Catholic Biblical Quarterly Monograph Series 6. Washington, D.C.: The Catholic Biblical Association of America, 1977.

Dewey, Joanna. *Markan Public Debate: Literary Technique, Concentric Structure, and Theology in Mark 2:1-2:6.* SBL Dissertation Series 48. Chico, CA: Scholars Press, 1980.

Standaert, Benoit. *L'Evangile selon Marc: Composition et Genre Litteraire.* Brugge: Sint Andriesabdij, 1978.

*L'Evangile selon Marc.* Lire la Bible 61. Paris: Cerf, 1983.

Stock, Augustine. *The Method and Message of Mark.* Wilmington, DE: Michael Glazier, 1989.

"The Structure of Mark." *Bible Today* 23 (September 1985) 291-96.

Tolbert, Mary Ann. *Sowing the Gospel: Mark's World in Literary-Historical Perspective.* Minneapolis: Fortress, 1989.

van Iersel, Bas. "Locality, Structure, and Meaning in Mark." *Linguistica Biblica* 53 (1983) 45-54.

*Reading Mark.* Translated by W.H. Bisscheroux. Collegeville, MN: Liturgical, 1988.

### Notes

1. Colossians 4:10.
2. *Against Heresies* 3.1.1.
3. *Ecclesiastical History* 3.39.15.
4. Mark 15:41 outlines the Galilee to Jerusalem movement.

5.  Several scholars have observed this fivefold circular (chiastic) movement in Mark. See, for example, Standaert, *Composition et Genre Litteraire*; *L'Evangile selon Marc*; van Iersel, "Locality, Structure, and Meaning," 45-54; *Reading Mark*, 18-26; Stock, *Method and Message*, 19-32; see Stock, "Structure of Mark," 291-96 for a view of the chiastic arrangement of Mark as a whole; and an online article ("A Bible Study of 'The Gospel according to Mark'") at www.Christviewmin.org (http://www.christviewmin.org/bible.study/bible.studies.gospel.mark.php) for an accessible example of working with the literary structure of Mark.

6.  We'll look at the question of Mark's ending (16:1-8/20) a little later.

7.  I find it more than interesting that the Levitical priesthood and the sacrificial system of Judaism was never restored after the destruction of Jerusalem and the temple by the Romans in AD 70—as Jesus predicted.

8.  I first learned of the pattern from Dr. Carroll D. Osburn while a student at Harding School of Theology in Memphis. See the Preface for some honorary comments regarding Dr. Osburn.

9.  I think the disproportionate length of the top, blue section may result from the focus of this material on the *beginning* of the good news about Jesus. It starts, in other words, with the ministry of John the baptizer, and we learn nothing more of John and his work until the description of his death in chapter 6. John's work culminates in his preparation for and testimony to the coming of Jesus. Though we receive testimony about Jesus from John and from the Father, and we learn that the Spirit leads Jesus into the desert to be tempted (with no specifics), we move into the actual ministry of Jesus by way of introduction and summary in Mark 1:14-15.

10. In early Christian theology, baptism became symbolic for the death, burial, and resurrection of Jesus (see, for example, Romans 6:1-11). The transfiguration scene of Mark 9:2-8 may also reflect baptism traditions, as early Christians were immediately clothed in white garments following their baptism (9:3: "and his clothes

became dazzling white"). The scene certainly connects with the baptism of Jesus in Mark 1:9-11 from a literary perspective with the Father's pronouncement of Jesus as his beloved son. The whole central section of Mark may in fact be a sort of catechesis (= instruction) about what it means to be baptized as a follower of Christ.

11. Dewey, *Markan Public Debate.*
12. See Boucher, *Mysterious Parable;* esp. 42-63 for this emphasis in Mark 4:1-34.
13. See Tolbert, *Sowing the Gospel;* esp. 121-26 for an example of one who interprets the parable of the Sower as a "plot synopsis" that functions "to assist its audience in following its aural narrative" (p. 124).

# Conclusion

# A Plan for the Church

My mother died while I was working on this book. She had a long term, chronic illness that resulted in many, sometimes mysterious, increasingly debilitating and painful symptoms. Her body and strength began going downhill rapidly in the last few years. By the time she died, her kidneys had failed; her lungs were weak and failing (she "smothered" a lot); her digestive system was broken (she often ate next to nothing); her heart and blood pressure, erratic . . . In some ways even worse, for the last couple of years, her muscles began to grow increasingly weak, to the point that in her last few months, she couldn't sit up or even turn over in bed. She could barely feed herself. The doctors kept treating all the symptoms . . . This medicine, that medicine; this side-effect, that side-effect. . . . never really knowing what was wrong. Everything was wrong. But why? (I believe it was partly the result of a long-term battle with chronic, systemic Candida—but that's another story.) After she died, the paperwork was delayed because they weren't quite sure what to put as the cause of death. Everything. Nothing. I'm grateful I got to spend some very meaningful time with her during her last months, and we rejoice in the replacement of frailty and tubes with dancing in the light and love of God.

I tell you that story not to sadden you at this point in our journey or to play on your sympathies, but to illustrate the effects of hidden illness. Yet what we are talking about concerns things more important than our physical bodies. We're talking about our eternal spirits and the accessibility of the light and healing power of God given to us by God in his written word, the Bible, while we live on the earth. The first step in treating any serious condition or illness, of course, is to know and admit it exists. The second is to make changes (chemical, physical, emotional, spiritual) that can affect and overcome the problem.

Despite her rapid deterioration over the last few years, Mom actually suffered from some of her problems for most of her life. She rarely felt well. At one point, she had chronic fatigue so severe that the doctors labeled it narcolepsy. Yet she pressed on, loving and serving us, always. Sometimes, I have to wonder what her life might have been like if she had felt well—if she had had the energy and strength to do the things she wanted to do, the way she wanted to do them. From my own health struggles, I've learned that it's hard to do good when you feel bad.

Now, complete the analogy: could we be facing similar symptoms in our churches and our lives today—lethargy, weakness, chronic fatigue, spiritual narcolepsy—because of a hidden illness: the loss of the books of God? But to look toward a bright future, can we, like Josiah in the temple, participate in a rediscovery of the word of God so personal, yet so pervasive and powerful that it revives us as individuals, ignites and empowers our churches, and ultimately changes the world? This is my prayer and purpose in writing this book.

# The Illness

The greatest threat to Christianity in America today is, in my opinion, the loss of the books of God. The greatest threat to Christianity today is the disintegration of the Bible. The greatest threat to Christianity today is the shattering of the Bible into thousands of pieces—verses that we read and interpret through the prisms of our own psychological, emotional, and spiritual matrices more than through the inspired contexts of the books themselves. Consequently, the church is sick with a fever. (*The Church* is healed and sound and whole and powerful through the blood and Spirit of our Lord Jesus Christ—since ultimately God's character and action is not diminished or threatened by our failings. My comments apply to our character and actions—our small-letter creations.)

We live in a time of great spiritual illness and attack by the enemy upon our persons and our health. All eras have such. What makes ours so dangerous, at this point and for the most part, is that it's hidden. It lies quiet in our spiritual settings and psyches, undetected in our devotional habits, snickering silently as it leads us by the hand to subtle forms of possession ultimately as debilitating as with those who couldn't hear or see or speak when Jesus walked the earth. Our temptation sprouts from a spirit of radical independence and freedom that extends both to individuals and groups (churches and denominations). Our vulnerability—the chink in our spiritual armor, so to speak—comes from a new form of biblical illiteracy that's caused, ironically, by the availability and proliferation of scripture (actually, pieces of scripture).

Inkblotitis—one of the most dangerous spiritual threats of the last few centuries and even more so now—is the condition that results when we go to "hear" from God, even to read and reflect on scripture, we often look upon images of ourselves because we have replaced the books of God with "the book" of God, disintegrated into thousands of independent verses and brief passages—spiritual inkblots, razor sharp tools—hijacked by the enemy to divide, cut, and dwarf us. In this, we replace the life-changing power of the inspiration of the Holy Spirit with the infinite (circular) reflection of our

311

own misinformed, underdeveloped, sometimes ugly thoughts and feelings. In short, inkblotitis is the potential for someone to learn more about us when we read or hear a verse of the Bible than we learn of God. What a terrible predicament, to look upon the word of God for God's great beauty, love, and power and come away the same. That's only possible if what we see is not God, but ourselves, or something even less or worse. The ultimate tragic irony: to look for God and find only myself. What a colossal disappointment! . . . for each of us, and for those who might otherwise be brought to God by us.

Of course, I'm exaggerating. But not completely. I believe the illness of inkblotitis to be a very serious condition facing the church today. It is the spiritual plague of the 20th and 21st centuries. It's Christianity's dangerous and hidden disease. This is why I tried to alert you to its existence and convince you of its seriousness in the first part of this book. "How to read the Bible to *miss* God's point"— tongue in cheek—was our overarching subject, as we explored the condition together. If previous generations lost sight of God in the darkness of authoritarian control and ignorance, we lose him in the blinding light of freedom and independence.

One of the great contributions of the Protestant Reformation to the history of the church was its emphasis on scripture. This emphasis led to the idea that every Christian ought to be able to read and interpret the Bible for himself or herself, in his or her own language—"Christianity's dangerous idea," Alister McGrath calls it. Many ultimate sacrifices were made so that people could read the Bible in their native languages; and now, like never before, the Bible is available for almost everyone to open, read, and explore. Just as no one stands between us and God, except the Lord Jesus, so no one stands between us and our Bibles—the opportunity to seek God through his written word. We have the freedom to read the books of God when and how we choose.

The belief that all Christians should be able to read and interpret the Bible—a view with which I strongly concur—is the origin of inkblotitis. Once planted into our spiritual culture, this seed of scriptural freedom carries with it, like all good things, a potential for abuse—the sharper the axe, the deeper the cut. Behind our backs, Satan has craftily exploited this opening to evil ends such that now we live in a culture replete with contextless Bible reading and—dare I say it—disarmed readers. But, as in all forms of evil, Satan uses us (he didn't pick the fruit and force-feed it to Adam and Eve). That's why what we do matters, and that's why the way we approach the Bible matters a lot—which leads us, first of all, to a question of motive. Why do we read the Bible? The answer to that question sets the stage for everything else.

If everything in and about the Bible were straightforward and simple, we wouldn't have a problem, would we? But it's not. So we looked briefly into the origin of the Bible, and at some of the reasons why reading and understanding the Bible can be difficult. The wide scope, ancient cultures, multiple genres, profound content, and the—let's say, "affected"—readers themselves all contribute to moments of "what in the world does this mean?" when we read the Bible. But that doesn't mean we can't read and understand it if we're aware of these things and especially if we make some effort to listen to God in scripture. On the other hand, the ways we read the Bible often cause us to miss God's point(s), creating a climate rife with subjective, personal understandings and a soil moist and fertile for the implanting and spread of Christianity's dangerous disease. To illustrate this, we looked at several not-so-good—but very popular—ways to read the Bible: *devotional*, *theological*, and *argumentative* Bible reading—though these are really just overlapping labels for anything that breaks the Bible apart into verses and snippets, producing out-of- or devoid-of-context standpoints and habits.

# The Treatment

In the second part, we looked at the treatment: how to read the Bible to get God's point. God did not give us his word without the means of receiving it! We've been reading and using the Bible in such small pieces, however, gradually (from a cultural and historical perspective) losing our knowledge of the contexts of each book, that what I'm proposing almost seems like a new way to read it. It's really not. We're simply trying to honor the way God chose to communicate to us. He did it in history, and he did it in individual writings or "books." Instead of Random Access Bible Reading (RABR)—reading a verse or two, or even a chapter or two, here and there—we need to learn to read each book carefully as an integrated whole. And then . . . to interpret the parts as they fit into that big-picture whole. Though perhaps a little forced or silly, I used the acronym SABR to contrast the approach that takes a verse or small sets of verses as though they inherently stand on their own. We need to read each book straight through from beginning to end—sometimes many times—in order to get a clear sense of the issues and purposes of the book. This is Sequential Access Bible Reading; or I like better the idea of Summit Access Bible Reading, as if we're climbing a God-indwelling mountain so that when we reach the top (get to the end of the book), we have a God-given perspective from which to look back and see the verses within their book-level context. Once we "see the picture," we put ourselves in much better position to "get the point." "See the picture, get the point."

Much of what I've been saying is in keeping with an age-old principle of Bible interpretation—a written passage or verse of scripture should be interpreted *in context*. Easy to say, not always easy to do, especially since we're not in the habit of doing it. Because each book of the Bible has a literary context (the writing itself, from beginning to end) and an historical context (the setting in life that gave rise to the writing), good Bible reading means reading each book within its own literary and historical contexts, which I've often shortened into the phrase "book-level context." Since God gave us his word this way, inspired by the Holy Spirit, I believe we can also say—

playing with our SABR acronym—that reading the Bible this way is actually Spirit Access Bible Reading.

To flesh out these ideas, we looked together at two fundamental principles of good Bible reading: "Context Rules" and "Rules of Context." "Context Rules" means that the exact meaning of a word or phrase is determined by its context—its surroundings—the meaning of which is determined by *its* surroundings, and so forth. We often give lip-service to the idea of context by reading a few verses before and a few verses after a text (the "immediate context") and then assume that "we've put it in context," while missing, often badly, the bigger question of how the verses fit and function in the book as a whole. To help with that task, we turned to the "Rules of Context," which I presented as "Ten Rules of Good Bible Reading," followed by two practical examples from the Bible books of Philemon and Mark. Here's the list of rules one last time:

1. Read the whole book, preferably several times.
2. View the verses in book-level focus.
3. Discover the shape of the text.
4. Highlight recurring words and ideas.
5. Appreciate the differences of genre.
6. Tune in to the historical setting.
7. Use commentaries and other study tools with discretion.
8. Digest your experiences in the word.
9. Live what you've learned.
10. Do it again.

The treatment for the illness of inkblotitis is no more complicated than rediscovering the books of the Bible on their own terms as part of God's inspired library, which is the Bible. It's that simple. It's as simple as reading Bible books and then reading them again. . . . building a book-level, big-picture perspective so that we can understand the verses and chapters within that Holy-Spirit inspired framework. It's not complicated, but that doesn't mean it's easy. It requires a sincere, seeking heart and in many cases a willingness to change—in some cases to change a lot.

In other words, inkblotitis is a form of biblical illiteracy (do you know how your favorite verses help to support the major message[s] of the book they came from?) that results from habits (and the leaders of the church not teaching us otherwise). And you know how hard some habits are to break. Throw in an addictive element like opium or nicotine, and they can seem next to impossible to break. Is there anything more addictive than not having to work hard, being comfortable and maybe even a little lazy, especially from a religious or spiritual perspective? Is there anything more addictive than not having to depend on the work, sacrifice, and community of others because God teaches us all we need to know privately and directly? Is there anything more addictive than believing that we think and behave as we ought, as when the Bible doesn't challenge us morally or theologically? . . . than having a well-defined set of religious dos and don'ts that provide a sense of periodic reassurance (a "snort" or "hit," so to speak) because they're concrete and measurable and help set us apart as the "true" followers of God? Is there anything more addictive than thinking that "me and God are tight, 'cause it says so right here" in this verse and that verse, and I've believed it all my life? Is there anything more addictive than me? . . . than my own reflection, to recall the Narcissus story? Inkblotitis is as easy as the selfish side of self-love that pervades all us sinners.

So . . . are you up for the challenge? Or is it too difficult? Will it take too much time and effort? Would you rather not have to worry with context and purpose and . . .? I'm being a little facetious because I honestly believe that the life-giving power of the Spirit of God within the word of God is self-propelling and self-compelling. Just read the book. Read the books, and ask God to guide you as you seek to know him and his will for your life. I'm not trying to make this hard. I'm just trying to break old habits, and you know how hard that can be. The treatment is the word of God. Not definitions, rules, methods, or anything else. "And the Word was made flesh . . ."— revealed to us in *the books* of the Bible.

# The Main Point (My Thesis)

In a broad sense, the whole question comes down to an issue of definition. Put simply, what is the Bible? In some ways, we've come to answer that question in our day by way of analogy. That is, we actually have several kinds of "books"—different genres and purposes that affect how the books are read, the content shaped and received. Many of those books are functional wholes, especially books of fiction or nonfictional stories. They tell one, sequentially developed, story. We also have reference books: dictionaries, encyclopedias, recipes, how-to manuals, etc. These are not designed to be read as a whole, in a single sitting or experience, but in small sections, bites, or pieces as one needs. Though they may have a broad, encompassing theme, educational books often function like this as well. You read a page or a section, learn what you need, then put it down 'till you need it again.

As the books of God were assembled into a single volume, which came to be known as "the book" (Bible) instead of "books," we've also come to treat it as such. But here's the problem: reading it as a single, integrated, story-book doesn't work. It can't because that's not what it is. Unless, of course, you know a whole lot about the historical settings and meanings of all the books and how they fit together in the unfolding history of God in the world—which is our ultimate goal, because in this sense *the Bible is the book of God*. But you can't read it this way as a beginner or young believer because that's not what the Bible is; consequently—and this is crucial—we begin to treat it more like a reference book, where we look up recipes or poems or themes or proverbs or good-sayings or . . . whatever. In other words, *because we can't read the Bible as a book, we read/use it as verses*. Or, to get to the same place, we quit reading and searching the scriptures for understanding, and substitute short passages or verses that summarize pieces of our faith for the experience of hearing from God. And herein lies the beginning of the end, the seeds of inkblotitis that lead to the goal of the enemy: the disintegration of the Bible. Turning the books of God into verses of "scripture" has the potential to tear away the Spirit's foundation from those verses. That's why

317

this is Christianity's *dangerous* disease. Turning the books of God into inkblots—little mirrors of the self—represents its festered, metastasized form.

The heart of the question, then, is an issue of definition: *What is the Bible?* When we stop to think about it for a minute, most will agree. The Bible is a collection of the books of God, each with its own historical setting and literary context, each with its own inspired message(s) from God. We've believed and taught this for years and years—in theory. It's orthodox. But the great impetus of Christianity's dangerous idea that all Christians have the right to read and understand the Bible for themselves helped to create a culture where we've never really lived up to it. To state the principle of context a little more boldly: It's not until we read and understand each book (and each verse as a part of that book) that we have put ourselves in position to see the divinely inspired and divinely inspiring, panoramic view of the whole (and of its parts). Otherwise, the picture will simply be too out of focus to discern. (Now, that doesn't mean that someone can't teach us about the things that help to fill in the gaps so we can get there faster—that's another subject. I certainly believe in the value of Spirit-guided teaching, but the question here has to do with how we read the Bible for ourselves.) *The Bible is indeed the book of God, but it was and is first the books of God. It is what it is, God made it that way, and that is how we must read it—book by book—if we are to get God's points and overcome the debilitating tendencies of inkblotitis.*

From a general perspective, my main point (or thesis) has been that we need to rediscover the Bible as a collection of inspired books (instead of disconnected verses of "scripture"). But that's just the starting point. Because of where we are in our culture when it comes to the Bible, that's easier said than done. The breaking apart ("disintegration") of the Bible has become so commonplace and so much the norm that we've developed a sort of random access approach to the Bible that results in what I've described as an illness or fever. Thus, in the first part of the book, we took time to look at the illness itself, at some of its causes and history. More specifically: Reading and using the Bible in short sections (verses or sets of verses) without knowledge of how the verses fit within the book as a whole creates a condition where something other than the inspired context controls the meaning and consequently leads to personal, subjective interpretations that often miss the purpose and point of the text. In short, we turn scripture into inkblots by reading and using it as isolated verses. And, to repeat myself, the treatment is the text, the complete text, and nothing but the text of each book (well, almost nothing).

To put it another way, the Bible is a collection of independent, sometimes interrelated and overlapping, contexts. Learning to work with a keen sense of book-level context is the key to understanding the Bible. To make this point, I've used several images throughout this book to present the idea that the individual books of the Bible each constitute an interrelated whole, which, when taken apart, may lose their ability to speak to us as intended. A mosaic is a good example. Each individual piece is meaningless on its own, but when put together becomes part of an artistic, even beautiful image. A human body cannot function without its cells and organs. Independently, they are pointless and lifeless; together, each contributes to the magnificent wonder of a heart-beating, blood-flowing, music-making, living being. Each part has its function in the body. I often used the idea of a puzzle to put forward this idea regarding the Bible. I find a puzzle to be an especially effective analogy because it's designed to be put together and taken apart. The points of connection (lines and curves) can still be seen in the finished product, and the pieces can then be pulled apart at the same places. The chapter and verse numbers in the Bible create a similar potential: they act as perforations, points of separation. Point to any puzzle-piece in an assembled puzzle, and the relational meaning of the piece is clear. Same with Bible verses. Separated into single pieces, without refreshed and remembered images of the whole, they become inkblots. This is the predominant analogy I've used to communicate the destructive potential of breaking the Bible into small pieces. Reading or using a verse or set of verses from the Bible doesn't automatically make it an inkblot. Not perceiving, understanding, and remembering how the passage functions in relation to its book-level context does.

319

Uncharacteristically and in conclusion, let me see if I can say it briefly. Replacing the books of God with verses from the Bible, we have thereby redefined the Bible. The exciting, life-changing remedy is a rediscovery of the Bible as the books of God. These are in essence the main points of the two halves of this book.

.

# Objections

Not everyone is going to agree with what I've said in this book. This is normal. It's part of what makes us who we are, the freedom to read and understand on our own, and to disagree. (On the other hand, what if someone read only a paragraph or two, and then disagreed, would he or she, in fact, be doing what we do to the Bible?) Some will disagree vehemently, perhaps calling me a heretic (more on this shortly). Others will oppose some things on theological grounds, especially perhaps my understanding of the work of the Spirit (more on this as well). Still others will likely react because what I've said hits too close to home, cutting irritatingly against the grain of their history and experience. I'll start with this group.

Those who gain a sense of identity and maybe even base their spiritual authority on subjective, personal experiences may respond emotionally to what I've written and reject the point outright—they probably won't read the book, or, if they start, they'll likely not read far. They believe that God meets them during their devotional times and that they don't need anything but a verse or two, or a word or two (or perhaps none) to "hear him clearly." Though they likely wouldn't think of themselves this way, they are, in a sense, modern mystics, holding strongly to the view that God talks to them directly and often. I'm not here to dispute this or to attack their belief, or to suggest that they don't find God in those quiet moments. Nothing I can say or do can limit God. So I really hope those with mystical tendencies won't put down this book because I'm emphasizing another side of our spiritual nature and history. I hope they can add the book-level experience to their quiet times with God, since the Holy Spirit put so much of himself into the circumstances and writings of the Bible, and because God has done so much to make it available to us in this form today. As I said early on, to neglect the Bible as delivered to us seems not to appreciate what God has given us; to read it and know it only in short verses seems to put one in a habit of interrupting or even ignoring God.

What are some points of objection that might be raised to what I've said? Of course, there are some—maybe many. Some will no doubt call me a heretic. They will say, "**You are denigrating God's book, the holy Bible.** It all fits together perfectly to form one great revelation of God. Because they all come from God, each verse helps to explain the others. The best method is to let one passage explain and interpret another. To call the Bible the 'books' of God is to threaten the idea of the inspiration of scripture and to miss the divine integrity and harmony of the plan of God for humankind—revealed in one complete, inerrant book. The Bible is the Bible, the book of God."

I agree with most of this. My point is not to desecrate or challenge the inspiration or harmony of the Bible, but to acknowledge and rediscover how it came to us through the revelatory work of God's Spirit at different times and places in individual, self-contained "books," which functioned perfectly for the people to whom they were written and which fit together perfectly for us today. I disagree vehemently, however, with the idea that you can read any verse in any order (or use any verse to explain any other verse) and get God's originally intended points from such a random approach to scripture. It's really rather nonsense. But it's often what we do. I believe in the Bible, the book of God, as a collection of books of God—which is undeniable—that should first be understood within their Holy Spirit-inspired contexts before they fit together into the completed book of God. In other words, the Bible, the book of God, is made up of the books of God, and it's only when we approach it in that order that we put ourselves in position to perceive correctly the marvelous and intricate grandeur of God's book. Reading and studying the Bible thus becomes a book-by-book venture, sort of like building a bridge or a building. You can't put on the roof before you pour the foundation and build the scaffolding. You can't suspend a bridge from nothing. I certainly believe in a Bible-level focus in addition to a book-level focus, but the two things cannot be poured into the same mixing bowl at the same time and expect the proper results. What you get is verse-level focus that results in inkblotitis.

Others will object to the idea that the Bible is sometimes difficult to understand. They will say, "**The Bible is not hard to understand.** How else can we expect God to make the gospel available to everyone? God's will and truth are simple. A child can understand it. We even have children's versions for them to read and understand." "You," they might say, "turn reading the Bible into an intellectual thing; you try to make scholars out of every Bible reader. It doesn't take that much work. Regular people aren't able to do what you say, anyway. The Bible says what it says and means what it means. So just read it."

Let me again say that I agree with some of this, especially that last line. I agree that the message of salvation is simple. It requires the faith of a child. Jesus told us this. And I agree that in one sense the most important values of the kingdom of God are simple, like love and faith and joy; but, on the other hand, too deep and hard for us adults to hold onto. Reading and understanding the Bible is a different matter, however, and on this point, we may just have to agree to disagree. I would ask one last question, though: what about people who speak a language into which the Bible has not yet been translated? Can they be saved? "Of course," we all say in unison. There is a clear difference between (1) the Bible as the written revelation of God and (2) the message(s) of the gospel of God. The earliest Christians didn't even have a copy of the New Testament for quite some time, but clearly heard the spoken message.

Similarly, some will reject the whole notion that we often turn Bible verses into inkblots. They will likely think this is impossible. They will say something like, "You're making way too big of a deal about this," contending that many, if not most, verses and statements in scripture stand on their own and communicate wonderful truths of God, with little to no context needed. (Our culture believes this—there can be no question that this is the way we most often use the Bible.) To this I say that some verses do stand on their own. I've never denied that. I have, however, tried to show that in many cases they do not because of the way words and sentences receive their meaning and because of the history, genres and styles of biblical documents. Yet some will say, "**The Holy Spirit did not inspire inkblots.**" With this I have to agree.

This actually raises a very important distinction between what I'm talking about—reading and understanding the Bible—and the

323

idea that short verses of scripture contain and can communicate truthful ideas. We so frequently cite and use Bible verses by themselves, with beautiful and powerful, divine sentiments, that it seems absurd to criticize the practice. We remember them and use them with great comfort and strength, as we should. And I heartily agree that brief expressions and verses from scripture do contain reminders and summaries of basic, even core values of our faith; and they communicate something of these core values, especially when heard by folks with little to no knowledge of the Bible. As such, they are tools for education and evangelism. I'm certainly not trying to say that verses by themselves can't communicate essential truths, like, for example, the existence of God, that God is love and gave his Son for us, that faith in Christ is the way to salvation, that God is with us and hears us when we pray. Any expression of truth about God is from the Holy Spirit and to be appreciated as such. *That we should read the Bible book by book does not mean that verses of scripture cannot or should not be used to summarize and present important pieces of our faith.* Please hear me when I say that.

On the other hand, I would suggest that *there is a vital difference between remembering, stating, or proclaiming a value or belief and reading the Bible in order to understand it.* And this is precisely the point. We turn verses that often have very nuanced shapes and shades of meaning in their Bible contexts—possibly meanings that don't quite fit the thinking and theology we bring to the table and with which we surround those verses—into summaries, reminders, and proclamations of our faith and theology. Of itself, that's not a bad thing, and in the end, our reading (for understanding) and our proclamation (for outreach and evangelism) should be in sync (in order words, we want to proclaim the true meaning of the text). As when Jesus quoted the beginning of Psalm 22 from the cross, we can't cite the whole book any time we want to reference a piece of it. My contention, however, is that the summary, cut-out method (often with reference to views we already have) is by far the most common way we use the Bible in our culture today—which means that *we rarely read in order to understand.* Let me ask The challenge Question one more time: pick your favorite verse or set of verses, those you might use to express some wonderful point of your Christian faith ("For God so loved the world . . ."), then ask yourself how these verses help to communicate the major point(s) of the book from which they came. Because of the pervasive habit in our culture and in our churches of reading/using the Bible as verses instead of books, most people can't answer the question. Verse-level Bible reading is the exclusive way many people know and use the Bible.

But—and this is a very important "but"—our subject is something else. Our subject is how we come to understand those verses. Our goal is reading and understanding the Bible, not using verses to verbalize general Christian beliefs and values. This is the difference between reading, listening to, and understanding the Bible and professing one's faith (not to mention the widely divergent potential understandings of the beliefs and values so expressed). It's the difference between interpretation and proclamation. It's the difference between learning and lecturing. It's using the Bible to speak *for* God versus hearing *from* God. It's the difference between listening and talking, between receiving and giving, inhaling and exhaling . . . And when listening becomes talking, what happens to the relationship? (This is the dawning of inkblotitis: isolated readings allow and promote subjective, personal interpretations so as to divide, weaken, and wound us—distancing us from life-giving encounters with the word of God.) When reading is simply reminding, repeating, and thus proclaiming (sometimes "preaching"), we arrive back at the place where, instead of hearing something *outside* ourselves—the divine word of God—we meet ourselves, see ourselves, hear ourselves. To the extent we have become transformed into the image of God, this is as it should be. To the extent we have not, it's the height of pride and arrogance. When inhaling becomes exhaling, we quickly run out of breath. If we do it for long, we will surely die. If all we do is exhale when it comes to the word of God, we also run out of breath—the very breath of life from the Spirit who gives life. Do that for a few months, a few years, a few decades and "the word of God" becomes buried under habits and layers of the exhaling of verses, citations, clichés and mantras. (Is it any wonder people often don't know if a quoted saying is from the Bible or Benjamin Franklin?)

These objections raise an important question concerning the role of one's mind when it comes to reading/understanding the Bible, which leads to another potential objection. From those who actually read and entertain the ideas presented in this book, I suspect that the strongest objection some will have comes on theological grounds. Some will likely object on the basis of pneumatology (= thinking or belief about the Holy Spirit). Some will say, **"You reject the work of the Holy Spirit and replace it with human reason."** They will accuse me of being a "rationalist." I reject the label. I reject the label if by "rationalist" they mean someone who places his or her faith in human reason instead of in God. I do not. I simply include reason and the rational side of things as part of what God, the Holy Spirit, is and does. Being a part of the image of God, thinking and reasoning (the mind) reflects and partakes of the work of God's Spirit. To exclude it is to diminish severely God's image, presence, and work. The Holy Spirit is not just the Spirit of the moment or of the emotions, in other words. He's the Spirit of all that is good in us, created in the image of God and recreated in Jesus Christ.

If, on the other hand, by "rationalist" they mean someone who criticizes an undefined and unrestrained mysticism, then I plead guilty. It's all too easy for moderns to fall into a pattern of lazy mysticism as a substitute for effort, discipline, and good ol' fashion (mental and emotional) hard work. Why do we assume that one of the most important things, learning and knowing truth, that which leads to life and health—a "pearl of great price"—should come at no cost or require no effort in light of our deep brokenness and powerful counter forces? Being saved by God is simple: he did all the hard part and offers salvation to us freely in Christ. Growing in God; maturing in Christ; replacing illusion with truth, egoism with humility, selfishness with love—these are not easy (as "the way" section of Mark's Gospel so patently teaches us).

The issue, then, is not one of mysticism or spiritualism versus rationalism. I'm not advocating or defending either view. The issue is how God's Spirit reveals the word of God to us in scripture. I do not deny God's ability to work whenever, wherever, and however he chooses, with a word or a verse or silence. On the contrary, I'm trying to remind us of an important one of those whenevers, of something God did with great, historical purpose and wonder through the inspiration of the Holy Spirit. To reject the importance of a contextual understanding of the Bible, seems to me, is like saying, "Ah, thanks God, but no thanks"; it's like saying, "It's really not my style; you can take it back" to someone who gives you an extraordinarily meaningful and expensive gift. I don't think we have the right to tell the Creator how he should have communicated with us. My effort is not to define or restrict how God's Spirit works in and among us—I couldn't if I wanted to. My desire is to awaken us to the incredible value of the gift God has given us in his written word, the Bible. Beyond Tischendorf's "treasure in the trash," the discovery and meaning is out of this world.

# Looking Ahead: A Plan for the Church

Only God sets *the* plan for the Church—his Plan for his Church, the bride and body of Christ; we await with anticipation his divine control and the execution of his will. When I speak of "a plan for the church," then, I'm using a very small letter "p" as it applies to the issue of a disintegrating Bible—a "treatment plan," if you will, for the illness of inkblotitis. Or perhaps "prayer" would be a better word: a prayer for the church. And, since her people constitute the church, so the plan/prayer relates to us as individuals and as communities or churches.

## 1. Rediscover the Books of God for Yourself

There are three things we need to do. Number 1: We need a revolution in Bible reading, not just or primarily in amount of reading, but an utter sense of anticipation and excitement at what God will reveal to us again through his word. We must rediscover the Bible as the word of God. We must rediscover the books of God. We need to learn to do this as individuals and as groups, and this means that many of us will have to make some significant changes in the way we read and use the Bible.

Do you remember the statement I made at the beginning: "I'm writing this book to change the way you read the Bible"? To effectively treat the condition of inkblotitis, this must be more than a good idea, more than a bold but merely theoretical statement. It must become a way of life. So, to describe our first task or course of action another way: we need to change the way we read the Bible. We must frequent the library of God and become Bible-book consumers, gradually cultivating a new sense of biblical literacy wherein reading in context becomes the normal way to do it—a way of life—and the contexts begin to go with us so that we are led by the Spirit whenever we hear or use verses from the Bible. Knowing one's Bible means encountering God book by book, knowing the context and content of each book's Spirit-guided encounter with God.

As with any condition or illness, the disorder has to be detected before it can be treated. We must be aware of the problem. Or, as in addictive behavior, we must admit we have a problem; otherwise and of course, we'll have no motivation to do things differently. In essence, these two things—(1) admitting there's a problem and (2) doing something about it—are the two major halves of this study. So, let me be the first to take the plunge: "I am a consumer and producer of Bible inkblots, but I am now committed to learning to let God lead when it comes to what he wants to say to me in his word, the Bible. I want to become a grateful receiver of God's books."

I believe that reading the Bible in context is something that most everyone can do. It's not so academic or so difficult that most Bible readers can't do it, at least to some extent. On the other hand, pastors and ministers/preachers, who are often more trained in these sorts of things, should certainly be able to do it. Consequently, though real change always begins with me, I believe pastors have a huge role to play in the rediscovery of God's word. Pastors must train their people to read the books of the Bible within their Spirit-inspired contexts. The shepherds are to lead the sheep by gentle guidance and by skillful example. If week after week, Sunday after Sunday, pastors model and teach good Bible reading, the recovery will spread like a blazing wild fire in a dry California forest. Shouldn't it be our leaders who rediscover the Bible first and then bring it to their people? On the other hand, maybe the sheep will instinctively lead the pastors.

Rediscovering the Bible as the books of God must be an individual experience—lay and clergy, sheep and shepherd alike—if it's to be effective. It must be *your* thing, *your* experience, *your* discovery. Hearing from God is a personal thing after all; in the end, we will all stand before God as individuals. So this is the first thing each of us must do: as an individual soul before God, commit yourself to silence and to listening to the voice of God in the books of God.

## 2. Rediscover the Books of God in Groups

We need to participate in a revolution in Bible reading as individuals. This is step one of the treatment plan. Just as much of true spirituality takes place in community, however, so the rediscovery also needs to be a group experience—after all, we live in families and groups and churches. We are the communities of God. Step two, then, is to incorporate our newfound passion for God's books into our groups.

Of course, our rediscovered focus on reading and understanding verses of the Bible within their own literary and historical contexts needs to be taught and modeled in the churches, which means that preachers, pastors, and teachers in the church will have a key role. In fact, if leaders in the churches don't teach their people the appropriateness and benefits of reading the Bible as books, it will likely never happen. To the extent that preachers model contextless Bible reading by using versus as springboards to subjects and issues, or as "mobile analogies," as we talked about, the people will, too. On the other hand, expository preaching should in fact be based on careful study of entire books, which should not only help the speaker put the emphasis where God does, but will also encourage the members to be good stewards of the word in scripture.

Perhaps we can witness and participate in a growing revolution of Bible reading within small groups in the church. Think how helpful it will be to apply the principles of good Bible reading with a friend. And then with several other friends, holding one another accountable to the messages of the text and seeking to apply those messages to our lives. We could then become small group communities of God's people, seeking him together in the Bible in ways that perhaps we never have. Two heads are often better than one, and when we get together with this goal of listening to God in his books, wonderful things will happen. When small group Bible studies become Spirit-led encounters with divine moments in history, limitless truths of a timeless God will fill our souls, touch our hearts, and change our lives.

Along that line, I'd like to make a suggestion. I'd like to suggest that we/you start this kind of Bible study group. Small group Bible studies have been around for years and years, but think how exciting it would be to rediscover the word of God together in such settings. Perhaps we can launch a whole new series of Bible Book Clubs, friends reading and working together to hear God in scripture: BBCs or BBSGs—small groups where we read and study books of the Bible, and work together to ask and answer questions of the content and meaning of the text. We're into small groups. We often have "Bible studies." I believe a great movement could awaken in the church where we acknowledge and renounce *versing* (verse-level Bible reading that leads to inkblotitis) as the first method of handling scripture and where we seek to receive God's word as his Spirit communicated it to us, listening again to God's first conversations with his people. Don't you think God will bless us tremendously if we were to say were sorry for interrupting him so often and we want to listen carefully and closely? I believe God will honor that sort of repentance and bless us with an outpouring of his Spirit perhaps like none we've seen.

I don't know if or when it will happen, but I'd love to get these sorts of small group Bible studies set up online—virtual small groups devoted to journeying with a group of people through books of the Bible. They'd last a predetermined set of weeks, have concrete start and end dates for people to sign up, guides to help apply the principles of good Bible reading, online meetings and chat sessions with fellow-group members and possibly with me or some other leader, encouragements for how to apply the major lessons of the books to our lives. Perhaps God will bless these idea and efforts, and perhaps I'll have the marvelous privilege of chatting with you about one of the most important things I know: what God says. (At the time of this writing, I've acquired the rights to

www.inkblotitis.com,
www.LibraryofGod.com, and
www.TheBooksofGod.com.

There's nothing there yet, but check back from time to time to see if this vision for virtual small group Bible studies has become a reality; or to find a link for a blog site where we can interact about *Inkblotitis* in general.)

Whether the online thing happens, let me encourage you to take your own personal revolution in Bible reading with you into your group settings; and remember, the question is not, "What does this mean to you?" but "What does this mean?" "What does it mean in its book-level context?" Community seeking to hear from God, to know and love God, to respond with worship and praise, to live in sync with his divine will—isn't this, in essence, what church is supposed to be?

## 3. Hold Your Leaders Accountable

This may be the most important step in the treatment plan and perhaps the most impactful thing you can do with the principles you've learned in this book. Step/Task #3 is to hold our leaders accountable in the churches. Make sure they are good stewards of the word of God given to us in the Bible. Hold them accountable to the big pictures of the books of the Bible and thus to God's most important points. Make sure that they're not just pulling out passages and using them as analogies, subject-springboards or topic-launchers, that they don't turn God's inspired pictures into personal or denominational proof-texts, that they live up to their responsibilities as leaders in the church to "feed the sheep." Hold them accountable for being examples in how they read and use scripture. Make them ask and answer The Question (maybe introduce them to this book or show them what a Bible-verse inkblot is yourself). That doesn't mean that every sermon has to be an in-depth, expository study of scripture. There's certainly room for theology and dealing with important topics and challenges of the day. What it does mean is that when our leaders use Bible verses, they've done their homework and they have some sense of the place of those verses in their book-level contexts, so that the points they make will be in keeping with the intended meaning of the texts. In other words, hold your leaders accountable to getting and delivering God's point(s) when they use and teach the Bible.

If we as individuals have a revolution in our own private reading and use of the Bible, and we begin to take those encounters with God into our small groups and church Bible studies, it's only natural that our leaders will want to keep pace, especially if the recovery movement is to spread. Even if for some reason you don't feel like you personally can do all the things we've talked about in this book, you can be a force for God in educating and encouraging your pastors to live up to them. I can see a sweet but feisty old lady stopping by to see the preacher on her way out of the church, saying something like "And how does that verse help Luke get across his main messages of . . .? How does it fit into the picture of Luke's story of Jesus?" I can hear a devoted young college student, with due respect, asking his pastor, "Is that really the meaning of these verses in the context of Mark's book? I thought Mark was about . . ." I can envision a hard-working, street-wise single mom helping her small group leader see how the love chapter of 1 Corinthians 13 helps a group of God's people deal with conflicts and potential divisions. In other words, *I can see the sheep steering the shepherds, at least to the point of letting them know, in love, what sort of shepherds they want—leaders who take full advantage of God's Holy Spirit, revealed and released to us in the books of God.*

To sum up: Revolution begins with the power of the people at the grassroots level. If you perform any action from having seen this book, let it be this: ask your leader/teacher the following question: "What is the main point of the book of . . .?" (Matthew, Mark—whatever book you are studying). Then follow up periodically with, "How does this verse [or group of verses] relate to . . . [Matthew's, Mark's, etc.] primary purpose?" When we begin to demand answers to these questions from our leaders, the revolution will have begun.

# A Bible Reader's Pledge

And that's it. That's my prescription for the church when it comes to rediscovering the power and Spirit of the books of God. It's not fancy. It's easy enough to say or predict. And *it starts and ends with you.* So let's put it in first person as a sort of pledge or commitment:

(1) "I will seek to rediscover the Spirit of the books of God by working to become a better reader of the Bible."

(2) "I will help others become better readers of the Bible by taking the awareness of God's Spirit in the books of God into my groups and small groups."

(3) "As humbly and lovingly as the Lord Jesus would want, I will hold my leaders and pastors accountable to the Spirit of God in the word of God."

In a word, "I pledge to create and support no inkblots." If you are able to make this pledge, then I have extreme joy at what God has done through our journey together, and I pray that God will take us all into the greatest encounters, the deepest knowledge, and the strongest empowerment of his Spirit through his books that we call the Bible.

May I give you two final exhortations? The first: Answer The Question. At least ask The Question. If you don't feel fully able or qualified to answer The Question, then hold your spiritual leaders accountable by making them ask and answer The Question. Make your leaders answer The Question—*how does this verse or set of verses fit in the big picture of the book?* How does it function in the pages of the text? Not for the sake of being smart, of literary and grammatical study—that's boring and lifeless—but for the sake of hearing God. That's life-giving. If they can't answer the questions, send them back to the word and tell them to go exploring. You depend on them, and you want to trust that what they are telling you comes from God, not from their own personal or psychological impressions evoked by an inkblot-like verse—no matter where it comes from. And together, let's listen to God's first conversations with his people; otherwise, we might be getting someone's personal conversations with God . . . or who knows what.

The second and final exhortation: Zoom out!

# Epilogue

# John 3:16

On several occasions in the course of this book, I've referenced the most frequently cited verse from the Bible, John 3:16, and asked the question, is such a beloved and powerful verse of scripture subject to inkblotitis? I'll let you answer that question by your own book-level reading of John's Gospel, but I'd like to close with a few observations from the literary context.

In John's Gospel, Jesus is presented as the expression of God. The "Word" of God, John calls him. He is the incarnation of God, which means the holy, awesome goodness and power of God put into human form. He "brought God down to us," so to speak, "so that he could bring us up to God." In Jesus God became human so that we could see what God is really like. "If you've seen me," Jesus said to Philip, "you've seen the Father" (John 14:9). John thus gives us an invitation: to come and see God in Jesus. That invitation is painted across the pages of his book.

For example, in his Introduction, John says, "The Word became flesh and made his dwelling among us. We have seen his glory, the glory of the one and only Son, who came from the Father, full of grace and truth" (1:14: NIV). During the calling of the first disciples in John, Jesus calls Philip to follow him, who promptly goes, finds his brother Nathanael, and says to him, "We have found him about whom Moses in the law and also the prophets wrote, Jesus son of Joseph from Nazareth." Nathanael responds with a revealing (about Nathanael) and evocative question: "Can anything good come out of Nazareth?" To which Philip replies, "Come and see" (1:44-46).

This theme of seeing, experiencing, understanding, and coming to know God in Jesus is one of John's predominant themes, and is, in fact, the overarching purpose of his book, as he invites us to come and see God, the Father, in Jesus, the Son. He wants us to see so that we will believe and have eternal life. These two themes—seeing God in Jesus and faith or belief—are thus intimately related. When Nathanael shows up and sees Jesus for the first time, Jesus says, "You believe because I told you I saw you under the fig tree. You will see greater things than that," adding, "Very truly I tell you, you will see heaven open, and the angels of God ascending and descending on the Son of Man" (1:50-51: NIV).

A careful reading of John's book and tracing of these themes reveal extraordinary truths ("heaven open") about Jesus and finding life in him (". . . whoever lives and believes in me will never die . . ."), as we come face to face with the character (= "glory") of God in Jesus. There is, moreover, a very interesting twist or reversal on this theme in the story of the death of Lazarus in chapter 11.

John portrays Lazarus and his sisters, Mary and Martha, as good friends of Jesus, going out of his way to describe them as persons whom Jesus loved (11:3, 5, 36). Lazarus got sick—very sick. So the sisters, believing that Jesus could heal, sent a message to him. But Jesus did a curious thing. He intentionally delayed his coming to them, knowing that Lazarus would die so Jesus could use the occasion to display something of the nature of God. When he finally arrived a few days later, Lazarus had died. When she heard that he was near, Martha went to meet Jesus and expressed her deep sorrow: "Lord, if you had been here, my brother would not have died" (11:21). Likewise, when she told her sister Mary that Jesus had arrived and was calling for her, Mary got up and went out to meet him. Seeing her get up quickly, thinking she was going to the tomb to weep, those who were comforting Mary and Martha in the house followed her. When Mary gets to Jesus, she kneels at his feet and in deep distress repeats the words of her sister, "Lord, if you had been here, my brother would not have died" (11:32).

The scene is intense and emotional. Both sisters have taken their great grief to Jesus—face to face. Mary is on her knees, weeping. The mourners who had come with her are weeping. It's as if they've brought the whole funeral-like scene, the pain and sorrow of their tremendous loss due to Jesus' absence, out to Jesus. In a dark and sad moment, the sorrows of earth—of being human, of loving and hurting so much over losing someone that we can't stand it—are intimately presented, face to face to the one who is from above the earth and who made the earth.

Now watch what happens: "When Jesus saw her weeping, and the Jews who came with her also weeping, he was greatly disturbed in spirit and deeply moved" (11:33). The very Word of God, the one who was with God in the beginning, the one who was and is God, is so deeply touched by their sadness and tears that almost as if he couldn't take it anymore, with passion and purpose, Jesus asked, "Where have you laid him?" (11:34).

They said, ". . . come and see" (11:34). (Linger here for a moment.)

Then we have what's known as the shortest verse in the English (KJV) Bible: "Jesus wept" (11:35).

See, the experience goes both ways. How profound is that!

In Jesus we experience God and the things of God. We see God and the things of God. This is how we come to know God and believe in Jesus so that we may be born again and have eternal life. But *in Jesus*—and this is the point—*God experienced what it means to be us*. I'll say that again: In Jesus God experienced what it means to be us. To be human. He experienced the things of earth, the broken and sad things. The hurtful things. Even to the point of dying on a cross in our place. Here he weeps in great sorrow and friendship with those who have lost one they love dearly.

But death is not the end, and it wasn't in the story of Lazarus. The text goes on to say that again being greatly distressed, Jesus goes to the tomb. "By now he already stinks," Martha said. Jesus says, "Didn't I tell you that if you believed, you would see the glory of God" (11:40). Then Jesus raises Lazarus from the dead. The result: "Many of the Jews, therefore, who had come with Mary and had seen what Jesus did, believed in him" (11:44). "Come and see."

I'd like to give you one more example of the experience of God in Jesus that John invites us to in his book. This one comes at the end, with Jesus' own death. (I'll highlight our theme words "come" and "see.") Early on the first day of the week while it was still dark, Mary Magdalene *came* to the tomb. She found the stone rolled away and the tomb empty. So she ran and told the disciples. Upon hearing the news, Peter and John didn't just go to the tomb, but they *ran*, with John outrunning Peter and arriving first. He bent down to look in and *saw* . . .

> Then Simon Peter *came*, following him, and went into the tomb. He *saw* the linen wrappings lying there, and the cloth that had been on Jesus' head, not lying with the linen wrappings but rolled up in a place by itself. Then the other disciple, who reached the tomb first, also went in, and he *saw and believed* . . . (20:6-8).

Mary stood outside the tomb weeping. When she bent over to look in, she *saw* two angels, sitting where the body of Jesus had been. They asked her why she was crying, and she said, "They've taken away my Lord, and I don't know where they have laid him" (20:13). She then turned around and *saw* Jesus standing there. Jesus also asks her why she was crying. Thinking he was the caretaker, she said, "Sir, if you have carried him away, tell me where you have laid him, and I will take him away" (20:15).

Then with one word, Jesus changes all of human history. In a voice she had heard many times, he says, "Mary!" Recognizing the sound, she exclaims, "Rabboni!" "Which means Teacher," John adds.

> Jesus said to her, "Don't hold on to me [you can imagine her impassioned grasp], because I have not yet ascended to the Father. But go to my brothers and say to them, 'I am ascending to my Father and your Father, to my God and your God.'" Mary Magdalene went and announced to the disciples, "I have *seen* the Lord"; . . . (20:16-18).

This experience—the ultimate experience of Jesus—continues in the next few paragraphs. Later that evening, the disciples were assembled behind closed and locked doors out of fear of the Jews, and Jesus *came*, stood among them, and said, "Peace be with you."

"After he said this, he *showed* them his hands and his side. The disciples rejoiced when they *saw* the Lord" (20:19-20). Then Jesus breathed on them (the "breath of new life," you might say), said "Receive the Holy Spirit," and sent them out (commissioned them) as the Father had sent him. (They were to become the continuation of God's presence on the earth.)

Thomas, who earned his nickname "doubting Thomas" on this occasion, wasn't there when Jesus *came*. Of course, they told him about it. "But he said to them, 'Unless I *see* the mark of the nails in his hands and put my finger in the mark of the nails and my hand in his side, I will not *believe*'" (20:25). A week later when the disciples were again assembled behind locked doors, Jesus appeared to them again. This time Thomas was there. "Then he said to Thomas, 'Put your finger here and *see* my hands. Reach out your hand and put it in my side. Do not doubt but *believe*'" (20:27). You can imagine his response: "My Lord and my God!" And don't miss Jesus' reply: "Have you *believed* because you have *seen* me? Blessed are those who have not *seen* and yet have *come* to *believe*" (20:29). John's conclusion highlights his inspired purpose:

> Now Jesus did many other signs in the presence of his disciples, which are not written in this book. But these are written so that you may come *to believe* that Jesus is the Messiah, the Son of God, and that through *believing* you may have life in his name (20:30-31).

Here Jesus and John speak about us. We cannot have the same firsthand experience the disciples did, but that doesn't mean we can't have *any* experience. It doesn't mean we can't come and see and experience God in the flesh. In fact, that's the whole point of John's book (and all the books of the Bible). It was written, John says, so that we too can come and see and come to believe in Jesus as the Son of God. In a sense, the book John wrote is God's replacement to us of the eye-witnesses, showing us the very presence of God on earth. Jesus came and called and walked and lived and died and rose so that we could see God and come to trust in him. *Seeing God in Jesus inspires faith.* This is John's premise and his purpose. Seeing God in Jesus inspires faith, which leads to life—eternal life. John wrote about that so the rest of us can make that journey as well.

The Spirit-inspired word of God invites us to experience the Spirit-filled Word of God (Jesus the Messiah) so that we too can believe and have life. I invite you to come and see the Son of God anew in the books of God we call the Bible.

And one more thing:

. . . .

For God so loved the world that he gave his only Son, so that everyone who believes in him may not perish but have eternal life (John 3:16).

. . . .

There is no doubt this makes a good summary of our faith, though I challenge you to come to see the important depths of meaning John gives to these words in the context of his book as a whole, like, for example, what he means by "eternal life."

But here's the bigger point. When we take these verses only, without their context, where goes the experience of God in Jesus that John says leads to faith? We can tell people all day that we believe God sent his son so that we could be saved or that they ought to believe in Jesus and be saved, but based on that statement alone—John 3:16—how many will have the deep conviction of heart that leads them to be born again and seek to know and follow God for the rest of their lives? *When we take the verses out,* in a sense, *we remove the experience of Jesus that John says produces faith.* Of course, the invitation to "come and see" is implied when we recite John 3:16—at least I hope it is—but the question remains, what have we done with John's Gospel that is the experience of Jesus, the Christ?

Sharing a verse of two from John as an invitation to faith in the Lord Jesus—even one as powerful as John 3:16—is a little like telling someone who's never had it what chocolate tastes like—only a thousand times more indescribable. Of course, we have to start somewhere and, like a well-known brand on a supermarket shelf (when you have a hankering for chocolate), an invitation is a great place to start. But how far do we go to see Jesus? To hear God? How far will *you* go?

Will you go to *the book* level?

May we be the tools of God to bring others to come to know God in Jesus, the Word of God. May we experience him together in the word and world of the books of God. May we be made new, and share his love and light, as the Spirit of God revives and instills the presence of God. Nothing matters much in comparison to these things.

Just as John invites us in his book, I invite you to the books of God with the same exhortation: "Come and see." The Spirit of God lives in and breathes on us through their pages.

# Appendix 2

# Special Paragraph Markers (Pauline Letter Forms and Themes)

## Thanksgivings

1. A Pauline Thanksgiving is the early part of a letter, usually occurring immediately following the salutation (A to B, greeting), in which Paul gives thanks to God for the readers.
2. In Paul's letters, the Thanksgiving prepares the audience for a positive hearing of the letter: secures the goodwill of the audience, introduces major themes, and prepares the listener for the following discussion and exhortations.
3. It typically proceeds into a report of Paul's prayers in behalf of the recipients which is directly connected to the purpose of the letter: it is the letter in a generalized nutshell.
4. As an introduction, the Thanksgiving usually comes immediately prior to the beginning of the body of the letter; thus, the opening of the body may be determined by finding the end of the Thanksgiving.
5. It is sometimes concluded with an emphatic reference to Jesus, particularly his second coming ("eschatological climax"), a blessing, or a doxology.
6. The Thanksgiving establishes a degree of mutuality between the recipients and the author of the letter.
7. The gospel, its initial coming to the recipients, or some aspect of their faith are often major themes and may be connected with the reason for the Thanksgiving.
8. Elements of the Thanksgiving:
   a. Verb of thanksgiving: "I thank"
   b. Modifier (optional): "always"

c. Object of thanksgiving (optional): "God"
d. Person(s) addressed (optional): "for you"
e. Substance of the thanksgiving: "because of your faith"
f. Prayer report
9. Examples: Romans 1:8-12/17; 1 Corinthians 1:4-8/9; Philippians 1:3-11; Colossians 1:3-12/14; Ephesians 1:15-19/23; 1 Thessalonians 1:2-10; 2:13-16; 2 Thessalonians 1:3-12; 1 Timothy 1:3-5/7; Philemon 1:4-7

# Disclosures

1. A disclosure is a statement by which information is made known ("disclosed") to the audience.
2. Reminders of something that the listeners already know sometimes have the same force as disclosure statements.
3. Disclosures often function as the background or basis for arguments (proofs) and/or exhortations, i.e., information on which the point depends. For example,
   Disclosure: "It's raining outside"
   Transition: "So/Therefore"
   Exhortation: "I ask you to take an umbrella"
4. A disclosure statement is usually the topic sentence for a paragraph or section of material, and an argument or exhortation may thus be based on all of the material in that section.
5. Its elements are
   a. Subject and verb of desire: "I want" or "We want"
   b. Person addressed: "you"
   c. Disclosure infinitive: "to know"
   d. Information disclosed: "that it's raining outside"
6. Examples: 1 Corinthians 10:1; Philippians 1:12; 1 Thessalonians 3:13

# Petitions/Requests

1. A petition is a request or exhortation for something to be done.
2. Petitions are highly significant in Pauline letters, and the first major petition of the letter may indicate the primary purpose of the letter.
3. In addition to its ethical implication, the primary petition reflects the main argumentative thesis or proposition of the letter, i.e., the main point.
4. Like the disclosure, the petition usually functions as a type of topic sentence for a larger block of material.
   a. Often the primary petition will occur at the beginning of the more ethical portion of a Pauline letter.
   b. Within these sections, major themes from the earlier part of the letter are brought together in summary fashion.
   c. Moreover, new ideas which will be important in the following part of the letter may be introduced.
   d. Thus, in addition to highlighting a major purpose of the letter, petitions help to clarify the relationship of some of the preceding themes and serve as transitions into subsequent material.
   e. The petition section is thus a pivotal, transition section in the makeup of the letter.
5. Petitions contain three basic and two optional elements:
   a. Petition verb (request, exhortation): "I beseech/ask/appeal/urge . . ."
   b. Addressee (optional): "you"
   c. Background
      (1) The background may be expressed by one sentence or, more often, by a larger block of material, such as is introduced by a disclosure.
      (2) The background is often pointed to by such inferential words as "therefore" and "wherefore."
   e. Divine authority phrase (optional): "by the mercies of God"
   f. Desired action: "to present your bodies as a living sacrifice"
   g. Examples: 1 Corinthians 1:10; Romans 12:1-2; Ephesians 4:1-3

# Prayers (Summaries/Conclusions/Transitions)

1. Prayers or prayer reports that include the content of the prayer in the body of a letter concern the major struggles of the audience which the letter has addressed.
2. Since the material prior to such prayers has also been designed to speak to the problems of the recipients, either through information or exhortation, the prayers tend to summarize and conclude major sections of material.
   a. They epitomize the dominant concerns of the previous material and thereby help to highlight the major concerns of the letter.
   b. When they occur in the middle of the letter, they also serve as a transition into new material.
3. Actual prayers (found in Romans and 1 Thessalonians) may include such things as
   a. Subject: "May the God of peace"
   b. Verb: "give"
   c. Objects: "you peace"
   d. Purpose or elaboration: "at all times in every way"
4. Examples: Romans 15:5-6; 1 Thessalonians 3:11-13; 5:23

# Expressions of Confidence in the Addressees

1. Pauline expressions of confidence in the addressees are expressions of Paul's belief that the readers will comply with the request(s) that he makes in the letter.
2. Such expressions have a persuasive function.
   a. They do so by increasing the likelihood of a favorable hearing and by creating a sense of obligation through praise.
   b. They thus support the general purpose for which the letter was written.
3. In some cases the expressions tend to imply favorable action even beyond the express terms of the letter.
4. These expressions can include up to five elements:

   a. Conjunction (linking the expression with what precedes): "and"
   b. Subject (1st person): "I"
   c. Confidence term(s): "have confidence"
   d. Reference to the addressee(s) (2nd person): "in you"
   e. Indication of the content of the confidence (often starting with the word "that"): "that you will take an umbrella"
5. Example: Philemon 21

## Commands of Attitude and Behavior

1. Imperatives of attitude and behavior, and answers to important questions were sometimes given in a stereotyped manner which helped to prove the reliability of what was urged or affirmed.
2. A clear indication of the behavior required, a reason why that behavior was required, and an indication of one or more of the consequences that might be expected were included.
3. The purpose of the form was to issue commands and answers to important questions in a way that would show the accuracy, reliability, and necessity of what was affirmed.
4. The form had three essential and two optional elements:
   a. Injunction: "let everyone take an umbrella"
   b. Reason: "because it's raining outside"
   c. Refutation (optional): "whoever doesn't will get wet"
   d. Analogous situation (optional): "as wet as if he took a shower"
   e. Discussion: "umbrellas are useful and inexpensive"
5. Example: Romans 13:1-5

## Apostolic Authority and Presence

1. Paul considered his presence with his converts of primary importance. The letter seems to have been a lesser substitute, yet still an effective means of expressing apostolic authority.
2. The letter was on some occasions seen as an anticipatory substitute for his presence.

3. There were at least four things Paul used in his letters to stress his apostolic authority:
   a. Emphatic references to himself
   b. References to his past conduct with his churches
   c. Expressions of his confidence in the addressee's compliance with the requests of the letter
   d. Visit Talk ("apostolic presence")
      (1) Visit talk is an expression within the letter of intentions for an upcoming visit.
      (2) It tends to appear at the closing of sections as incentive for compliance with the requests of the letter.
4. Expressions of apostolic authority tend to occur in the latter part of a letter or a section of a letter as support for its message.
5. Such expressions of authority may be somewhat suppressed when an emissary is sent along with the letter.

## Expressions of Self-Confidence

1. An expression of self-confidence is an assertion by the author about the virtue of some aspect or aspects of his character (usually relating to his credibility or competence to advise).
2. Most of the expressions contain a word or a phrase with the meaning "confidence" or "to be confident."
3. The major elements are the assertion of confidence and the descriptive reference to an aspect of the writer's worthy character.
4. Such expressions normally function to highlight the opinion that the author hopes the listeners will have toward him, which, for some reason, may be deficient.
   a. The author is thus trying to create or restore a good, perhaps authoritative, relationship with his readers in order to obtain a favorable hearing for his advice.
   b. Expressions of self-confidence are therefore often followed (or preceded) by a section of advice.

5. Such expressions may also function as thematic statements, joining the attitude that the author hopes the readers will have toward him with the major point of a particular section or the letter as a whole.
6. Example: Romans 1:16-17

# Greetings

1. The greeting form is the form that usually occurs at the end of a letter and is an emotional expression establishing or highlighting a bond of friendship (not to be confused with the "greeting" of the salutation).
2. It helps to show the intended readership of the letter and the relationships of the people involved.
3. Its elements include,
   a. Greeting verb: "greet," "greets"
   b. Indication of who is to do the greeting: "You," "Luke"
   c. Indication of who is to be greeted: "one another," "you"
   d. Elaborating phrases (optional): "with a holy kiss"
4. Examples: Romans 16:3-16; 1 Corinthians 16:19-20